The Brandywine Battlefield: The Untold Story of Its History and Preservation

1. **Exploring the Battlefield:** This photo of 90-year-old Amos Brinton pointing to the former location of the wooden posts connected to Chads' Ferry, appears in the 1912 book *Along the Western Brandywine*. The author, Wilmer MacElree, typically solicited residents when exploring the battlefield.

Brinton, who was related to the family of Brinton's Mill, left behind extensive notes and documents on the battle now housed at the Delaware Historical Society in Wilmington, Delaware. *Author's collection.*

The Brandywine Battlefield: The Untold Story of Its History and Preservation

The generational effort to save the
vanishing battlefield
of September 11, 1777,
now spanning Chester and Delaware Counties,
Pennsylvania

By Catherine C. Quillman

Hedgerow Press/Quillman Publications

2023

Library of Congress Cataloging-in-Publication-Data

Quillman, Catherine C.

The Brandywine Battlefield: The Untold Story of Its History and Preservation

The generational effort to save the vanishing battlefield of September 11, 1777, now spanning Chester and Delaware Counties, Pennsylvania

Brandywine, Battle of, 1777. 2. Pennsylvania—History—American Revolution, 1775-1783—Philadelphia Campaign of 1777-78.

ISBN 979-8-218-04210-3

Copyright © 2023 by Catherine C. Quillman

All rights reserved including the right to reproduce this book in any form or by any means such as photocopying or scanning. Brief quotations from the book are accepted if credit is listed. All inquiries should be sent to the address or email below.

Published by Hedgerow Press

info@catherinequillman.com

Cover & map design: Linda Clark, Art Station, P.O. Box 87, Unionville, PA 19375

Illustrations of landmarks by Ann Bedrick ; portraits by the author

Cover details: The background map is a topographical map created in 1863 by Henry L. Whiting of a team called the U.S. Coast Survey for the Defense of Philadelphia. The map illustrated fortifications and landmarks dating to the Battle of Brandywine, which might serve the Union Army in case of a Confederate invasion. Main photo: A circa 1909 postcard of Washington's Headquarters (the Ring House) in Chadds Ford. Note the hand-painted sign nailed to the tree. . *Photo courtesy of the Christian C. Sanderson Museum, Chadds Ford, PA © 2016*

For battlefield preservationists & advocates of open space

Other books by Catherine C. Quillman

100 Artists of the Brandywine Valley

Between the Brandywines

Walking the East End

Walking the Uptown

The Story of Milford Mills and the Marsh Creek Valley

The Brandywine Valley: A Pictorial History

The History of the Conestoga Turnpike

10 | The Brandywine Battlefield:

2. **Osborne Hill:** Douglas E. Brinton issued two photographs of the British gathering point known as Osborne Hill in 1899. Both naturally illustrate the distant view Generals Howe and Cornwallis had of the open countryside surrounding Birmingham Meeting. *Courtesy of CCHC.*

Table of Contents

Author's Note	15
Maps: Upper Ford & Lower Ford	18-19

Part One: Research & Preservation Efforts

Beginnings	20
A Broader Reach	23
A Battle of Terrain	24
Historic Markers	27
Battlefield Observers & Recorders	28
The British Left Hook	33
Chads' Ferry vs Chads' Ford	35
A Study of "Firsts:" A Historical Perspective	38
An Endangered Battlefield	39
Defining the Battlefield	63
Battle Hill	69
Historic Districts	72
Discovering Fords & Colonial Roads	78
The Animated Battlefield	79
Battlefield Tourists	82
Patriots & Relic Seekers	84
Battlefield Promoters	88
Present-day Battlefield Explorers	94

12 | The Brandywine Battlefield:

Anniversary Celebrations	99
A National Trend	103
Early Preservation Efforts	110

Part Two: Historic Narratives & Community Anecdotes

War Comes to the Brandywine Valley	116
Washington's Officers	120
Washington's Multicultural Army	124
Spies & Traitors	127
Knyphausen's Diversion	128
Waiting for the Crown Forces	130
Proctor's Artillery Brigade	132
A Record of the Day	136
A String of Dispatches	138
The Sighting	139
The Storm Above John Chads' House	141
General Washington's Sniper	142
Battle at the Fence Lines	143
The "Eminences"	145
Entrenched at the Second Eminence	147
The American Revolution Remembered	149
Lafayette's Tree in John Bennett's Field	152
Lafayette's "Other" Tree	154
The Lafayette Monument of 1895	155
Fêting Lafayette	155

Part Three: Historic Sites & Military Landmarks

Martin's Tavern	160
Welch's Tavern	161
Trimble's Ford	163
Jefferis' Ford	168
Sconnelltown	170
Respite at Strode's Mill	172
The Royal Forces at Osborne Hill	173
Poised for Battle	174
Proctor's Hill	175
Washington's Headquarters	181
Gilpin's House	182
Kuerner Farm or "Washington's Hill"	183
Brinton's Ford	184
The "Ravine" at Chadds Ford	186
The Orchard at the Ring House	186
Closing Action at the 1704 House	188
British Takeover of Dilworthtown	190
The Rear Guard South: "The Sun Shown"	191
Retreat to Chester	193
Acknowledgments	198
Endnotes	199
Bibliography	212

14 | The Brandywine Battlefield:

3. Historic Crossroads: The photographer Douglas E. Brinton did not identify the road in this photograph taken for his Battle of Brandywine series of 1899, but he may have wanted a distant view to show the size of the village he identified as Dilworthtown. *Courtesy of CCHC.*

Author's Note

Judging from more conventional military histories, I suspect that readers believe that a history is not complete without an index, appendix, and even a glossary of terms. My book lacks those features, but here's my disclaimer: while readers will find plenty of descriptions of military tactics and troop movements in these pages, I was more interested in highlighting the stories that can't be found in the excellent books about the Philadelphia Campaign of 1777 and those about the Battle of Brandywine in particular.

In other words, the "history" of this history may seem anecdotal compared to more academic books, but that may be the result of my focus on local places and landmarks that we can still see today and the military outcomes connected to them. I also wanted to "unpack," as the journalistic saying goes, those community stories or legends that have continued to persist as reliable sources documenting the Battle of Brandywine. I thought the best way to do that was to read accounts published in 19th-century newspapers as well as the so-called "Bible" of local history, the *History of Chester County, Pennsylvania, with Genealogical and Biographical Sketches* (1881), by J. Smith Futhey & Gilbert Cope.

Futhey, a distinguished Chester County judge, and Cope, the author of numerous genealogies, had the advantage of knowing the "who's who" of Chester County, interviewing residents or in the lingo of the day, "teasing" tales and legends from local farmers.

Compared to the historians of today, Futhey & Cope (to use the abbreviation found throughout this book) may have relied too heavily on community stories and legends. Still, their habit of citing the location or historic setting (in 1881) of each battle-related story no doubt helped fix their importance in the collective memory of Chester County residents. More to the point, Futhey & Cope inspired a respect and love of local history, which lead to the preservation efforts of the people described in this book.

 Note: Numbers marked within parentheses such as (1) indicate that a photo is included elsewhere in this book.

Commonly used abbreviations: Chester County History Center (CCHS); Chadds Ford Historical Society (CFHS)

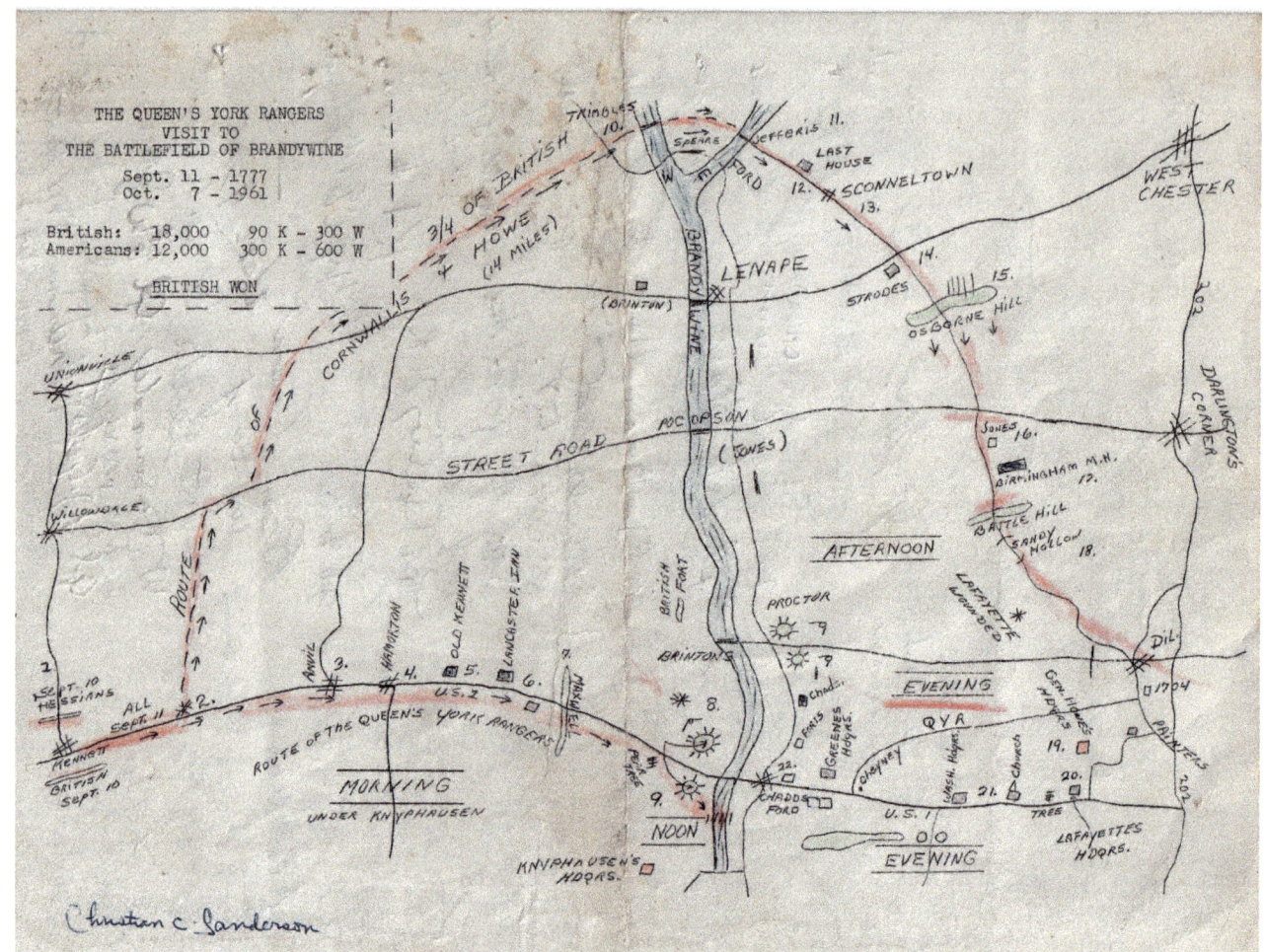

4. The Queen's Rangers map. The esteemed Chadds Ford historian Chris Sanderson created many maps of the battlefield over the years, but he made this one specifically for a Canadian regiment known as the Queen's York Rangers. When they visited on October 7, 1961, they followed the course of the British Queen's Rangers down Nottingham Road. *Photo courtesy of the Christian C. Sanderson Museum, Chadds Ford, PA © 2020.*

About the Maps Featuring the Route of Howe & Cornwallis
(See next page)

Maps depicting the route of the so-called "British Flanking Column" or "British Left Hook" have varied over the years, but the one published here is based on the latest research of the Brandywine Battlefield Task Force. Beginning at Kennett Square, the Howe's & Cornwallis' troops (aka the British Left Hook) traveled north by way of the c. 1720 Unionville Road (Route 82) before turning east on the c. 1775 (resurveyed) East Doe Run Road (which now includes a turnabout shown on the map).

The troops continued in a southeasterly direction, seemingly traveling out of their way before coming to modern Northbrook Road off Street Road, (which derives its name from the c.1707 Marlborough Street Road). Modern Northbrook and Red Lion Roads roughly followed a former road the British took to the Upper Fords called the "Great Valley Road" or the "Road to the Great Valley," (explained elsewhere in this book).

In addition to showing the Flanking Column route, this map was designed to feature the fords of the Brandywine River in 1777 and to give a sense of the scope and broad placement of Washington's Army.

On the east side of the Brandywine, the map illustrates Washington's main focal point –Chads' Ford and Chads' Ferry – and the secondary fords protected by troops extending from Buffington's Ford (just south of present-day Route 842) to the southernmost post, Gibson's Ford (17), a crossing near the Wilson's Run, two miles south of Chads' Ford.

On the west side of the Brandywine, a select infantry corps known as "Maxwell's Men" posted at four sites, all of them located in equal intervals along the Great Nottingham Road, a circa 1743 road that roughly followed the present-day Baltimore Pike (22). The posts were as follows: just east of Welch's Tavern (62); at the junction of Kennett Pike (Rt. 52); just west of Old Kennett Meeting (8); and at the intersection of the present-day Brinton's Bridge Road (27).

Additional troop locations shown on the Upper Fords map are explained in the Proctor's Artillery Brigade chapter.

18 | The Brandywine Battlefield:

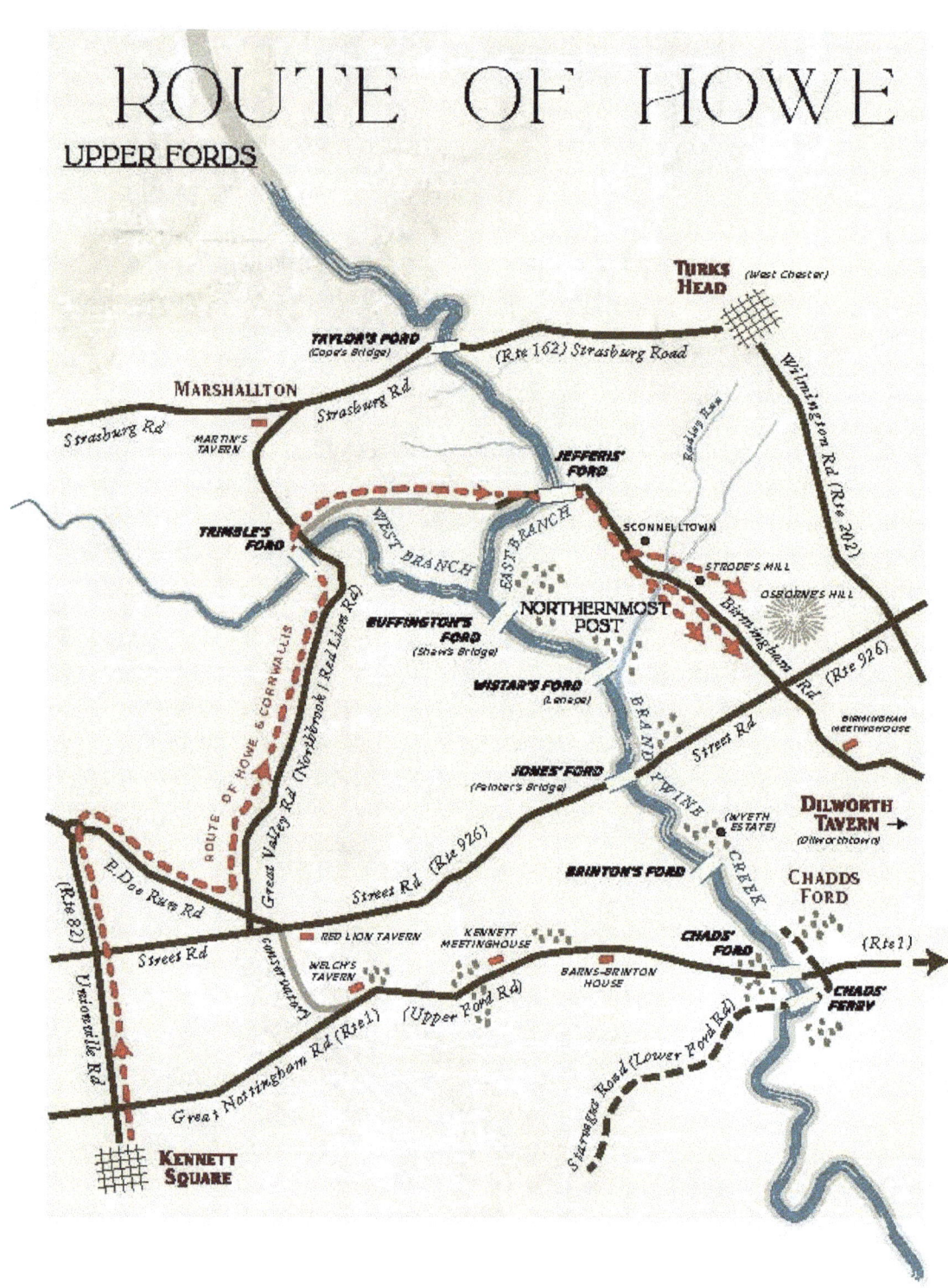

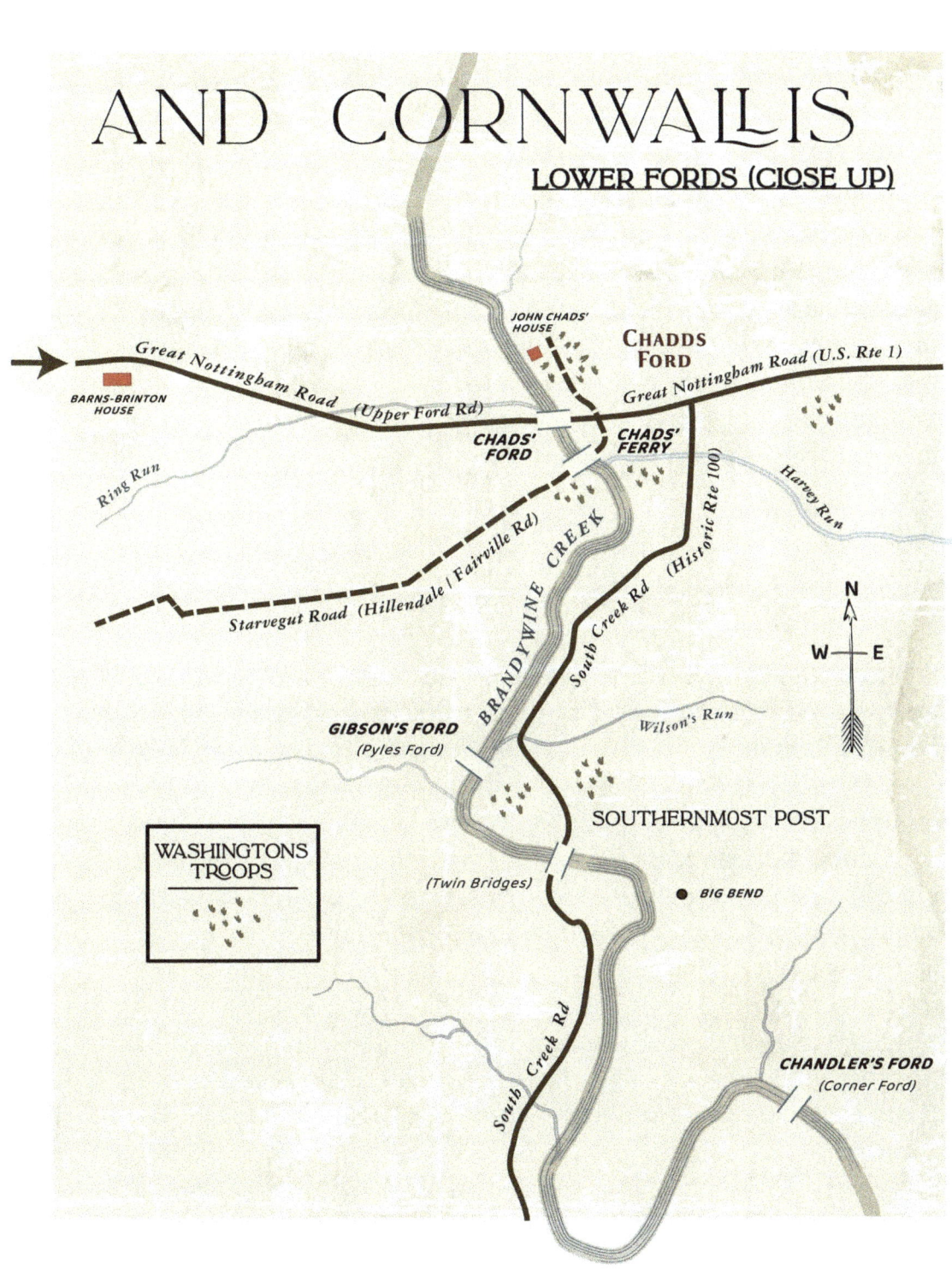

Part One
Research & Preservation Efforts
Beginnings

    The history of the Brandywine Valley is filled with events that have made a difference in American life. One was the Revolutionary War struggle at what is now known as the Battle of Brandywine. The dramatic and final encounter of the Brandywine battle did not occur in Chadds Ford, Pennsylvania – a place many tourists today assume to be the core battlefield site – but a small region of Chester County that borders South New Street and Birmingham Road.

    Generations of battlefield explorers would come to know this bit of hard-won territory as Sandy Hollow, (5) especially after 1895, when a small memorial column at the nearby Birmingham Meetinghouse (47) (known to soldiers on both sides as the "church" at "Birmingham Hill") was unveiled (58). It honored the Marquis de Lafayette, the 19-year-old soldier of French nobility who famously volunteered to serve as Washington's aide-de-camp.

    In the final hours of the Battle of Brandywine, Lafayette was wounded with a shot to the left thigh soon after he dismounted from his horse near the Meetinghouse or perhaps at Sandy Hollow – the exact spot has never been determined – but his injury was surprisingly minor compared to what could have happened during the chaos that erupted on September 11, 1777. On that day an estimated 30,000 American and British soldiers clashed at Sandy Hollow and took part in what many call the bloodiest and largest single-day land battle of any other military engagement in the American Revolution.

    The Hessian and British soldiers were told to engage or "amuse" the Americans as a diversionary tactic at Chadds Ford, but they did so at a heavy loss and without disrupting the Americans more than momentarily. Mainly because both armies were spread over a vast area, either positioned for combat or left behind as detachments to guard certain areas, the exact number of casualties may never be known.

    This is particularly true of the Continental Army, which never issued a casualty report – neither officially nor informally – although some figures became known soon after the battle when British records were seized. These records gave only rough estimates, but they may be fairly accurate since the Crown Forces not only stayed behind for five days on the field, they also oversaw many

Sandy Hollow, scene of last fighting Battle of Brandywine, and right of the American line

5. Sandy Hollow: A c. 1905 postcard of the Sandy Hollow site, the "right of the American line."

Author's collection.

of the American burials. One British report noted that "400 rebels were buried on the field by the victors," though other officers counted "502 [Rebels] dead in the field" and 750 wounded.

Major General Nathanael Greene is the only American officer to commit his estimates to paper, and he gave a range from 1,200 to 1,300 Continental troops – a significant figure considering that an estimated 14,600 American soldiers alone fought in Chadds Ford. An additional 300 to 400 soldiers may have deserted the cause or were captured, as British reports suggest. [1]

Curiously, all the recorded losses including those published by London newspapers focused on the Continental statistics. The British losses generally only appeared in the official military reports and they were often relatively low figures compared to what the Americans believed. [2] Thomas J. McGuire writes that the "American estimates of British losses run as high as 2,000, based on distant observation and sketchy, unreliable reports."

One of the earliest studies of the Brandywine battlefield, spearheaded by a group of women in 1989 – a battlefield historian, an archaeologist, and an architectural historian – attempted to locate the burial sites that have been historically tied to certain areas. [3] They included mass burial sites created in old roadbeds by caving in

6. A Historic Ruin. The historic ruin of Martin's Tavern is located on Northbrook Road, about 100 ft. west of the Strasburg Road (Rt 162) in village of Marshallton. The site is maintained by the Friends of Martin's Tavern, a nonprofit group that named the Revolutionary War site after the first owner, Joseph Martin, who built the tavern in 1764. *Illustration by Ann Bedrick*

the high embankments, presumably a quick way to bury the dead on what was a blistering hot day in September.

The exact location of these discoveries were not available to the public at the time – fear of looting was a concern in 1989 – but researchers have recently speculated that as a many as 1,600 soldiers lie in unmarked graves including those in and around Birmingham Meetinghouse (47) and the Old Kennett Meetinghouse (8). Both meetinghouses saw heated engagements and were, in the words of one commemorative marker, "engulfed in a hail of bullets." Elsewhere burial sites have been discovered at what was described as "seemingly random" locations around the battlefield as well as a "few smaller grave sites" scattered in or near the "core" battlefield region in Birmingham and Thornbury Townships.

As a *Philadelphia Inquirer* feature story related, Nancy Webster, the battlefield historian of the study group, spent much of her time trying to document not only the core battlefield site but "hidden" sites such as former field hospitals, British redoubts, wagon routes, and encampments. The study also looked at area homes that stood in 1777. Webster and her colleagues searched nearly each one "from attic to basement." The women were among the first to interview the homeowners as well as historians (including British historians) to compare "local folklore and historic fact." The benchmark study of 1989 was not merely about discovering historic landmarks and burial sites. The researchers saw it as an end to the old way of seeing battlefields as vanished landscapes of the past, offering little of interest accept when a burial or military artifact was discovered. In terms of beginnings, it marked a renewed interest in defining the scope of the battlefield.

A Broader Reach

To the casual student of history, the significance of the Battle of Brandywine may not be immediately apparent especially since nearly all the military encounters on that single day in September of 1777 occurred on a far-flung range of privately-owned properties in the Brandywine Valley. Enter a Chester County preservation group called the Brandywine Battlefield Task Force (the "Task Force"). The group has worked for decades to promote the battlefield's history beyond driving tours and anniversary events.

The core members of the Task Force are part of the Delaware and Chester County Planning Commissions, a connection that serves to ensure that future comprehensive plans and township zoning works in conjunction with battlefield preservation.

Along with a broader reach for the Task Force, the so-called "battlefield landscape" has been expanded in recent years to include army encampments, former hospitals, and burial sites as well as historic villages and homes plundered by the British. The territory of interest so to speak now spans approximately 35,000 acres. The expanded territory helps to explain why the Task Force is now comprised of an army of representatives in 15 townships and historic commissions in two counties (Chester and Delaware). In 1777, Chester County was a much larger territory and included parts of Lancaster County and Delaware County where the county seat, Chester, was based.

By 2006, the Task Force had identified about 800 individual parcels in Chester and Delaware Counties that were part of the September 11th battlefield including historic sites related to the battle's interpretation. 4 One of these is a 50-acre easement placed on a property in Pennsbury Township that helped to protect the viewshed of an area bordering Hillendale Road, where British supply wagons rolled through fields near Kennett Square (51).

Another important part of Hillendale Road that is not formally protected but remains open space is where the road meets Hickory Hill Road. The Task Force cites the area as one of the few places not directly related to the battle but one that contributes to the interpretation of the "behind-the-lines" life of the British military support staff and civilian camp followers. This open corner of land is believed to be the main area where the British forces parked their baggage train during the Battle of Brandywine.

The Task Force also included parcels where key action sites occurred even if not much can be seen of an original structure. The so-called first shots of the Battlefield of Brandywine, for instance, took place at the Welch's Tavern (2) – later known as the Anvil Tavern – before it was converted in the 1930s into a boarding house for workers from nearby Longwood Gardens. Perhaps the most interesting stone "ruin" is Martin's Tavern (6,61), a historic site maintained by the Friends of Martin's Tavern in Marshallton. In 1777, it was a short distance by horse from the British route through Trimble's Ford (59) south of the village.

In the months leading up to the Brandywine Battle, the tavern was a popular gathering place for local colonists, especially among members of the Chester County Militia. On the morning of the battle, the guests included scouts as well as "Squire" Thomas Cheyney, who was later celebrated as the man who spotted the British flanking movement and galloped on to warn Gen. Washington. The focus on terrain also underscores an idea long promoted by the Task Force: that the character of the land is inextricably tied to its history.

A Battle of Terrain

Exploring the terrain outdoors – or virtually, in the case of online animated maps – is one way to understand how every battlefield landscape configuration is unique. Thanks to renewed discoveries such as a diary written by the Hessian captain Johann Ewald, who recorded troop movements and encampments (often on both armies), the Battle of Brandywine is now seen as a struggle of terrain since each army had to cope with an endless series of military obstacles – steep embankments, soft limestone soils, and river gorges, among them.

Other aspects of the terrain have also been re-considered. Earlier historians typically focused on the "Brandywine" of the battle, for instance, but battlefield studies now consider the region's numerous creeks (many of them tributaries of the Brandywine) that played a role in skirmishes and encampments.

Historic structures aka historic resources are also now considered part of the military terrain, especially if they shielded troops in battle. Perhaps the best examples are all found along the Great Road to Nottingham (13). The famous American

7. **Landmarks of the Battlefield.** The present-day "Kuerner's Hill" was identified as "Washington's Hill" on a topographical map created in 1863 by the U.S. Coast Guard.

patrol known as "Maxwell's Men," as well as detachments from the Virginia line, tried to avoid being exposed in open areas and so they sought out shielded posts along the road, west of the Brandywine, including the Old Kennett Meetinghouse (8) and Welch's Tavern (62). 5

During the morning fighting, which began at 6 a.m. and continued for most of the morning, the open and straight stretch of the Nottingham Road determined military tactics. There were no posts at the circa 1725 John Hope House nor its neighbor to the east, the circa 1714 Barns-Brinton House (15), but both armies may have used the structures to shield troops and to dodge artillery. 6

In other parts of the Nottingham Road a stretch of wooded and marshy ground on either side of the road was used by Maxwell's Men to unleash an ambuscade, meaning an ambush from a forest or grove, that took the Crown Forces by surprise in the early morning and left "nearly half of the two corps . . . either killed or wounded," as one Hessian witness observed.

A map issued in 1778 by the London publisher William Faden is particularly useful in understanding the importance the British placed on documenting not only terrain but features that might pose obstacles for an advancing army. For instance, the map was not only published as a detailed survey, it is said to be one of the few maps to provide such field boundaries as hedges, hills, and swaths of woods, drawn as dense collections of individual trees.

Perhaps the most interesting mention of a woodland inhibiting the Crown Forces is summed up in the map's accompanying narrative as *"The 1st British Grenadiers, the Hessian Grenadiers, and the Guards entangled in the woods."*

The letter *"G"* is found southwest of Dilworth (3), identifying an encounter that took place late in the battle at Sandy Hollow (5). Although by that time, the Grenadiers were said to be virtually out of ammunition and had to struggle to drive off the Rebels with bayonets, the map's narrative solely focused on a pivotal moment when British Grenadiers and three battalions of Hessian grenadiers as well as a brigade of Guards were unable to pursue the Continentals due to the dense woods.

Another important source: The journal of Sgt. Thomas Sullivan, a British infantryman who later deserted to the American side. One entry noted that the "rebels" were found in a *"close valley covered in wood,"* an area now believed to be the Ring Run Valley in Pennsbury Township and named for the watershed of the Ring Run, a feeder stream of the Brandywine. In the early hours of the battle, which began around 8:30 a.m., the British were ambushed there by volleys of cannon and continuous gunfire that rained down from a hilltop recently identified as Chadds Peak, a former family-owned ski run that had a vertical drop of 200 to 300 feet.

Today the area can be reached by taking the Old Baltimore Pike (a narrow road of deep embankments resembling its colonial counterpart) off of Baltimore Pike and traveling south on McFadden Road, which now dead ends at 100 McFadden Road, but once led to Chadds Peak near the Ring Run. Here an artillery unit under Maxwell are said to have constructed a large log and earth battery, one that included a breastwork of seized fence rails that snaked across the fields.

As it turned out, the fourth encounter of the morning – sometimes called the Bombardment of the Ring Run Valley –took place near the battery when Ferguson's Rifles and the Queen's Rangers tried to approach the Brandywine and were blocked by Maxwell's troops. After about two hours, the fighting was said to have abruptly ended when the Rangers — an unusual opponent since a majority of the troops were American Loyalists and New York Tories along with Hessian and Highlander detachments—were able to gain the upper-hand by forcing Maxwell's men to abandon the battery and withdraw east across the Brandywine while still under fire.[7]

The engagement is now considered to be an important prelude to the battles at Chadds Ford since Maxwell's men, though defeated in the last fight on this side of the

Brandywine, had managed to delay the Hessian advance by more than two hours, inflicting more than 300 casualties by 10 o'clock in the morning.

The military terrain characterized by such places as Chadds Peake was one reason why it was considered still relevant during the Civil War. In 1863, the region was studied by the U.S. Coast Guard and a contoured map was created that introduced the defense positions of the Battle of Brandywine based on the idea that the same sites might be of service if there were a northern invasion by the Confederates. 8

Curiously, many of the place names recorded by the British and the Continental Armies are used, but there is no map key or explanation of how they were employed in 1777.

Some of the high elevations surrounding Chadds Ford, for instance, were cited such as Rocky Hill, near Gibson's Ford (17); Chadds Ford Hill, known as Proctor's Hill because it was one of the main Continental redoubts in 1777; and Washington's Hill, now known as Kuerner's Hill overlooking Ring Road (7,68). 9 Similar landmarks are found throughout this book, and those that have vanished can perhaps be re-imagined through the accounts of 1777.

Historic Markers

Today one cannot travel through Birmingham Township and other areas of the Brandywine Valley without seeing a historic marker commemorating the battle. The earliest date to 1910 (46) while the first to be funded privately was placed near Trimble's Ford (59) in 2016. 10

More signs are planned by the Task Force, which launched its educational program –The Brandywine Battlefield Interpretive Signage Program –a few years ago with the help of a challenge grant of $45,000 from the Pennsylvania Society of Sons of the Revolution and its Color Guard. The sixth of 15 proposed signs were unveiled in 2021 at the Church of the Loving Shepherd on New Street, the crossing site for the British Left Flank when the center of the action was at Birmingham Meeting. 11

The Task Force calls the signage the first step in implementing its educational and interpretive plan, which will be augmented by a series of "Heritage Centers" (many of them kiosks) as well as signs marking the core boundaries of the Brandywine Battle. The latter is comprised of dark blue signs that announce you are "entering" a National Historic Landmark (NHL), or the 10-square-mile area of the Brandywine NHL.

The Task Force's interpretive plan is especially needed in and around Chadds Ford and Birmingham. According to Michael C. Harris, nearly half of the original 1900-era markers are now missing, with the greatest losses occurring along four important roads: The Great Road to Nottingham (Baltimore Pike) (22) and three roads designated as "Scenic Byways" in 2005: Birmingham, Meetinghouse, and Wylie Roads.

The Nottingham Road markers that went missing were especially important to understanding the string of engagements that occurred in the early morning of Sept. 11th, as the Hessians advanced towards Chadds Ford. The former markers included one that stood just east of Kennett Square (51) near the intersection of Schoolhouse Road; a marker near the Chadds Ford Elementary School honoring the American Light Infantry; and a nearby marker at the Rt. 1 bridge over the Brandywine; and marker near the Harvey Run marking the place where Gen. Wayne's troops were attacked in the late afternoon. 12 It is believed that all these markers were erected in 1952 by the Pennsylvania Historical and Museum Commission (PHMC).

Battlefield Observers & Recorders

Some of the officers who could be described as professional recorders have helped the Task Force document what is described as military terrain. On the British side, they range from the Hessian *Jäger* captain Johann Ewald, who lost an eye in a duel but nonetheless was an astute observer of the region's geography and topography, to the 23-year-old Captain Friedrich von Muenchhausen, who was appointed Howe's aide-de-camp after it was discovered that very few British officers including Howe spoke German.

Although Lt. Col. Alexander Hamilton saw action before and after the Battle of Brandywine, his chief assets as Washington's senior aide were his fluency in French and communication skills in interpreting the flurry of dispatches that were delivered to Washington's Headquarters (16) throughout the day of the battle.

As a recorder, Hamilton was often blunt and opinionated but nonetheless he kept Washington informed. Almost from the moment the British arrived by ship at the Head of the Elk (Elkton, Maryland), for instance, Hamilton wrote about Howe's slovenly movements and the devastating loss of some 400 horses at sea. He even found fault with the landscape of New Castle County, Delaware, which he deemed too flat for a Seat of War. 13

Washington's adjunct general, Timothy Pickering, was another observer who noted that the Continental Army's failures in New Jersey in the spring of 1777 was the result of the army's lack of a good spy network and skilled advance troops who could expose the enemy's plans.

It would help to know the terrain, but Pickering, who penned a manual for the colonial militia in 1776 titled, *An Easy Plan of Discipline for the Militia*, felt the first

8. Maxwell's Post. This c. 1713 Quaker meeting became "Old Kennett Meeting," after another meetinghouse was built in nearby Kennett Square. It's now the oldest extant Friends meetinghouse in the Brandywine Valley, with additions made in 1719 and 1731.

9. The Brandywine Road: No postcard or image was ever issued of the Great Valley Road – the route of the British flanking troops – but images of the Brandywine Road such as this one depicting the road near Trimbleville suggest its likely meandering course. *Both photos Author's collection.*

10. The Northmost Post: Buffington's Ford, aka Brandywine Junction and The Forks of the Brandywine, was named after a colonial family who were so prominent, Benjamin Franklin featured the family's reunion in 1739 in his newspaper, *The Pennsylvania Gazette*. It was the furthest crossing on the Brandywine protected by Continental troops. Wistar's Ford (Lenape) was right below it. Both fords were guarded without incident by Gen. Moses Hazen's 2nd Canadian Regiment, part of Sullivan's Division. *Author's collection*

order of business was training the troops, which of course, wasn't fulfilled until the Valley Forge encampment. There are also accounts from ordinary foot soldiers such as John Nagle who, at 13, was one of the youngest members of Washington's multicultural army.

As a member of Proctor's artillery at Chadds Ford, Nagle typically wrote his observations from his hilltop view of the action along the Brandywine. In many entries, Nagle writes of the ford crossing in a visual way. His spelling and grammar intact, one diary passage reads, "A cross the road on the left was a buckwheat field opposit [sic] to a wood and the Brandewine between them."

From his high location, Nagle had a bird's eye view of the field and a nearby woods where Hessians and Maxwell's riflemen unexpectedly clashed. In his words "The Hessions [sic] and Morgans [sic] riflemen being both in this wood." Tall stands of buckwheat were in bloom and shielded a lone soldier, Nagle writes, noting that "I took notice of one in a white frock laying on his back [with one leg crossed] to lead his gun."

The Crown Forces were famously devoted to maps and local guides, especially

11. Wistar's: The former ford is best identified today by the seven-arch stone bridge at "Lenape."

It was built in 1912 using stone from the razed Bower's paper mill. *Author's collection.*

those who could be trusted to know the best routes through a region fraught with roller-coaster hills and wooded areas of dense vegetation. The British map now called the Windsor map – it was discovered by Thomas McGuire in the royal archives of Windsor Castle – is still in use today by the Task Force.

In contrast to period maps drawn from memory or copied from dated sources, the Windsor map was created on the spot by Capt. Archibald Robertson, the chief Royal engineer. He had five days to complete his job because that was the length of time Gen. Howe rested his troops after the battle.

Many historians, as well as the Task Force, consider the Windsor map to be the most detailed, large-scale survey than any other extant map of the Battle of Brandywine. The map's graphics included certain field boundaries such as hedges and rail fencing as well as natural obstacles such as the wetlands Howe called the "swampy morass." (40)

The completed map, which cannot be published in its original form today, was accompanied by a corresponding narrative peppered with alphabet letters to indicate important battlefield sites or features. For instance, lowercase letters denoted the Knyphausens' positions in Chadds Ford, especially along the Nottingham Road (22), and uppercase letters were used to document the action of the Royal Forces at Birmingham Meeting and Sandy Hollow.

While the "Enemy's" actions are recorded in the narrative, their positions are understandably cited only in relation to that of the Royal Forces. For instance, it's easy to discern the British columns at Birmingham Hill; they are labeled in large caps "*D*" and "*E*," but the Americans' position is only suggested with the sentence, "Attack of the Guards and Hessian Grenadiers who forced the Enemy on the

12. The Route of the "Flanking Party": This 1899 image by Douglas E. Brinton is described as the road to Jefferis' Ford. The building at the right is believed to be the 1714/1760 homestead of Emmor Jefferis,
Courtesy of CCHC

first onset."

Robertson was understandably biased in labeling areas where the "Rebels" were defeated, but his impressive narrative nonetheless underscores the British officer's understanding of the battlefield terrain that offered opportunities to see and displace the American troops. For instance, Robertson writes in the map's narrative that after "advancing to the high Ground mark'd A [Osborne's Hill] in the Plan, the Enemy were observed at Birmingham Meeting...."

The section of the map and narrative detailing Knyphausen troops' movements specifically cite the Americans' positions including the Continental batteries but that is may be because Robertson wanted to indicate that enemy was prepared for battle. A single narrative line sums up the morning action along the Nottingham Road (labeled "g"), but it takes a knowledge of present-day research to interpret why Robertson would consider the road filled with "Defiles," or narrow passages between hills or steep embankments. (24)

The day before, Maxwell's Men posted at areas that had relatively high elevations (since then long removed) such as Welch's Tavern and Kennett Meeting.

Indeed, Robertson seems to have recorded an entire stretch of defiles along the Nottingham Road. 14 The narrative reads: *"Knyphausen in a march at g in the morning, his Van having drove back the Rebel Detachments, which attempted to defend the Defiles from Welch's Tavern to the Heights of Chadsford."*

The British Left Hook

Historians over the decades have examined the infamous flanking maneuver known as "British Left Hook" as the key to the British victory – and the obligatory part of any narrative about the Battle of Brandywine. Marching at least 14 miles out of their way on a 9 to 10 hour trek through rugged countryside, the Crown Forces made a large loop above Washington's troops at Chadds Ford, crossing the Brandywine at two fords before they were spotted.

The authors of *The History of Chester County* (1881), J. Smith Futhey & Gilbert Cope, simplify the tactic as a "circuitous route, traversing portions of the townships of Kennet [sic], East Marlborough, Newlin, West Bradford, East Bradford, and Birmingham." The author W. Barksdale Maynard calls it "one of the more ingenious flanking maneuvers in military history" in part because the British were able to trick the Americans into believing they faced the entire Royal Forces at Chadds Ford.

Among the mistakes made: Washington did not investigate the claim made by only one local farmer who insisted that the Upper Fords, or those above "the Forks" (10,11) of the East and West Branches of the Brandywine (about twelve miles above Chadds Ford) were inaccessible due to the terrible condition of the area roads. (12)

In the words of the farmer, never identified, one crossing alone named Trimble's Ford demanded a particularly "long circuit through a very Bad Road (9)." The statement reportedly convinced Washington that he should place men along the middle and lower Brandywine near Chadds Ford to protect only those fordable points reached by good roads.

As a result, on Sept. 11th, Washington not only didn't anticipate Howe's two-pronged attack – the rarely advised splitting of one's entire army – there were just too many crossing points to adequately defend. Ironically, the two fords that were presumably unknown to Washington – Trimble's Ford and Jeffries' Ford – were both relatively shallow crossing areas, unmanned by any appointed gatekeeper or ferryman.

At one point after the battle, Washington's chief consultant, American Brig. Mj.Gen. John Sullivan, was given the hopeless task of explaining to Congress how the surprise attack occurred. Speaking of the Upper Fords, Sullivan recalled that he inquired of "his Excellency [Washington] whether there were no Fords still higher up," but was given no answer.

Placing the blame on Washington, he added that he "had no Orders, or even Hints to look at any other places, but those mentioned…."

The American officer Timothy Pickering seemed to concede with Sullivan when he wrote in his diary that he had learned "two or three important lessons" after enduring the Battle of Brandywine. The first was to "reconnoitre throughly" or as he described it, "before the battle of Brandywine we had time to have viewed all the ground several miles on our right but did not do it."

Pickering mentioned the lack of "correct" maps and detailed the third lesson as "you should have guides perfectly acquainted with every road. These men should be timely procured beforehand, and not be sought for just at the critical moment when you want them."

Curiously, flanking maneuvers seems to have been Howe's preferred military tactic, and yet Washington failed again and again to anticipate them. His army was flanked during the New York Campaign (Aug. 26 & 27, 1777) and at the Red Clay Creek (Sept. 9, 1777) and along the Schuylkill River (Sept. 22, 1777).

Still, nothing came close to the Left Hook at the Brandywine in terms of scale and scope. It is one reason the Battle of Brandywine has been called the turning point of the American Revolution since it led to the realization that the British could never be defeated until the Continental Army received proper training – and that only happened at Valley Forge.

The Crossing. A c. 1938 view taken from the same perspective as photo 13.
Photo courtesy of the Christian C. Sanderson Museum, Chadds Ford, PA © 2022

The Untold Story of Its History and Preservation |35

13. The Old Covered Bridge: This colored 1915 postcard depicts the 1860 covered bridge along Baltimore Pike (looking south) and the railroad tracks of the old Reading Railroad line that ran past the present-day Chadds Ford Elementary School. The bridge was used as marker to locate the former Chads' Ford just north of it.
From the Thomas C. Marshall collection at the Hagley Museum and Library.

Chads' Ferry vs. Chads' Ford

To identify the two crossings known as Chads' Ferry (1) and Chads' Ford (13) – both named for the ferryman John Chads – generations of historians have cited a bridge over the Brandywine on the Nottingham Road (Baltimore Pike). The bridge, though it changed location over the years, served as a marker for the crossing. In recent years, the Task Force has worked with the Delaware archaeologist Wade P. Catts to confirm the historic locations of both crossings.

In the early 1700s, Chads' Ferry was one of the few crossings on the Brandywine where deep waters required a ferry or small wooden raft, guided by an operator who pulled the vessel along with a rope slung between the two riverbanks. John Chads for the first to establish the ferry when he obtained his license in 1736, seven years after his marriage to Elizabeth Richardson. He obtained a tavern license the same year.

Surprisingly, the ferry service continued for more than 90 years; it was owned by Chads but others ran it beginning in the early 1740s, including his neighbors, Ben jamin Ring (16) and Gideon Gilpin (29).

Chads relinquished ownership of both the ferry and tavern in 1746, fourteen years before his death, to his cousin-in-law James House, father of Amos House (introduced later in this book).15

The ferry crossing can be visualized today by standing at the rear of the Brandywine River Museum and looking south, beyond the current railroad trestle bridge. (23) Other than this trestle marker, it is difficult to envision the crossing though it is now described as being located just above the mouth of the Harvey Run and north of a bend in the Brandywine. In addition to the ferry, the former Starvegut Road (21) and much of the surrounding area used by the Hessians to advance to the Brandywine, were completely obliterated by the construction of a railroad in the late 1800s (23).

Historians in the 1900s described the crossing known as Chads' Ford or Chads' Crossing as being located about 300 feet north of the bridge that crossed Baltimore Pike at the time. On the British maps, the crossing is shown to be directly on the Nottingham Road. By the 19th century, however, none of the bridges crossed at the ford. Two bridges—an open wooden structure built in 1829 and a covered bridge built in 1860— occupied the same site. But when the covered bridge was demolished in 1921 (13) and replaced with a two-span concrete arch bridge (14), it was located slightly upstream or closer to the ford.

The road had also changed considerably from its former colonial one. Four years before the concrete bridge was built, a new concrete "highway" (24) was laid so that it ran into the bridge where the road now known as the Fairview Road curved to follow the Brandywine and then traveled across what is now a parking lot of the Brandywine River Museum. The approach changed again in 1938 (19) when the road was widened to three lanes and the 1921 bridge (14) was replaced with new open span steel and concrete bridge (25), which was located even further north.

In the 1920s, travelers reportedly could travel down from the Nottingham Road on a foot path that lead to a small approach bridge that crossed the mill race for Hoffman's Mill (now the Brandywine River Museum) (23). One can imagine that historians such as Christian "Chris" Carmack Sanderson (38) frequented the approach bridge to get a better view of the former ferry.

Judging from accounts at the time, the historic location of Chads' Ford held little interest, perhaps because there were many former fords on the Brandywine, and only one ferry crossing – Chads' Ferry – in all of the region. As mentioned previously, the ford crossing, described by MacElree as being 300 feet north of the 1860 covered bridge, was near a dam (14) and was surrounded by wetlands that grew during "times of freshets." The same was no doubt true in colonial times, and so it was easier to

14. The Chadds Ford Dam: The author MacElree wrote about the dam and the marshy areas near the ford.

The Bridge at the Ford (right): This photograph (looking north) may have been taken to illustrate the location of the 1921 two-span concrete arch bridge prior to its partial demolishment in 1938.

Note the construction crane on the other side of the bridge, as well as the c. 1890 Darlington's Creamery, now Taylor's service station. *Courtesy of CFHS*

take the ferry across the Brandywine. Curiously that didn't seem to be a consideration in 1777, since one of the best equipped batteries – later called "Proctor's Hill" – was established on a hill northwest of the present-day Christian C. Sanderson Museum in order to protect Chads' Ford. 16 Along the road, close to the ford, Washington's troops placed a barricade of felled trees.

Downstream, the ferry crossing was supported by Greene's troops and a four-gun battery. The site was not as heavily fortified as Proctor's Hill, which is believed to have had additional support from artillery near the c. 1725 John Chads' House (18).

The ferry crossing was also shielded by steep hills and the dense forest on the west side of the Brandywine – just one reason why General Knyphausen planned to cross there. But the main reason was that his troops could take the Starvegut Road directly to the ferry, avoiding what was described as the "morass" or wetlands, and the "causeway-like" Nottingham Road (22, 40).

Unfortunately, too, for Washington's troops, it was assumed that Chads' Ford would be the main crossing and so the Ferry and Lower Fords were manned with either inexperienced troops, or troops assigned to a broad area. In the words of McGuire, five hundred yards northeast of the ferry crossing, "the two Pennsylvanian brigades of Wayne's Division, nine regiments totaling about 2,000 men, were spread thin in one battle line, with high hills on both flanks."

Today it is difficult to trace the Chads' Ferry (21)crossing or to determine the exact placement of the Hessians on the hillsides above the Brandywine since the area is no longer accessible by any road. However, both the ford and ferry have been re-examined in recent years to understand Knyphausen's motives.

The general is believed to have focused his diversionary tactics at Chads' Ferry since there were steep wooded hillsides that made it easier to embed his troops and to trick Washington into thinking he was opposing Howe's entire army.

Historians have pointed out that Washington's army outnumbered Knyphausen's division two to one, and thus the Hessian general did not want to risk a total confrontation. Instead, Harris writes that Howe "marched his various units one way and then back again, using the hills and swales to show them or hide them as he saw fit, all in an effort to artificially swell his numbers." In Howe's words, the idea was to "amuse" the enemy with cannon and false fording crossings "until the attack upon the enemy's right should take place."

Situated primarily in the hills west of Chads' Ferry, Knyphausen's frontal division positioned the artillery to fire on the American positions across the Brandywine. The artillery fire was most severe just after 12 noon when Washington briefly attacked Knyphausen's flank. After an afternoon lull, the long-range artillery fire resumed at 4:00 p.m., when troops on both sides heard that the attack had begun at Birmingham Hill. By then, Harris writes, most of the American gunners in Proctor's batteries had "either withdrawn out of harm's way or were desperately attempting to save the guns."

Paradoxically, it was not the Ferry crossing but Chads' Ford (13) that became the site of the most violent action. Beginning as early as 9 a.m., there was a near constant "Cannonade on both sides," as the British Major General James Grant put it. Then suddenly, a little after four in the afternoon, it ended as the Continentals were directed north to Birmingham. "Presently a total silence ensued," Lt-Col. Francis Downman of the Royal Horse Artillery recalled, "General Knyphausen ordered us to leave off."

A Study of "Firsts": A Historical Perspective

In addition to the British Left Hook, the Battle of Brandywine broke new groundwork in the number of "firsts" that occurred. McGuire calls it a case study in "strategy, generalship, and lost opportunities." There are also several military milestones . The battle is now seen as the first – and possibly the last – to fully engage a new type of breech-loading, rapid-firing rifle named for its inventor, Patrick Ferguson.

A captain who led the Queen's Rangers in the early morning skirmishes, Ferguson became part of community lore when he was described as the man who nearly shot General Washington and then, moments later, was wounded in his shooting arm.

Ferguson recovered, but it was said that neither he nor his rifle corps saw much action until late in the war. In fact, the Ferguson rifle may have been used only one time again, in the Siege of Charleston in the spring of 1780. That fall Ferguson was killed while leading a group of Loyalists on King's Mountain in South Carolina.

The Battle of Brandywine has been called the first major artillery battle to take place on American soil. That claim partly rests on recent studies that document the action along the Great Road to Nottingham. The road is no longer thought to be the place where a series of isolated skirmishes took place before the main clash in Chadds Ford. Instead, historians now promote the road as being the scene of a running battle that included nearly continuous artillery fire, long-range cannon duels, and storms of exploding shells or canister shot. 17

Another new outlook: Washington was taken by surprise by the British Left Hook, (12) but that didn't mean he had no pre-battle strategy. Recent research has shown that Washington carefully chose the location of the American batteries as early as August 1777. The placement and construction of these batteries – built solidly of fence posts or earthworks made of packed dirt and logs to absorb British cannon fire – is one reason why some historians say that that the Battle of Brandywine saw the first major use of established defense lines.

The white flag of surrender had been used for centuries, but it was especially needed at the Battle of Brandywine, which involved a surprisingly number of inexperienced troops and placed even top American commanders at risk.

Lastly, a "first" that has never been fully documented: The Battle of Brandywine may be the best historic example of the ups and downs of battlefield preservation. Indeed, compared to Gettysburg, which captured the attention of preservationists even before the Civil War was over, the amount of preserved acreage and signage in the Brandywine Valley seems almost negligible. Gettysburg is now a 3,965-acre national park and preserves a battlefield that had at least five times more soldiers than the Battle of Brandywine.

That transpired to generations of relatives who personally cared about memorializing the battles of the Civil War. The historian W. Barksdale Maynard suspects that the disparity between the preservation efforts of the Brandywine battlefield and

Gettysburg has more to do with the fact that the Americans lost the Battle of Brandywine and "defeats rarely get commemorated."

An Endangered Battlefield

Perhaps complicating the history of battlefield protection is the long route it took to get to the present-day state of the "front line." The Task Force was organized in 1993 for the purpose of researching and documenting a 10-square-mile area that officially became the Brandywine Battlefield National Historic Landmark on January 20, 1961, but was not thoroughly examined until the late 1980s.

As of this writing, there are more than two thousand National Historic Landmarks (NHL), 126 of which are in Pennsylvania. In the 1960s, the program was only beginning to take shape, and after the National Register of Historic Places program was established in 1966, historic landmarks were automatically put on the NHL list as well. As a result, the Brandywine Landmark – centered in Birmingham, Thornbury, Chadds Ford, and Pennsbury Townships – was the first to be protected by both federal programs.

Unfortunately, it was a designation that was largely forgotten for more than twenty years – perhaps because the Landmark's boundaries were not actually confirmed until 1977 (and then re-considered in 2010). A clerical error also caused unusual delays in getting recognition for the Landmark. Until it was corrected in the early 1980s, anyone looking for the Landmark in the National Register of Historic Places saw only a description of the Battlefield State Park, not the federal landmark designation.

Ironically, the Brandywine Battlefield saw the most development in the decades after it was designated a NHL, from 1961 to 1981. Those years also saw rapid growth for most of southeastern Pennsylvania and other areas on the East Coast. According to a recent survey by the National Parks Service, more than 100 nationally significant sites related to the American Revolution and the War of 1812 are now gone, and an additional 245 are fragmented by development and 222 sites are deemed "at risk" because they are in the path of development or in areas that are expected to see explosive growth in the next decade.

Today the Brandywine battlefield remains the only Revolutionary War battlefield designated as a NHL landmark – most are protected as state and federal parks—but the area of concern has also been expanded. The benchmark study of 1989, for instance, focused solely on what is called the "core" battlefield site of 6,400 acres, or 10 square miles. Despite the 1989 study's published findings, three housing developments were built in the area of study. Those closest to Sandy Hollow (5) and Birmingham Meetinghouse (47) were given names that played a kind of tribute to the battle, such as "Revolutionary Farms" and "Fieldpoint."

A 1991 *Philadelphia Inquirer* story headlined "Battling Development at War Site" cited Radley Run, a 300-house development that began in 1965, as the region's first residential subdivision. Mainly because it was built in the path of the infamous British Left Hook, (12) and set the stage for subsequent housing developments that took up large swaths of land, the development was later dubbed "Radley Ruin" by preservationists and history buffs.

Photographed by Keith S. Smith of CFHS, 2011

On the positive side, Radley Run led to the realization that very few homeowners knew that they were living in the middle of a National Historic Landmark, and the Task Force worked to include an educational component to its projects.

Meanwhile preservationists began to think of new ways to preserve the landscape. In the mid-1990s that included using newly available federal funding.

Thanks to the American Battlefield Protection Act, passed by Congress in 1996, the National Parks Service now has the authority to issue preservation grants through the American Battlefield Protection Program (ABPP).

The grants have helped support research projects such as a 2007 study that examined the condition of 243 battlefields significant to the American Revolution and the War of 1812. Of these, only 100 sites in 2007 retained a "historic integrity" or enough open space to visualize troop engagement. The Brandywine battlefield was identified as one of only four intact – but largely unprotected – regions known as "battlefield landscapes," earning it a "Class A /Priority 1" category.

The Patriot Act of 1999 was another preservation victory since it led to the protection of a 290-acre swath where the British formed a half-mile-wide column along Meetinghouse Road in Birmingham Township. The battlefield land is now called the Meetinghouse Road Corridor and was protected with the help of government officials and landowners working with the Brandywine Conservancy in Chadds Ford and what is now the Natural Lands. The two organizations were named beneficiaries and overseers of $3 million in ABPP funds.

By 2007, the Conservancy and its partners had raised more than $16 million in public and private funds to acquire additional properties and/or place conservation easements with landowners, resulting in the permanent protection of 485 acres along the Corridor. In 2018, the last remaining key property was obtained (a 13-acre parcel

An Artist Paints. Noted artist Barclay Rubincan painted the c. 1714 Barnes-Brinton house in 1976. *Courtesy of Chester County History Center (CCHC).*

15. The Old Tavern. Commissioned by the Chester County Historical Society (now the History Center), photographer Ned Goode took this photo of the front façade of the Barns-Brinton House in 1959. In 1961, it became the subject of a painting, "Tenant Farmer" by Andrew Wyeth. *Courtesy of Library of Congress.*

Artistic License. The title of Rubincan's painting "Hessians Marching Past the Barns-Brinton House at the Battle of Brandywine" suggests that the battle took place further down the road. Today historians believe that the tavern was not merely passed by but witnessed the beginning actions of the Battle of Brandywine. *Courtesy of the CFHS*.

15. On The Great Road. This circa 1905 photo of Barns-Brinton House shows the unpaved Nottingham Road and the tavern's decorative brickwork. In 1938, the road was relocated to the north (back) side of the house. James Brinton was the property owner when hundreds of Hessian and British troops advanced to the Brandywine. *CFHS*.

44 | The Brandywine Battlefield:

Washington's Headquarters, Battle of Brandywine, September 11, 1777, near Chadd's Ford, Pa
(Destroyed by Fire, September, 1931)

16. A Perennial Favorite: This c. 1909 image was re-issued after Washington's former headquarters burned down. Hence, the postcard's caption. Note the house in relation to the road. The present-day Baltimore Pike lies much lower, making the front yard a steeper incline.

Courtesy of CFHS

16. A Restored Landmark: This c. 1950 photograph shows the recently restored Washington's Headquarters. The surrounding 50-acre Brandywine Battlefield Park was created in 1948.

Courtesy of CFHS

17. **Below Gibson's Ford.** This c. 1910 photo looks towards the historic George A. "Frolic" Weymouth estate, "The Big Bend," named for its location on the Brandywine. The ford is out of view to the right of Locust Knoll Farm. On the day of the battle, this region was guarded by 2000 of Gen. James Potter's Pennsylvania Militia. The troops' defense line extended from today's Bullock Road to Rocky Hill Road. *Photo courtesy of CFHS.*

18. The Ferryman's House: This undated photo shows the C. 1725 John Chads' House as it looked when it was a tenant farmstead, with open fields and a slight incline, where one can imagine Gen. Washington reviewed his troops. *Photo courtesy of the Christian C. Sanderson Museum, Chadds Ford, PA © 2022*

Right: Along Creek Road. An undated photo of the John Chads' House looking toward Nottingham Road. This embankment has been changed and the house now features a restored beehive oven on the wall closest to the road. The building was restored soon after the Chadds Ford Historical Society was founded in 1968.
Courtesy of CFHS.

48| The Brandywine Battlefield:

19. From A Single Lane. This 1938 view of the Baltimore Pike looking east shows the c. 1781 "Pyle Barn," one of the few structures that was moved instead of razed during the 1936-1938 state road improvement program. The Pyle family (not related to famous illustrator Howard Pyle) lived across the highway in a homestead that may have served as Gen. Greene's headquarters. They were said to have insisted that the state highway commission move the barn to its current location. *Courtesy of CFHS*

21. Above Chads' Ferry: This 1960s view of Chadds Ford depicts Hillendale/Fairville Road and the railroad trestle bridge that serves today to envision the former Starvegut Road and Chads' Ferry that crossed just north of the bend in the Brandywine. *Courtesy of CFHS*

The Untold Story of Its History and Preservation | 49

19. Building a State Highway. This undated photo depicts the state's widening project on an unidentified section of Baltimore Pike. The road-widening project radically changed many of the properties and villages along what was once the Great Road to Nottingham.

Courtesy of CCHC.

22. The Nottingham Road (below): a 1900s view of the same road looking towards Chadds Ford.

THE VILLAGE OF CHADD'S FORD FROM THE ROAD TO KENNETT.

50 | The Brandywine Battlefield:

23. Chadds Ford Junction: This 1925 view recalls Wilmer MacElree's quote that much of the battlefield landscape was being altered by "dam, bridge, and railroad embankments." The junction, once marked by a tower (shown here north of a collection of buildings still standing today) was the meeting point of two different railroad lines. **Below: The Railroad Trestle Bridge**: This c. 1920 view shows a distance view of Hoffman's Mill (see insert) hidden on the left behind the trees. The next stop was the Chadd Ford Station, which once stood at the end of the present-day Station Way. *Both courtesy of CFHS.*

24. The Concrete Highway: An unidentified stretch of Baltimore Pike after the road was paved with concrete during the 1917-`18 state road improvement project. Courtesy of CCHC.
Below: An undated view of Chadds Ford Junction Station. *Courtesy of CFHS*.

24. **Steep Embankments:** This house (right) still stands across from the Chadds Ford Elementary School along the Baltimore Pike. The photo captures the 1938 widening of the road from two lanes to three and the leveling of steep embankments. It is included here to provide a visual explanation in understanding why the British complained of the road's series of "defiles" that cut through the hills. *Courtesy of CFHS.*

25. Inspecting the Damage: Chris Sanderson donned his raincoat and waders in this undated photo when a flood interrupted the construction of the open span steel and concrete bridge at Chadds Ford. *Photo courtesy of the Christian C. Sanderson Museum, Chadds Ford, PA © 2022*

Top left: Another undated view of the same flood damage. *Courtesy of CFHS.*

54 | The Brandywine Battlefield:

Chadd's Ford Inn (side view). "BRANDYWINE BATTLEFIELD" SEPT. 11, 1777. Chadd's Ford, Pa.

26. A Stop on The Battlefield: This 1930 postcard advertised the Chadds Ford Inn in connection to the battlefield.

Stationary from 1915 when the place operated as the Chadds Ford Hotel. The hotel proprietor wrote to Chris Sanderson to inform him that he had "taken the liberty" to arrange a drag fox hunt beginning at Sanderson's home, then Washington's Headquarters. *Courtesy of CFHS.*

27. A Motorist Landmark:
The restaurant, Dario's, (right) was a tourists' mecca when this photo was taken in 1950. Built on the site of a pre-Revolutionary War home, it is now the Gables restaurant. The caption placed on this postcard is correct: Knyhausen's troops posted to the west of the American line, extending in a vertical formation across Nottingham Road to the crossroads here at Brinton Bridge Road. *CFHS.*

The Battlefield Tea Room: This c. 1928 photo of Baldwin's Store includes a sign advertising the "Battlefield Tea Room." The second line, "This is Chadds Ford," suggests that passing motorists might not immediately realize that they were at the site of a historic battleground. The tea room, along with a community meeting hall, were added after the building (which housed the Chadds Ford post office) was rebuilt after a major fire in 1915. *Photo courtesy of the Christian C. Sanderson Museum, Chadds Ford, PA © 2022*

56 | The Brandywine Battlefield:

The "Ham": Chris Sanderson is shown in his costume in 1937, when he played the part of Rip Van Winkle at Longwood's open air theatre. The shop's barber, Pete Zimmerman, seems to pretend for the camera to cut Rip's hair. *Photo courtesy of the Christian C. Sanderson Museum, Chadds Ford, PA © 2022*

28. **A Close Shave:** Right, another 1930s view of the sign N.C. Wyeth created for the Chadds Ford Barber Shop, which once stood next door to the Ceresota sales barn. The sign reads: "This is the place where Washington & Lafayette had a very close shave." The sign, now displayed at the Christian Sanderson Museum, suggests that the community could easily get the word play, given Chadds Ford's importance in the Battle of Brandywine. *Courtesy of CFHS*

The Continental Soldier Sign: This c.1930 shows the former Ceresota Sales Barn along Baltimore Pike. Farmers who came to the barn for livestock sales were greeted by a sign that served as a reminder that the village was a former battlefield. *Photo courtesy of the Christian C. Sanderson Museum, Chadds Ford, PA © 2022*

58| The Brandywine Battlefield:

29. **Lafayette Farm:** In Brinton's photography series of 1899, he cites this homestead as Lafayette's Headquarters. *Courtesy of CCHC.*

Above right: None of the postcards depicting Lafayette Farm in the 1900s mention Gideon Gilpin, the owner in 1777 who forced to open a tavern to reclaim his financial losses (more than 500 pounds) after the war. Curiously, the property's most famous landmark — the ancient American Sycamore tree — is just out of view to the left of the homestead.

Below right: The photographer Ned Goode may have taken this shot for a 1958 Historic American Buildings Survey (HABS) complied by Bart Anderson of the Chester County Historical Society (now the Chester County History Center). In the survey, he estimated that the stone section of the house dated to 1695. He described the addition as a rare example of an English-style frame house covered with clapboards typically found in homes of the late 1600s.

Both Courtesy of CFHS.

Gen. Lafayette's Headquarters, Battle of Brandywine, Sept. 11, 1777

owned by the Odell estate), ending the Conservancy's 25-year effort to preserve more than 500 contiguous acres in the Corridor.

As many Task Force members see it, protection of the Meetinghouse Road Corridor marked a significant and a far-reaching acknowledgment of the battlefield land. Previously, it had been up to the individual townships to follow through in protecting land and historic sites. For instance, the grounds considered to be part of Sandy Hollow (5) – some say it was the bloodiest battlefield of that September day – were acquired by Birmingham Township in 1994 as a trade-off for approving what was then a Toll Brothers subdivision.

That same year a group called Preservation Pennsylvania listed the Brandywine Battlefield as an "at-risk site," and it was designated as the first Pennsylvania Commonwealth Treasure. The designation was soon followed by the first ABPP-funded study of the battlefield, and the creation of the 42-acre Sandy Hollow Heritage Park in 2002.

In a 2012 congressional hearing, David Hackett Fischer, the Pulitzer Prize-winning historian and author, described the endangered battlefields as mostly located on "open land in suburban or exurban areas" outside of cities and large towns. 18 It is a description that fits the landscape of the Brandywine battlefield, which Fischer specifically mentioned at the hearing along with three threatened sites in New Jersey ranging from lands where Washington crossed the Delaware River on Christmas night, 1776, to the battlefields at Trenton and Princeton.

The preservation of the New Jersey battlefield sites continues to be challenged as of this writing, but major preservation efforts in the Brandywine Valley have been successful.

One battlefield landscape that matches Fischer's "exurban" description was saved from development: the Dilworth Farm at 1370 Birmingham Road. The 10-acre property is adjacent to the Dilworthtown (3) (added to the National Register in 1973). The property is not far from the commercial Route 202 corridor but it was never protected until 2017, the year of the 240th anniversary celebrations of the Battle of Brandywine.

The property was willed through the James Dilworth family beginning in 1769 and remained in the family for generations. Sadly, the Dilworth farmhouse was razed a few years before the Task Force received ABPP funding to acquire the property. The original barn still stands and overlooks a landscape that saw the closing action, when Greene's Rear Guard Defense made its retreat from Sandy Hollow (5) to the colonial seat of Chester.

From a preservationist standpoint, the acquisition of the Dilworth Farm marked the first time the Task Force was able to use ABPP's program called the Battlefield Land Acquisition Grant, which was funded through the federal land and water conservation funds. It was the first American Revolutionary War battlefield protected in this way in Pennsylvania. The ABPP grant was supplemented by grants from Chester County and was matched by private donations from the Civil War Trust's Campaign of 1776. [19]

In 2018, a similar process occurred with the help of the Natural Lands Trust: a nearby 88-acre tract, part of the privately owned Osborne Hill Farm, was preserved (2). [20] Early 20th-century driving tours tended to downplay the significance of the farm, located just north of Birmingham Meeting, describing it merely as a place where the British stopped for tea on the northwestern upper slope of the farm, known in 1777 as "Osborne's Hill (2)." However, it is now considered a strategic spot where the British generals directed the action below, at Birmingham Heights, an area described by the historian John Reed as a "natural redoubt made by the heights at Birmingham."

Natural Lands is currently assisting Westtown Township to purchase another key battlefield site – Crebilly Farm, a 309-acre landmark farm owned by the same family since 1937. The preservation group has already achieved their goal of completing 7 percent of its funding through a mix of state and federal grants and private fundraising as of March of 2023. That included state grants from the Department of Conservation and Natural Resources (DCNR).

In order to meet certain grant criteria, Westtown Township is required to raise the remaining 30 percent of the land cost, or up to $7.5 million. To date, the township has received Chester County open space funds totaling $6.35 million.

The land "save" was perhaps the most unusual in Chester County's history of preserving open space, mainly because it was sparked by public outcry, including the formation of two community activist groups, and six years of hearings that ended in 2022 only after the Toll Brothers corporation decided not to develop the property.

Public support continued that fall with a campaign, "Vote Yes to Save Crebilly," resulting in open space fund referendum. Township residents voted overwhelmingly—two votes to one—in favor of saving the Crebilly farm even though the tax levy increased both their earned income and real estate taxes.

Another important preservation project was initiated by the owner of some farmland opposite of the Brinton 1704 House (31) and acquired by the North American Land Trust to become a public space called Brinton Run Preserve. [21] In addition to giving the historic 1704 House a protected viewshed, the Preserve is part of battlefield landscape where the Continental's so-called "Rear Guard Defense" occurred from about 5:30 to 9:00 p.m., according to the Task Force's animated maps.

Robertson's 1777 map also documents this American defense, and although his accompanying narrative is difficult to decipher, it does suggest considerable movement towards Dilworth. It reads that after a group of British light infantry "gained

30. The 150th Anniversary: As this 1927 photo indicates, the anniversary celebration of the Battle of Brandywine featured a Navy blimp overhead. Along with an Army blimp, the airships circled in and out of a cloud-filled sky, according to the *New York Times* and drew crowds that included "representatives from Great Britain and France."

Courtesy of CCHC.

the Hill [Battle Hill]" and "drove the Rebels and took their two Pieces of Cannon," the "Rebels retreated to their right seemingly with an intention to outflank our Left." Judging from Robertson's narrative, the spot marked "N" or the "Hedge N," may have been just south of present-day Webb Road and its intersection with Oakland Road.

It was the place where the Continentals were said to have "retired" before "they again cannonaded the 4th Brigade." Meanwhile the 33rd and 46th British regiments "were ordered to scour the village of Dillworth [sic], and then formed in the field o." At least three fields marked O, P, and Q were in the vicinity of Oakland Road, not far south from the 1704 House.

Another important area near the Brinton Run Preserve – marked *"Woods R"* – may have been what is now called the "Rising Ground" between Oakland Road and the former Wilmington Road (Rt. 202). The Task Force have identified this area – where there's still a slight rise in the landscape – as the place where the Continentals positioned two cannons and fired at British troops approaching Dilworth from Sandy Hollow (5).

Defining The Battlefield

In recent years, the Task Force's orderly study of the battlefield landscape has led historians to reconsider the scope of the battlefield. The Task Force's 2017 publication called the *Military Terrain Analysis* highlighted colonial and British diaries that told of the difficulties of fighting in the flood plains of the Brandywine and marching through the soft ground of the limestone-rich area south of Kennett Square. (51) On September 10th, for instance, several British regiments not only had to make their way north in a downpour at night, but they also had to prevent their cannon and baggage trains from sinking into the mud and soggy soils.

British engineer Capt. John Montrésor evidently tried to recall something positive about the route to Kennett Square, noting that the rugged terrain made it "an amazingly strong country." The beauty of a distant view, though, was different than actually traversing down narrow roads that unexpectedly rose and fell in a hilly landscape. After six miles on foot, Montrésor experienced what he famously noted was a difficult terrain, filled with a "succession of large hills, rather sudden, with narrow vales …in short, an entire defile."

For the Crown Forces, defiles were avoided mainly because they forced the troops to break from a column formation and to march in single file. The Hessian captain Johann Ewald was an acute observer when it came to scoping out terrain obstacles. 22 The march through the White and Red Clay Creeks region of Upper Delaware, for instance, took place along narrow, twisting lanes or "bye" roads bordered by

64 | The Brandywine Battlefield:

31. The Brinton 1704 House: This view of the house along Oakland Road was taken in July, 1958 by Ned Goode. The same architect who restored the Gilpin and Ring homesteads at the Brandywine Battlefield Park, G. Edwin Brumbaugh, restored the 1704 House beginning the following year, from 1954 to '55. *Courtesy of Library of Congress, Historic American Buildings Survey (HABS)*

"precipitous rocks" that formed narrow passes he also called "defiles."

On Sept. 8th, when Ewald led his advance *Jäegers* unit beyond Newark and into the White Clay Creek area, he provided one of the few descriptions of the terrain difficulties including one stretch of the creek that was "surrounded on both sides by steep rocky heights that formed a most frightful defile half an hour in length." Understandably, Ewald writes that such a route made the troops vulnerable to attack, since a "hundred riflemen could have held up the army a whole day and killed many men." His troops also got through without incident, as they would with other defiles they would encounter in the Brandywine Valley.23

The Americans tended to be less observant about their home turf, although a few Pennsylvania officers considered the terrain when setting up advance posts. Col. Walter Stewart of the Pennsylvania State Regiment wrote of the inconclusive skirmishes that took place at the end of August and the beginning of September when the Americans "pushed down" about three thousand of British soldiers from the White Clay Creek Valley to a "post about a mile from them, called Iron Hill" [Newark, Del.]

Writing on September 2nd, Stewart observed "Here the country is, one would imagine, formed by Nature for defense, having a great quantity of woods, large morasses they must pass through, and many commanding hills, which the Malitia [sic] may take post upon."

The Birmingham battlefield site known as Sandy Hollow sounds like the ultimate trap, but no early accounts mention it as terrain feature – legend has it that its

31. Before Restoration. This 1940s view of the same front of the 1704 House indicates the extensive changes the house underwent during its renovation including the removal of 1830s peaked roof. The Brinton family lost ownership of the property in 1860, but they were able to purchase it back in 1947 and subsequently formed the Brinton Family Association to open the site to the public. A 1960 guidebook features the 1704 House, giving the limited hours and 50 cents admission. *Courtesy of CCHC.*

name had more to do with the muted, hollow sounds made by cannon balls landing in a shallow area of what is now Thornbury Farm. Still, even though two geophysical studies conducted on the farm now suggest that at least part of Sandy Hollow may have been located on the farm, the Hollow's traditional location seems to prevail. In fact, it may date to the 1877 Battle Centennial when several artillery pieces were placed at an intersection facing Birmingham Meetinghouse.

One cannon was marked with a bronze label stating that the site was where Lafayette was believed to have been wounded at Sandy Hollow. Perhaps typical of the times, the location was selected by local historians and government officials who had conceded it was the place where the "main battle" took place.

The arrangement of the cannons reportedly replicated the five light field pieces that protected Stirling's and Stephen's divisions, which historian Michael Harris describes as being on an "open knoll in the center of the two divisions about 200 yards south of the road intersection" of Birmingham and Wylie Ter Roads.(34) Harris doesn't identify Sandy Hollow as being part of the knoll, but the spot is just west of Sandy Hollow Heritage Park. The fact that the park is also found on an elevated area only adds to the mystery of the origin of the "Hollow" moniker.

32. Taylor-Cope District: A Northern Chester County physician named J. Max Mueller, who liked to fish in the nearby Brandywine, took this rare winter scene of the Abiah Taylor property, looking towards Creek Road from the Strasburg. It shows the c. 1724 brick homestead, now of the oldest extant brick house in Chester County, as well as the Taylor's c. 1753 English-style barn. *Author's collection.*

Below: Author's photo showing a closer view of the same scene.

The centennial issue of *Lippincott's* magazine evidently followed the description given by the 1877 battlefield committee, who cited both Sandy "Hill" and Sandy Hollow. Still, the writer recommended that the "historic narrative" or "best descriptions of the battle" should be "compared carefully" by interested readers since ultimately the traditional locations will be "found vague and to some degree conflicting." The exception was "Greene's positions."

Recent studies have confirmed that Greene's Rear Guard Defense took place near the 1704 House (31), but it may be understandable that the *Lippincott* writer would associate Greene with Sandy Hollow. These "known" positions were found at the "Second Eminence," or in the *Lippincott* writer's words, marked on a "military map" as the "Second Position." 24

While it's unclear if the writer meant Street Road, he states that the second position was "south of a road" and a "half a mile east of the meeting house, on a hill-slope descending toward the west." The passage is of particular interest because the writer goes on to observe that the second known position was in a steep valley – at least not a knoll or hill – perhaps southeast of Birmingham Road "at a ravine now known as Sandy Hollow."

Despite the celebration in 1877, it seems that the name "Sandy Hollow" wasn't routinely used by the public until after 1915 when a West Chester firm began publishing postcards based on the 16 bronze tablets put up the same year in a far-flung area by the Commonwealth of Pennsylvania.

Legends and 19th-century accounts in many ways helped keep the American Revolution alive in the minds of Brandywine Valley residents. At least, it made it easier for later generations to identity the location of an old tavern or a property touched by the war. That educational course continues today as the Task Force has completed its parcel inventory of 1777 properties and has made the inventory more widely accessible through digital technology and online resources.

One digital atlas identifies resources that are considered outside the battlefield but closely associated with it. In East Bradford, for instance, the c. 1760 homestead of Col. John Hannum, on Frank Road just off Route 322, near the East Branch of the Brandywine, was listed on a study of historic resources in 2010, partly because of Hannum's role in overseeing the patrols at Martin's Tavern (6,61).

Hannum was reportedly with Cheyney when they first spotted the British while riding south from the tavern. Hannum's importance also rests on his actions as a commander of the 1st Battalion of the Chester County Militia. He also among the handful of Chester County residents (including Lieut. Col. Persifor Frazer) who were captured by the British and spent many months imprisoned in Independence Hall. In a strange twist of circumstances, Hannum was held in the same hallowed halls where the colo-

68| The Brandywine Battlefield:

33. **Copes Bridge:** Built in 1807 spanning the East Branch of the Brandywine, this bridge was once one of the most photographed stone bridges in Chester County, despite its location next to an early industrial complex . Below: a view of the Cope's bridge from the other direction. The photographer and historian Gilbert Cope took this photo of his family's namesake in June of 1888. A timber bridge was built seven years before the Battle of Brandywine, but it was still called "Taylor's Ford," an unmanned crossing named for the nearby Taylor family. *Author's collection.*

nists spoke of freedom in the years before the British occupation.

Legend has it that Hannum was seized from his own home, but a 1779 inquiry only stated that he was "made prisoner by the Enemy on their way from Brandiwine to Philadelphia."

The inquiry reported that he escaped the Independence Hall jail after he was transferred to a nearby tavern for health reasons and he "took the opportunity of a dark night of making his escape."

Battle Hill

In one of the Task Force's research studies, a U.S. geological and topographic map helped to clarify what was described as the "Second Eminence" – a ridge that is slightly higher than the Birmingham Meetinghouse grounds. (47) The historian John F. Reed has written that after the Americans retreated from the Meetinghouse, they reformed "on a higher eminence, since known as Battle Hill, a scant half-mile to the rear."

This ridge is likely the place where the second and final American defense line formed. The British officer John Montrésor's description of a "large body" of the "Enemy" no doubt included Stirling's and Stephen's divisions that formed in region now bordered by Thornbury, South New, and Birmingham Roads.

Several accounts, including that of Montrésor, speak of the severe fighting that took place beyond the Meetinghouse, in a region that is believed to be Thornbury Farm (called the Spackman farm in recent studies). The natural *"glacis"* or sloping bank, is cited by Montrésor as follows (the use of parathesis is by researcher Bruce W. Bevan): "This position of the Enemy was remarkably strong, having a large body advanced, smaller bodies still further advanced...their Rear covered by wood" [while] "their main body was posted (the south edge of the Spackman property) with a natural *glacis* of ¾ of a mile."

Much like Sandy Hollow, the fighting at Battle Hill was brief but intense, lasting fifty-one minutes and nearly decimating the 9th Pennsylvania Regiment, a unit that saw its first major engagement at the Brandywine. The American Major General John Sullivan called it an "almost Muzzle to Muzzle" encounter and quoted the 9th's brigade commander, Gen Thomas Conway, who claimed that he "never saw so close and severe a fire," though he was a veteran of several European wars.

The 2006 study of the Spackman farm cites a similar terrain shown in a 1777 watercolor by the young British ensign, William Augustus West, aka the Viscount Cantelupe, who recorded the scene in his journal soon after the action (his first major battle). The historian McGuire, who discovered the journal in a British collection, calls the illustration the only known contemporary image of the Battle of Brandywine.

Although the title of Cantelupe's watercolor sketch uses a common term for the elevation at Birmingham Meeting (the "heights"), it's likely that the Viscount included Battle Hill or the Second Eminence in *"A Battery of the Rebels opened on Brandywine heights the 11th of September 1777, in the county of Birmingham."*

According to McGuire, the sketch is a remarkable record of specific troop formations such as the "line of redcoats behind a fence along a road" (believed to be modern Street Road) as they "fire a volley up a hill." It is also a reminder that Revolutionary warfare—partly depicted in McGuire's words as "muzzle flashes of three cannons" and a "thick column of smoke" – took place in the midst of a peaceful countryside. "Farm buildings flank the battle line, and Cantaloupe carefully delineated plowed fields, fences, even a haystack," McGuire writes.

Given the fact that both armies needed to cross the landscape of the Thornbury Farm, it's not surprising that many military relics were found there over the decades and that the farm has historically thought to have burial grounds.

Another independent study, completed in 2006, looked for possible mass burial sites on three separate areas of Thornbury Farm, and concluded that at least two areas likely contain "several hundred battle casualties." 25 Noting that "archaeological testing" was primarily limited to one excavated pit and the rest to ground-penetrating radar, two of the study areas were confirmed as the traditional burial grounds. 26

34. The Main Position: This Civil War cannon was placed at the corner of Birmingham and Wiley Roads to mark what was described as the "main position of Washington's Army."

Author's collection.

35. A Great View: his undated photograph depicts the observation tower that was placed at "Mount Joy," as the main section of Valley Forge National Historic Park was called in the 1900s.

A similar tower was planned for the Sandy Hollow region.
Author's collection.

One site in one of Thornbury Farm's unplowed horse pasture was revealed by the radar survey to be part of "filled-in, shallow ravines." Much like the caved-in road embankments previously cited, the old quarry ravines presumably made ideal mass burial sites since the numerous fallen soldiers could be buried at once.

The second area of importance – identified by the 2006 study as mass grave site or "E area (Woods)" – is likely to be the area where a group of school children in 1924 (possibly under the direction of their teacher, Chris Sanderson) were part of a tree-planting ceremony. The remains of a group of pine trees — they once stood like sentinels guarding a "500-foot-long burial trench" — are found today along the between Thornbury Farm and Sandy Hollow Heritage Park.

Newspaper reporters at the time noted that the trench had been "unearthed in an alfalfa field" "near Sandy Hollow." Alluding to final stage of the battle that was also most ruthless, one reporter at the time estimated that it was the mass grave for "hundreds of Revolutionary soldiers who fell in the fight." Interestingly, a prior news story was published on June 13, 1924, in the Wilmington-based *Evening Journal* with the headline "*Death Trench Is Neglected.*"

Although the burial trench was described as being in an "oat field" and not in an alfalfa field, it's unclear if this meant that either the pine trees hadn't been planted yet, or this was another trench. At any rate, it is described as being bordered by a line of small American flags, which "marked the spot in a field of oats."

Paradoxically, Sandy Hollow is not mentioned but instead "Sandy Hill" is described as the "depression between Battle Hill and the Birmingham Meeting House." This is where the "trench" was dug since there were too many Continentals to be buried, the news story reads.

Chris Sanderson makes an appearance in the story and is quoted at length, being the "final authority" on the battlefield. He seems to identify Battle Hill only as a place where the Continentals "fought hand to hand and in forty-five minutes [and] the [Battle] hill was taken, lost, and retaken eleven times." Judging from the narrative, Sanderson was interviewed as he stood in the midst of the open fields at the rear of the Birmingham Meetinghouse . At least he is quoted as if he was standing beyond the Meeting where "the fight raged down the hill and towards that rise over there known as Battle Hill."

From a preservationist's standpoint, the most intriguing part of the article is focused on a man who lived a "half a mile" from the trench named W.H. Sheffield. Described as the president of the Brandywine Battlefield Association, Sheffield outlined the extensive plans being made to make the battlefield more of a tourist destination.

After noting the American Legion was pushing to purchase Washington's Headquarters in Chadds Ford, (16) Sheffield announced that his group was working to raise funds "through private subscriptions" to purchase the "trench" property and honor the dead by "dedicating" it as a preserved burial ground.

Other plans included building an observation tower at Osborne Hill (35,50) and for "improving" a battlefield road called "Patriot's Highway" so that visitors could drive past the place where Lafayette was wounded, then continue through the "heart of the battlefield" and to historic Dilworthtown.

The article ends with the line that "meanwhile" visitors are "becoming more and more numerous, and on Sundays, [one] finds the roads filled with motor cars heading" for the battlefield. Obviously, except for the restoration of Washington's Headquarters, none of the Association's plans materialized. Still, the story underscores what historians now believe: that a battlefield landscape is not merely a place of random landmarks but a place to be visited in person to understand the historic outcome of that battle.

Historic Districts

Nearly from the start of its historic atlas project, the Task Force has relied on numerous historic resource surveys that were generally undertaken by township historic commissions throughout Chester County beginning in the late 1970s and early 1980s. Another important element to the historic interpretation of the battlefield is the inclusion of Historic Districts, areas that are on the National Register of Historic Places.

Two historic districts not only preserve battle-related landscapes but still recall the rural character of Chester County when it was known as the "Breadbasket" and "Butter-belt" of the colonies. The relatively recent registered district, the Worth–

The Untold Story of Its History and Preservation | 73

36. The Gilpin Homestead: In the 1900s, this home appeared on postcards as "Lafayette's Headquarters," a notion disputed by the owners, the Arthur Cleveland family. The farm buildings that appear in the background of these slightly different postcards indicate that the property was then a working farm known as Lafayette's Farms. *Author's collection.*

74 | The Brandywine Battlefield:

37. The Oldest Mill. Strode's Mill as it looks today, with the pre-Revolutionary War-era barn at left, along Lenape Road, East Bradford. *Illustration by Ann Bedrick.*

Jefferis Rural (1994) District, spans East and West Bradford Townships and contains a high number of historic resources – nearly 50 structures such as the vernacular stone farmhouses and old bank barns artists have long been painted by area artists as quintessential Chester County.

While many of these structures reflect the wealth of the 1700s, only a few farmsteads are associated with the British flanking maneuver. The Crown Forces went through the center of the District, on now vanished roads, which makes the historic farmsteads that stand near Jefferis' Ford (63) that more important. Among them is the c.1714/1760 homestead of Emmor Jefferis, (12) an unassuming Quaker farmer who became part of community lore after a large stash of liquor stored in his cellar was plundered by the British flanking troops. As luck would have it, the liquor had been brought there by a group of Wilmington merchants who feared the British would occupy their city.

The second district associated with the wheat trade and agricultural wealth, the Taylor-Cope District (1987) (32), is confined to East Bradford Township and includes many early commerce sites along the Strasburg Road near Marshallton (another Historic District).

The Taylor-Cope District was named for two colonial-era Quaker families whose farmland once extended along the Strasburg Road. The oldest structure is the c. 1724 brick homestead of Abiah Taylor. The oldest extant brick house in Chester County, the home stands opposite the Natural Lands' Stroud Preserve and along the Taylor Run (which once ran the Taylor Mill). The property's c. 1753 English-style barn, which has no threshing floor but dates to a time when workers broke the wheat down by hand in the fields, is considered the oldest barn of its type in the state.

The Cope family gave their name to the nearby 1807 Cope's bridge (33) (listed separately on the National Register). It is now the oldest stone-arch bridge in Chester County, but during the American Revolution it was made of timber (erected in 1770) and reportedly saw much traffic by the militia drawn to Martin's Tavern (6,61) in Marshallton.

After the British occupied Philadelphia, members of the Continental Congress were said to have crossed the bridge on their way to the settlement of Lancaster, which became the colonial capitol for one day on September 27, 1777. It was an event recorded by Capt. John Montrésor's journal as "the Rebel congress precipitately [sic] abandoned Philadelphia, owing to a false alarm."

The Strode's Mill District (1989) is also located in East Bradford and has a similar agricultural history. However, perhaps because the district's visual history is no longer immediately apparent – speeding passersby may not even realize they are passing through a former colonial settlement – the preservation of the district has been at risk until recent years.

The centerpiece of this district is the c. 1721 Strode's Mill (64), which stands at the intersection with many not so visible structures such as the two historic homes perched on high elevations on either side of Birmingham Road. Shrouded by trees is the c. 1772 Richard Strode homestead (which later became a prominent school known as the East Bradford Boarding School for Boys).

Two early vernacular stone tenant houses are nearby: one on the west side of Lenape Road, and the c. 1777 Strode tenant house in part ruin across the street. The district also includes the c.1740 barn complex that is managed by the Friends of Strode's Mill. The importance of the district rests on its history as on a mill seat and crossroads settlement that thrived during the period when wheat farmers brought their crops to Strode's Mill. 27

Very few Historic Districts in the Brandywine Valley have direct connections to the American Revolution. The Strode's Mill District is not only one the largest districts, two important events happened there: it was the former resting place for the British Left Hook (12) and was part the British pre-battle staging area. In addition, it is one of the few historic districts centered around a mill – not a tavern or place of worship. Finally, the Strode's Mill District earned its listing in part because the mill is a rare survivor of the American Revolution – and it's the oldest extant mill on the Brandywine and its tributaries. 28

Thanks to the Strode family, who lived at the crossroads for more than 200 years, the mill retains its vernacular architecture as a banked, two-and-a-half story

76 | The Brandywine Battlefield:

38. **The Historian:** For some unknown reason, Chris Sanderson was not invited to serve on any committee for the much lauded 150th anniversary of the battle in 1927.

As usual, he persevered and created his own historic markers. Sanderson famously never learned to drive, but was able to solicit a friend with a car to distribute the markers throughout the battlefield.

Photo courtesy of the Christian C. Sanderson Museum, Chadds Ford, PA © 2020

structure. Its foundation may have been built as early as 1721 and was an example of a jointly owned custom grist mill. It was established by joint partnership by three neighbors, John Willis, George Carter, and Samuel Scott, who agreed that a mill built on Willis' land would be well located since it could be powered by a strong flowing tributary of the Brandywine — the Plum Run — and because it stood at the intersection of two well established roads.

Richard Strode ran a store and a blacksmith shop in nearby Sconnelltown (65), but he may have been associated with the mill prior to purchasing it in 1784 since the mill was known as Strode's Mill in 1777. The Strode family kept ownership of the mill until 1893.

The mill was listed separately on the National Register in 1974 as the Strode-Entriken mill; it was named for an Irish immigrant named George Entrikin, the first miller, who settled on a 128-acre property (small for its time in 1746) just west of the mill. Entriken was said to have acquired the mill in 1735 and saw it through various incarnations, first as a corn and grain mill, and later with a saw and cider mill addition.

In recent years Entriken's former home—once a picturesque working farm with rolling pastures bordered by hedgerows— was owned by the Tigue family who called their farm "Berryhedge" and gave their name to a road that now runs through the property. The site is now literally unrecognizable as a former farm, having been developed into a Toll Brothers townhouse complex called Darlington's Ridge. 29

Fortunately, East Bradford Township is going forward with plans to create a nature preserve and trail that will include Strode's Mill and a future Heritage Center that will focus on the area's Revolutionary War connections.

The mill is said to have supplied Washington's Army with flour during the Valley Forge encampment, but the complex is best known as one of the few resting places for the thousands of water-soaked British soldiers who marched in the flanking maneuver from Jeffries' Ford.

The British troops were finally able to stop, but only for about 30 minutes, after more than 9 to 11 hours of almost ceaseless marching on a scorching day. The site was also the staging ground for the British three-prong attack at Birmingham. (See Respite at Strode's Mill.)

The route from Sconnelltown to Osborne's Hill is also generally believed to be the place where many residents first caught sight of Cornwallis, who, in contrast to the portly and unkept Howe, had a dignified and commanding presence. Riding high on his horse, Cornwallis was said to have astonished farmers working in the fields.

The key account was by a young Quaker resident named Joseph Townsend (1756-1841), who lived near Jones' Ford. (See A Record of the Day). He noticed the general's rich scarlet uniform and his glittering metals that stood out among the greenery. The sighting, Townsend recorded, took place "between the dwelling of Richard Strode and Osborne's Hill." He also identified the location of the Crown Forces as moving toward the homes of the "Widows" Davis (also cited by Washington's scout Col. Theodoric Bland) who lived on neighboring farms near Birmingham Meeting.

With the exception of the graffiti reportedly scrawled on the interior walls of Strode's Mill, it appears that the British flanking party departed from the region without any incidents. However, one community legend concerns Richard Strode. He did not own the mill until 1784, but he had a blacksmith shop and store in Sconnelltown that may have been damaged. At least, Strode was the sole resident of what is now East Bradford to file a damage claim (for 125 pounds and five shillings).

After the battle, Townsend witnessed and recorded another incident involving Strode. Townsend is unclear whether a local man named Simon Kerns was wounded by enemy fire because he had been talking "freely" about the American defeat, or whether he was shot "in the thigh" because he was in the way of a British scouting party. Regardless, Townsend suggests that the incident took place in Sconnelltown or at Strode's Mill since Strode is described as the "kind neighbor" who assisted in carrying the wounded man into a "small house."

The local surgeons were all busy at Birmingham and so the man was treated by another neighbor, Thomas Darlington, and he survived to carry the musket ball until his death about 1850.

Discovering Fords & Colonial Roads

In 2020, the Task Force began "Phase Three" of its five-year preservation project. It includes a battlefield public-awareness initiative, or "heritage interpretation plan," involving the core battlefield site at Birmingham Township and four other townships. The plan includes trails and interpretive signage, but also continued research using a military mapping technique known as KOCOA. The technique looks at battlefields in a systemic way, using the five steps suggested by the acronym for key terrain, observation, cover/concealment, obstacles, and avenues of approach.

One important finding: KOCOA was used to pinpoint a previously unknown crossing used in the British Left Hook. It is located just below the traditional crossing, designated as Trimble's Ford (59) by a 1915 historical marker along Camp Linden Road in West Bradford Township. The discovery does not dismiss the ford named for two Irish brothers, William and James Trimble, who operated a grist mill that still stands along the Broad Run, a meandering stream that runs into the Brandywine.

The second possible British crossing was discovered close to where an unnamed tributary of the Brandywine flows into the West Branch. In 2020, a prominent archaeologist, Wade P. Catts, decided to work with a geophysicist at the site after they noticed a dark band of debris visible along the sides of the creek bank – a good sign that had been a colonial-era crossing.

In those days, iron shavings from a blacksmith shop were typically spread over a creek at certain crossing points. "If you're going up and down through that crossing, you're going to be churning up stuff so the more you can do to protect that riverbed, the better your footing will be," Catts said in an interview with this book's author.

To pinpoint the crossing at Trimble's Ford, Catts looked for an avenue of approach which may have split and led to both crossings. "KOCOA is really an organizing principle so that you are looking at a key military terrain as say, an 18th century officer or an enlisted man would see it," Catts said, "You are looking at viewsheds and imagining roads where someone can go to point A to point B."

A now vanished, circa 1728 road called Great Valley Road (9) or the Road to the Great Valley – it eventually led to the Great Valley – is now considered a key avenue of approach through West Bradford, perhaps second only to the c. 1743 Great Road to Nottingham in importance. Described as the "Nottingham Road" in this book, the road roughly followed today's Baltimore Pike.

Michael Harris uses another colonial name for the road, the Great Post Road, so named because it was part of a measured route from Boston to Savannah. Another formal-sounding name, the Great Road to Nottingham, is a nod to the road's origin in northeastern Maryland where the Nottingham family owned large tracts of land.

Beginning around 5 a.m., when the Hessians departed Kennett Square (51), the Nottingham Road became the most traveled thoroughfare during the Battle of Brandywine. It was not merely the site of a few morning skirmishes but played a key role in the Hessians' push toward the Brandywine. British records indicate that the "gros" of the British army – anywhere between 11,000 and 17,000 men – traveled along the road on that single day on September 11, 1777.

Today anyone interested in exploring the battlefield can do so without even stepping outside their door. The Task Force's on-going mapping project gives the public online access to 1777-era maps — that is maps that show the colonial landscape in a contemporary context. Cliff Parker, the director of the Chester County Archives, created the maps by cross referencing 1777 road petitions (required in colonial days to build a road) with British damage claims.

These new/old maps will serve as a good public awareness tool since homeowners will now know for sure if any troops, whether British or Continental, passed by their door in 1777. Ironically, Washington could have used such a map himself, ideally to prevent the British surprise attack that set in motion a string of attacks and patriot counter-charges – one accumulating in the bloodiest engagement of the American Revolution at Sandy Hollow. (5)

The Animated Battlefield

Battlefield tours and the occasional discovery of a Revolutionary-era relic unearthed in a plowed field have long inspired an interest in the battlefield landscape. Yet it's only been in recent years that the Task Force's focus on animated maps and the tradition of Staff Rides – named for officers on horseback— has led to a greater understanding of the military significance of a particular terrain or route.

The animated digital maps, based on early British military maps, have proven to be especially revelatory in the study of the Battle of Brandywine. The maps are part of an organized means of studying the battlefield, which because there was so much give and take and confusion on both sides, it's taken decades to document. Indeed, the Task Force now follows the latest in technological research but has focused on the Crown Forces for a reason: the British documented their battles in a way that provides a visual history that is easier to follow.

An extensive 2017 *Military Terrain Analysis*, for instance, is centered on the movements of the Crown Forces as they departed Maryland and headed for Kennett Square, Pennsylvania. 30 Numerous period documents are quoted, especially those by the British and Hessians' diarists who tended to remark about the difficult terrain and the choices the British made in selecting routes through the countryside in their overall mission to occupy Philadelphia.

Recreated in animated digital maps, Staff Rides are now seen as the best means of documenting a battlefield landscape—and are therefore part of the preservation process. The digital maps that were developed as part of the 2010 study were funded with ABPP grants. At the time, the maps were created by a member of the Chester County GIS department, Sean Moir, and soon became a national model.

Moir has gone onto to create other animated maps through his company, Western Heritage Mapping, so that they now include most of the troop movements of the Philadelphia Campaign from September 11th to Sept. 21, 1777, as well as special features such as a 3-D terrain analysis of the battle engagements around Birmingham Meeting.

According to Moir, the animated maps provide an hour-by-hour look at the troops' progression and help to simplify a battle that typified the give and take of 18th-century warfare. This is especially eye-opening when one sees the unfolding of what is termed the Continental's final "Rear Guard Defense" in the animated section near the Brinton 1704 House (31), which overlooks Brinton's Run Preserve.

The timeline given in the Brinton Run animation begins at 5:45 in the afternoon and ends around 9:30 p.m., when the Continentals were on the retreat to Chester. Despite period references to the setting sun including Robertson's note that when the Americans "retired," "it being by this time almost Dark...." the animation reveals the fighting continued until the bitter end, in the gloom of the setting sun.

By illustrating a Staff Rides approach, the animated maps help to highlight past military decisions and aptly illustrate how troop movements are shaped by the battlefield's terrain and topography. This is one reason why, before the creation of the animated maps, the Task Force studied the location of colonial roads according to the aforementioned mapping technique known as KOCOA.

The key "Avenues of Approach" were the Nottingham Road (for the Hessians) and the Great Valley Road and the other routes used by Howe and Cornwallis on the British Left Hook. As for the Key Terrain, historians now see the battles at Birmingham as taking place on two (and perhaps three) separate ridges the British called "eminences."

One ridge was at Birmingham Meeting variously described by both armies as the "Heights at Birmingham" or "Birmingham Hill." The second eminence may have been an eastern extension of the first ridge, and the third, known as Battle Hill, may have been located at the rear of the Birmingham Meetinghouse (47), perhaps on an

39. A Tragedy: The fire that destroyed Washington's Headquarters, the longtime home of Chris Sanderson pictured here, was all the more upsetting because he had been forced to move after his lease was not renewed.

As a newspaper reporter in 1923 observed, Sanderson, "patiently, and at great sacrifice of time and personal means," maintained the headquarters as a "historic shrine" to George Washington and his heroic efforts in the Battle of Brandywine.

Photo courtesy of the Christian C. Sanderson Museum, Chadds Ford, PA © 2022.

A 1931 photo of the gutted remains of the headquarters shortly after the devastating fire on Sept. 16th.
Courtesy of CFHS.

elevated area on nearby Thornbury Farm. (See the "Eminences" section in this book).

The Hessian Major Karl von Baumeister was not part of this latter phase of the battle, but he nonetheless was aware of his advance patrols and the constant shifting of battlelines. At first, he writes "the enemy's position" on "the hill beyond the Meeting House" was "a corps of about 1000 men and a party of enemy cavalry somewhat nearer our left wing." He later noted that the Hessian advance patrols reported that "a corps of 200 men and five guns [were] making for these hills in great haste to join the 1000 [Continentals] men already posted there." [31]

Interestingly, a separate geographical study completed in 1999 by the independent geologist Bruce W. Bevan confirmed that there is still a hill or "wooded ridge," on the "south edge" that is likely to be the same one cited by Baurmeister beyond the Meetinghouse. Bevan describes it being part of a sloping pastureland that marks the southern boundary of the present-day Thornbury Farm (known in Bevan's reports as "Spackman's Farm.")

Another elevation rising from the Thornbury Farm's pasture (and joining a preserved area that is part of Sandy Hollow Heritage Park) may be the region cited in recent years as Sandy Hill – and described as an excellent defense position for the Americans since it was high ground covered with trees.

Battlefield Tourists

Discovering the landscape of what has been called the military nadir of the American Revolution has been a pursuit since the early days of battlefield tourism. Many outsiders who felt the urge explore the battlefield on foot were inspired by the popular account of Joseph Townsend. He was a 21-year-old son of a Quaker farmer in 1777 – thus some early historians called his account the reminisces of a "Quaker boy" – but it soon became **the** go-to source for readers interested in the Battle of Brandywine. [32]

First published in 1846, the account may be the only surviving record documenting the movements of the Royal Forces on Sept. 11, 1777, from a non-combatant's point of view. It was originally published posthumously and privately with the title that began, *"Some account of the British army, under the command of General Howe; and of the battle of Brandywine, on the memorable September 11, 1777, and the adventures of that day."*

Thanks largely to the historians J. Smith Futhey and John S. Bowen, who helped usher the manuscript into print, Townsend's book enabled battlefield enthusiasts to envision the day's events visually—in other words, to examine the battlefield through its landmarks and terrain features.

40. Below Chadds Ford. The author MacElree used the same title for this photo published in *Along the Western Brandywine*, but it could have been also used to illustrate "the morass."

In addition, the nation's Centennial Exhibition – held in Philadelphia in 1876 – may have set the course for a widespread interest in the colonial period since it featured many exhibits that focused on the heritage as well as the industrial power of America. By promoting a positive sense of identity for the nation, early battlefield enthusiasts were able to reach a broader following.

Certainly, one of the high points for tourism may have been Lafayette's celebrated return to America beginning in 1824. At least, the tributes that followed led to a renewed regard for the material relics of the American Revolution, especially since the local newspapers avidly followed Lafayette's travels to area landmarks and villages he was known to have visited in 1777.

The historian Maynard writes that Lafayette's visit to the Brandywine battlefield on July 26, 1825, included lunch in the "cannon-scarred Samuel Jones mansion (55) north of the meetinghouse [where] he was shown a collection of military relics dug up by farmer Abraham Darlington on the surrounding battlefield."

Lafayette also famously visited the Gilpin (36) and Ring homes (16,44)– a fact that may have added to the confusion that Lafayette used the former home as a headquarters. Maynard writes that the Ring house, or Washington's Headquarters (16), has long been a "perennial favorite" for tourists, and he jokingly suggests that Lafayette was the first tourist "even before the war was over."

In December of 1780, Lafayette and a group of French friends that included a fellow officer named Marquis de Chastellux rode down from Philadelphia and visited the battlefields at Chadds Ford and Birmingham.

In Chastellux's now classic travelogue, *Travels in North America, In The Years 1780-1782*, he describes Lafayette's search for the place where he had been wounded, somewhere south of Birmingham Hill. It was a place where Chastellux observed that day "most of the trees [still] bear the marks of bullets or cannon shots." The group brought along a 1778 map published in London with a title that began, *"The Battle of Brandywine in which the Rebels Were Defeated...."* 33

Described as "drawn on the spot by a Hessian lieutenant," the map was hand-colored to illustrate the headquarters, deployment, and movements of all three forces with the colors as the British (red), Hessian (blue) and the Continentals (yellow).

Determined to find the place where Lafayette had been wounded, the group sought out the guidance of a former [unnamed] American officer who was living in a house overlooking Sandy Hollow. (5) Yet "already just three years after the battle," Maynard writes, "they expressed perplexity and disagreement about what had happened where." As for the 1778 map, it may have illustrated with landmarks, but parts of it were so inaccurate, Maynard writes, it "ultimately sowed much confusion about the events of the battle, which historians are still trying to disentangle."

Patriots & Relic Seekers

Tourism in the Brandywine Valley and the popularity of exploring the battlefield landscape —with or without a British map in hand – was particularly strong after the Civil War. Popular works of literature such as Bayard Taylor's *The Story of Kennett* (1866) also boosted tourism and respect for the battlefield.

Although the novel was a fictionalized account of Quaker life after the American Revolution, Taylor may have been inspired by a trip he made to Chadds Ford, taking a day off from school with two fellow classmates in 1840. The trip was documented by a local newspaper even though the "memorialization" of the battle, as it was described, was at a low point.

Both Taylor and one of his companions, the future historian John Smith Futhey, were not ones to follow convention. They walked for several miles from their school in Unionville, East Marlborough Township, for the sole purpose of examining the battlefield and "teasing" tales and legends from local farmers. In retrospect, the newspaper account suggests that the pair began their literary careers by learning to dramatize the accounts they heard into battlefield tales.

41. The Brandywine Road: The Great Valley Road enabled the British flanking troops to cut a direct course to the Upper Fords, and although it did not completely follow the Brandywine, such as the road pictured here, it was likely narrow and winding. Judging from the given address, this section of the road may have roughly followed today's South Creek Road (Rt. 842) near West Chester.

Below: Another section of the Brandywine Road. *Author's collection.*

42. A Relic Minefield. This 1900s postcard shows the octagonal schoolhouse built in 1819, the year of a major expansion of the Birmingham Meetinghouse on the same property when many battlefield artifacts were unearthed. *Author's collection.*

When they reached an area in Birmingham "north of the woods" – perhaps Sandy Hollow – they learned, for instance, that it was a sacred place "where the blood was shed in the greatest profusion, [and] an abundant growth of thyme sprung up spontaneously." Who told this story to them is not revealed, but Futhey went onto record many stories about the Battle of Brandywine as co-author of the 1881 book *The History of Chester County*.

While fictional accounts of the battle continued to be published, newspapers tended to offer hints about the downside to battlefield tourism, especially in the mid-1800s when visitors seemed to have little concern for protecting the battlefield landscape – one that was still scarred by wagon wheels and pocketed with sunken areas suggesting where a redoubt or artillery battery had been. Local newspapers, in fact, seemed to encourage relic-seekers, offering details, for instance, about the location and circumstances of a find.

Indeed, the stories were seemingly endless and covered a far-ranging territory such as the coin unearthed by a farmer that was stamped with the date 1776 along with a Prussian coat of arms. The coin was found in the Southern Chester County settlement of Landenburg, where there was no record of any British or Hessian troops.

Some of the more unusual discoveries in Chadds Ford included sprays of grapeshot found by workmen when the c. 1718 log walls of the Brandywine Baptist Church were being replaced to build a stone church in 1808; the discovery of a brass piece engraved with the English Crown, found by a fisherman on the "American side" of the Brandywine; and a cannon ball embedded in a tree trunk that nearly destroyed the blades of a sawmill.

The Centennial of 1877 also brought a spate of newspaper recollections about relics found and graves discovered. Only one story seemed to have focused on the actual battle, but that was because it was published in the Philadelphia-based magazine *Lippincott*'s, which had the subtitle "*Popular Literature & Science.*" Tucked between poetry and travelogues, the magazine's account of the Battle of Brandywine began with the British landing at the Head of the Elk in Maryland and quoted Joseph Townsend's account of following the "Redcoats" for much of the day.

To modern readers, the magazine story may seem relatively free from hyperbole and romance – with a few exceptions. General Washington makes an appearance in the narrative: he is described as "resting" in the shade of a "cherry tree (which fell in a storm a few years ago)," that grew south of the Nottingham Road below Chads' Ford. It was here that "Squire Cheyney" found him. [34]

Curiously, other accounts including a map drawn by Chris Sanderson document the same location but indicate that it was a pear tree. (4) Regardless, *Lippincott*'s writer may have wanted a segue into the tree's former location, since that was the general vicinity where the Centennial celebration took place during the reporter's visit that same day.

It was near the train station and evidently convenient to the some 1,200 to 1,500 celebrators, who came by a "special train" and then to "a grove" after bringing their bags to the Chadds Ford Hotel (26), as one paper reported. It was noted that a 12-piece City Cornet Band arrived by the 9 a.m. train. Then "everyone followed the band to the grove southeast of the village, known as Rocky Hill." [35]

Perhaps the most alarming account (to our modern eyes) was one written in an epistolary style by an anonymous writer in 1828. Partly titled "*A Letter From Chester County,*" the writer urged readers to dismiss the "rage for steam boats" and take a "jaunt to Chester County" to see the local American Revolutionary landmarks not merely in Valley Forge but in Kennett Square, Paoli, and Chadds Ford. The latter village was deemed a particular delight for relic-seekers since the landscape was little changed. The reporter cited that there was still evidence of a "little redoubt," "on a hill above the Brandywine" where visitors might "pick up an occasional bullet or grape-shot."

Although it's unclear whether the writer discovered any relics himself, he writes seemingly without any concern for what others would later call "sacred" battlefield land, the scenes of destruction and carnage. Not to be missed, he adds, is a visit to Birmingham Meetinghouse (47), where the "Sexton," with a shovel in hand, may be willing to turn up "some two feet below the surface, the bones of a British soldier."

The blood stains left by wounded soldiers on the Meetinghouse floor are not mentioned, but it evidently was a customary part of any tour. The year after Chadds Ford Hotel opened in 1860 – advertising that it was located in the center of the battlefield grounds – vandalism forced the overseers of the Meetinghouse to "decline the use of the key to visitors," as it was termed, since the bloodstained floor had been "scarred and chipped so much by pocket knives," presumably by relic-seekers, according to a period newspaper.

Battlefield Promoters

While exploring the battlefield on foot remained a popular pursuit for writers and historians, residents could also obtain an armchair tour through books and lectures. Chris Sanderson offered the latter beginning in the 1920s and right up until his death in 1966, both in the classroom and at outdoor events. He often presented what he called his "bedsheet" lectures on the Battle of Brandywine, using an actual bedsheet marked with a black pen to illustrate the 1777 locations of not only the fords but

Tourists on the Battlefield. *Courtesy of CFHS*

Restoration Begun: Chris Sanderson's death in 1966 prompted friends and neighbors to form the Chadds Ford Historical Society, mainly because they feared local historic structures such as the John Chads' House (pictured here) might be razed without Sanderson, the overseer. The Society soon acquired the house and it was restored by the prominent architect John Milner. *Courtesy of CFHS.*

now vanished hamlets such as Sconnelltown (65) and Trimbleville (59).

Today Sanderson's idiosyncratic collection, housed in the Christian C. Sanderson Museum in Chadds Ford, sheds light on the battle in interesting ways. One treasure is a 1797 edition of *Encyclopedia Britannica*; it was one of the first books to feature an entry about the Battle of Brandywine.

Several framed newspaper stories tell of Sanderson's interest in battlefield preservation such as *The Public Ledger*'s 1923 story titled *"Brandywine Battlefield To Be A National Shrine."* He also favored objects that reflected the community knowledge of the battle, such as the amusing sign, painted by the illustrator N.C. Wyeth, that once hung above the door of a local barbershop. (28) The sign read, "This Is the Place Where Washington and Lafayette Had a Very Close Shave."

Decades before Sanderson and his bedsheet lectures, audiences could enjoy slightly more academic "caulk-board" lectures given by Wilmer MacElree, a West Chester author and trial lawyer. In 1912, he traveled to Chadds Ford with a group of fellow historians and looked for significant spots worthy of a historic marker.

The group examined the same hilltop behind the John Chads' House (18) where Washington reportedly stood until cannon balls "began to fall," MacElree writes, repeating an oft-told story first related by Townsend's brother-in-law, Amos House. Overlooking the village of Chadds Ford, the hilltop offered views of the surrounding area, MacElree noted, and showed a "variegated landscape [that] extends as far as the eye can reach in all directions."

Much like Sanderson, MacElree believed that the Brandywine battlefield was best explored on foot, especially along the Brandywine in and around Chadds Ford, which had been radically altered by "dam, bridge, and railroad embankments." (23)

In his 1912 book *Along the Western Brandywine,* MacElree includes an entire chapter on Chads' Ferry, but he mostly explains the progression of its existence by citing colonial road dockets and does not answer such questions as why it fell out of use as a crossing. Equally confusing is the fact that MacElree includes scattered illustrations of a few random crossings, but he did not publish a complete map of the Brandywine crossings.

Even in his day, all nine of the so-called Lower Fords of the Brandywine had different names than those in 1777. In addition, many of the crossings were no longer used – Corner Ford and Richling's Ford below Chads' Ford, among them – and yet, MacElree anticipated the public's desire to explore the old fords by encouraging his readers to trace the former colonial roads. 36 For instance, MacElree writes that with the exception of the c. 1743 Nottingham Road, one of the most traveled roads in 1777 was the c. 1754 Brandywine Road.

MacElree refers to this road by its nickname— the "Starvegut" Road— and explains that it was so named because there were no taverns along it. Today the road is believed to have roughly followed the current Hillendale and Fairville Roads, southwest of the village center of Chadds Ford. 37

Long before MacElree encouraged readers to study these colonial roads, however, both crossings as well as much of the surrounding area were obliterated by the construction of the Philadelphia & Baltimore Central (P&BC) (21). Indeed, considering that the Starvegut was the main route used by Hessians to cross Chads' Ford, it's not surprising that the railroad construction also unearthed what one newspaper termed "sacred relics," or bones of soldiers. 38

MacElree does not mention any specific destructive results of modern progress, but unfortunately, he does not explain why such a small settlement as Chadds

43. The William Harvey Homestead: Ned Goode took this photo in the late 1950s. It is believed that he captured this southwest angle to highlight a part of the house that received the most cannon fire in 1777.

The original staircase was still intact in the 1950s. *Courtesy of Library of Congress, Historic American Buildings Survey. (HABS)*

Ford – once centered around the Sign of the Three Compasses Tavern – came to have both a ford and a ferry. ₃₉ He also muddies the waters, so to speak, by describing these crossings by their alternative names: The Upper and Lower Fords, which he described as being located "within six hundred feet of each other," which seems to be the closest distance between any of the ford crossings on the Brandywine.

Going further into the weeds (pun intended), MacElree cites a former covered bridge (built in 1828 and rebuilt in 1860) along the Nottingham Road to mark the location of the two crossings. (13) He writes that hose colonial travelers along the Nottingham Road crossed the ford "300 north of the present bridge" while travelers on the Starvegut Road (the "Lower Ford" Road) were able to cross the Brandywine "150 feet south of the present bridge."₄₀

Apparently, by the time the 1860 covered bridge was demolished and replaced by a two-span concrete bridge in 1921 (slightly closer to the ford), the old Starvegut was forgotten. Indeed, one map created after the 1938 widening of Baltimore Pike (19) erroneously lumped both the ford and ferry together as part of the "Upper Ford," while a crossing called "Lower Ford" was depicted just below it.

The ferry may have been forgotten by that time since it had been destroyed by a railroad track bed that ran close to the former Starvegut Road as well as by a railroad trestle bridge that crossed a mill race belonging to Hoffman's Mill (23), now the Brandywine River Museum.

In his book, MacElree does not clear up the locations of the confusing fords but he does suggest that Chadds Ford's first bridge – the 1828 covered bridge – was built between a small "dam" (still evident today) (13) and the Upper Ford in a narrow stretch of the Brandywine, its "width [a] little less than one hundred and fifty feet."

This part of the Brandywine may have been the area the Hessian general Knyphausen called the "swampy morass" (40) and what the chief Royal engineer, Archibald Robertson, marked on a map as "a swath of swampy terrain extending some 200 yards wide on both sides" of the Nottingham Road. MacElree saw it as dense wetlands that grew during "times of freshets" when the "tussocky meadow of a thousand feet" between the dam and John Chads' House "is frequently covered with water."

MacElree also cites a few early bridge petitions that suggest that Chads Ford and its swampy terrain were found unsuitable for bridge pilings. In 1801, a bridge-building jury comprised of residents did not even consider the ford crossing as a good location for a bridge. Instead, they recommended the "place most convenient and least expensive was about 13 perches below the said ford."

Apparently, John Chads didn't consider northern crossing either, even though it was near his home and the tavern he established in 1736.₄₁ When Chads borrowed money from the Provincial Court in 1737, he didn't mention the ford, but instead specified that a ferry be placed several perches south of "Great Road leading from Chester to Nottingham, on ye land of John Chads."

Chads' Ferry was soon forgotten in the years after Chadds Ford earned a stop on the railroad. Around the same time, MacElree's 1912 book helped to spur tourism, mainly because of his directions to look for the "redoubt [that] directly faced and commanded the passage of Chads's Ford," as MacElree described Proctor's Hill, Washington's main artillery position.

Still, the real surge in tourism did not occur until after the construction of a concrete highway (24), situated just north of the old Nottingham Road, around 1917. A few years later, in 1921, nine thousand people visited Washington's Headquarters alone. (16) The exact count was thanks to Sanderson, then a local schoolteacher and antiquarian who kept a record of the visitors during the time he rented the house from 1906 to 1922.

Postcards from this period suggest that Sanderson's visitors were drawn to the house by a simple hand-painted wooden sign nailed to a tree in the front yard. No doubt Sanderson put up the sign: he not only gave free personal tours of the house to anyone who requested one, he organized anniversaries and erected historic markers throughout the battlefield.

Sanderson famously never had a driver's license during his lifetime, but he was known to have created countless maps that could be used as driving tours. In fact, Sanderson may have assisted the writer of a 1922 *Keystone Motorist* article who swept through the area and wrote about the historical markers recently placed in the area by the Brandywine Valley Farmers' Club.

There were not as many historic markers as those in Valley Forge or Gettysburg, the writer observed, but a visitor "is able to identify principal points of interests," a vast improvement from "10 or more years ago."

Ten years later, another writer for the same magazine, a former clergyman named John T. Faris, became a popular writer of local histories based on his excursions. In one story, he echoed many writers before him when he compared the present to that "autumn day so long ago" and noted "the [Brandywine] creek, the meadows, the woods, the fields, some of the houses – yes, even the roads, in places – are not so much changed."

In many ways, Sanderson improved upon a state marker program begun in the 1900s but had stalled in the 1920s, just around the time of the 150th anniversary of the battle in 1927 (30). At least, Sanderson may have thought the marker program was incomplete since he was known to have made numerous cardboard cutouts, each resembling the design style of the state's Keystone battlefield markers (38).

On more than one occasion, Sanderson guided visitors with historic markers he placed throughout the 35,000 acre battlefield area, such as one in the middle of Kennett Square that read *"Where the divisions of Cornwallis and Knyphausen separated the morning of Sept. 11, 1777."*

Sanderson's more formal efforts to commemorate the Battle of Brandywine was said to have begun in early 1910 when he raised funds for a boulder marker placed near his front door. Working with the Delaware County Historical Society, Sanderson placed a bronze plaque on the boulder with the dates Sept. 10, 1910, identifying the house as Washington's Headquarters. (46)

Sadly, when Sanderson's rental agreement came to an end, in 1922, the house was converted into a tearoom – a progression that led to disaster. As the author Barksdale Maynard writes, Sanderson "had reluctantly moved away when, in 1931, news came that the venerable house had burned. (39) What stands today is a reconstruction."

The headquarters reconstruction did not occur until a few years after the Brandywine Battlefield Park was established as a state park in 1949. Sanderson did not attend the grand opening, and indeed, some of his supporters say he deliberately avoided the ceremony, choosing instead to give a lecture to a packed schoolroom in Chadds Ford Elementary. 42

Sanderson was reportedly disappointed that no government official had asked him to join a historic committee, nor did they even inquire about the history of battlefield, let alone the former headquarters where he had lived for so many years. A brief diary entry, now displayed at the Sanderson Museum, records the news he heard on "The Close of Monday, Nov. 17th, 1947."

Sanderson wrote of receiving a "personal blow" when he learned that he had not been appointed to the commission formed to oversee the establishment of a state park in Chadds Ford. He concluded his account by citing the "hard work" that his mother had completed and his own memories of the many visitors who learned about the history of Washington's Headquarters, their beloved former home.

Present-day Battlefield Explorers

Thanks to a group of residents and historians who created the Brandywine Battlefield Park in 1949, visitors now can get an insider's feel for what life was like for residents of the Brandywine Valley in 1777. The former homes of Benjamin Ring and Gideon Gilpin are furnished in an authentic colonial manner and preserve what a park history calls the lifestyle of wealthy, open-minded Friends (both had family members who were so-called "Fighting Quakers") as well as "a good house, good land, and good-size family."

Of the two historic homes, the circa 1731 Ring House is of special interest to battlefield enthusiasts, especially since it served as the former headquarters for General George Washington, and its period rooms, though reconstructed, give visitors a sense of the close arrangement and perhaps tense atmosphere that Washington endured conducting the business of war.

Although Washington's famous tent may have stood on the grounds, (45) the house reportedly was a place where Washington's War Council developed their strategy to defend the area fords and where the general received the "chilling word that the British were suddenly on his right," as the historian Maynard writes.

A few of the officers who gathered in the Ring parlor would go onto become well-known American figures such as the young Lieutenant Colonel Alexander Hamilton and Charles C. Pinckney, the future U.S. ambassador to France and a presidential candidate.

During the years Chris Sanderson and his mother rented the colonial stone house, they lived by the belief that the best way to preserve the Brandywine battlefield was to educate the public of its importance. To that end, Sanderson not only collected relics and artifacts about the battle, he logged what he called 20,000 "pilgrims of visitation ."

To accommodate those visitors, Sanderson created several hand-drawn maps over the years including one used by a Canadian regiment, the Queen's York Rangers, that visited the battlefield on October 7, 1961 (4).

Today there are a handful of historians and residents who follow Sanderson's method of walking the battlefield or – or in a more sophisticated level, exploring the battlefield landscape in the military tradition of Staff Rides to experience the terrain in person. They include Ken Lawson, a former board officer for the Chadds Ford Historical Society, who sees the Battle of Brandywine as a study of military strategy – or lack of it.

It's a battle known for its many unknowns, despite its importance as the "largest single-day battle against a foreign army in the history of the nation," as Lawson describes it. Lawson embarked on the first of several battle anniversary hikes in 2014. From the start, he focused on scouting out the whereabouts of early roads the British might have taken after splitting their forces at Kennett Square and marching north on the flanking maneuver.

On April 22, 2017, Lawson was joined by several local historians including Phil Duffy, a West Bradford resident and former reconnaissance officer, to complete a hike designed to find traces of the now vanished route above the Forks of the Brandywine (10) known as the circa 1728 Road to the Great Valley. (9)

During the colonial era, when main roads were typically named for their main destination, the Great Valley Road linked residents in Kennett and the Bradfords to the Great Valley, once described as "four miles north of Turk's Head (West Chester)."

Military historians have long created maps of the British Left Hook, but the maps tended to be barebones, depicting the road as going straight up from Kennett Square, for instance, and looping to the right over both Trimble's and Jeffries' fords.

Today the maps created by the Task Force are based on specific research and such conclusions as the belief that the Great Valley Road did **not** cross Trimble's Ford but instead had a different course, turning northwest. As Michael Harris writes, the road "continued north to Martin's Tavern – away from the American right flank – while a branch road curved eastward to Jeffries's Ford." 43

In 1777, a detachment of about 70 American Light Infantry under Lt. Col. James Ross left Chadds Ford and traveled as far as the Northbrook region, south of Trimble's Ford, and although his troops skirmished with the enemy, his subsequent dispatch to Gen. Washington was not acted upon. 44 In his dispatch, which had the dateline of "Sept. 11. '77. Great Valley Road, Eleven o'clock A.M.," Ross erroneously reported that the Great Valley Road – the exact route "He was marching upon" – led from "Taylor's" [sic] and "Jeffries ferries on the Brandywine."

Ross, who assumed that the crossing was manned by ferries, also mentioned skirmishing. However, he underestimated the number of enemy troops, in part because he only saw a cloud of dust (as did Col. Theodoric Bland) rising on the horizon above Trimble's Ford – a cloud that could only be caused, he reported, by "no less" than five thousand soldiers. 45

For Lawson and his fellow hikers that April day, the most likely spot where Ross's patrol briefly engaged the rear of Cornwallis' column was along Red Lion Road, perhaps at its intersection with present-day Corinne Road, just south of the Brandywine Red Clay Alliance at 1760 Unionville-Wawaset Road.

Another purpose of the hike was to determine the course of the Great Valley Road by filling in the gaps between the Red Lion Road and Trimble's Ford. Traditionally, it was believed that the British followed the Great Valley north from Kennett Square. Once one of the main east-west routes of Chester County, the road may have followed at least part of the present-day Northbrook Road off of modern Street Road, west of Longwood Gardens, and another section of Red Lion Road.

This road (named for the Red Lion Inn) now dead ends at modern Unionville-Wawaset Road (Rt. 842). However, recent research has confirmed what many older residents remember: an old farm road continued northwest and may have been part of the Great Valley Road connecting the Red Lion Tavern to Martin's Tavern (6,61) in the village of Marshallton.

On the day of the hike, Lawson's group tried to find this lost section of the Great Valley Road by passing through the roller-coaster hills of a preserve managed by

The Untold Story of Its History and Preservation | 97

44. Brandywine Day: Washington's Headquarters as it looked when it was occupied by Chris Sanderson, who no doubt decorated the porch and the pair of trees for the 150th anniversary of the Battle of Brandywine, on Sept. 11, 1927.
Courtesy of CFHS.

45. Washington's War Tent: This 1911 postcard was created from a watercolor commissioned by W. Herbert Burk, a clergyman from Norristown who founded the Valley Forge Historical Society. Burk purchased the tent in 1909 from Mary Curtis Lee, daughter of the Confederate general Robert E. Lee, and granddaughter of Mj. Gen. Henry Lee. The original tent is now owned by the Museum of the American Revolution in Philadelphia.

46. Spreading the Word: A young Sanderson, right, poses with member of the Delaware County Historical Society with a historic marker installed in front of Washington's Headquarters in 1910. In 1915, Sanderson was asked to help with another marker project carried out by the Chester County Historical Society. Below: Sanderson and his mother, Hanna, at home.
Photos courtesy of the Christian C. Sanderson Museum, Chadds Ford, PA © 2020

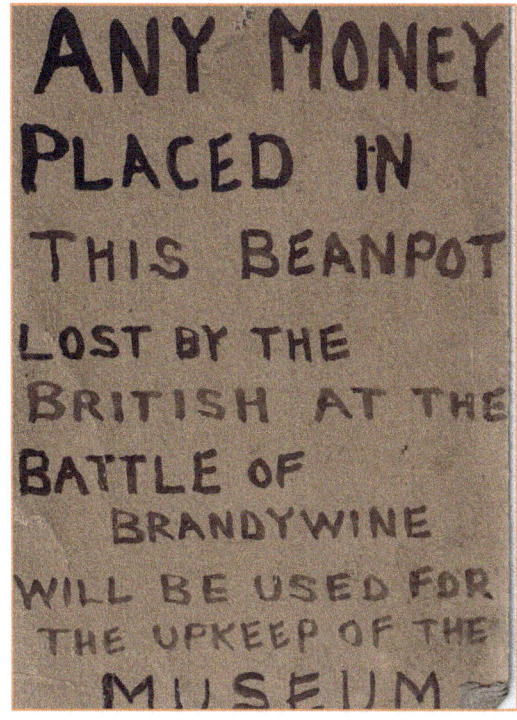 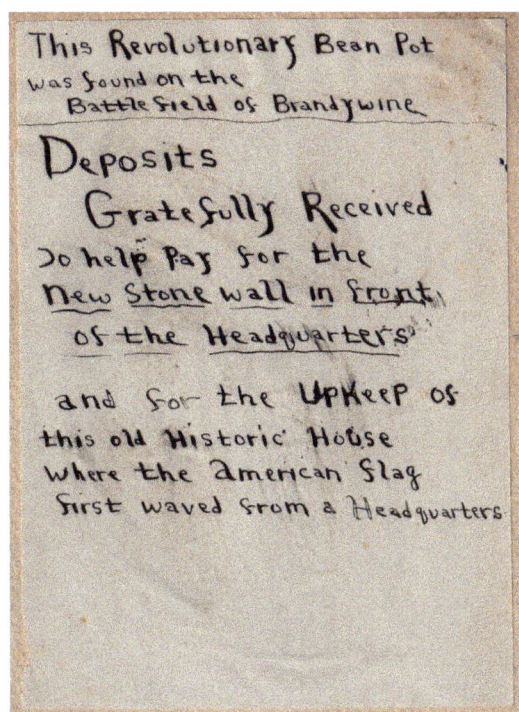

Gratefully Received: The two surviving signs that were once placed on the porch of Washington's Headquarters, propped up against a British bean pot excavated at Osborne Hill and obtained by Chris Sanderson. Many of the signs requested donations to help with the upkeep of the house, but Sanderson's supporters have long contended that he barely covered his expenses. *Photos courtesy of the Christian C. Sanderson Museum, Chadds Ford, PA © 2020.*

the Brandywine Red Clay Alliance. The hills and the distant ford prompted the hikers to commiserate and wonder how the British, burdened with thick uniforms and heavy arms and equipment, could make such a trek before any battle.

In the end, the "consensus," as Duffy called it in a report written a few weeks later, was the belief that the Great Valley Road may have continued north in a fairly straight path to a point that is now near the dead end of Bragg Hill Road. (60) In other words, the Great Valley Road continued alongside the eastern bank of the West Branch of the Brandywine and reached a crossing somewhere near Bragg Hill Road.

This route now crosses private properties, but the group had permission to continue along the riverbank until they found a small tributary that flows into the West Branch. Remarkably, many of the fords along the Brandywine are found at a creek junction and this was no exception, the group concluded.

The Task Force calls it the second crossing at Trimble's Ford (59) to distinguish it from the traditional crossing site designated by a 1915 historic marker placed at today's Camp Linden Road.

Anniversary Celebrations

Until the 100th anniversary of the Battle of Brandywine in 1877, yearly events to recognize the battle were typically confined to a low-key community event known as Brandywine Day (44). For the participants, the event kept the memory of the battle alive even after the visual reminders began to disappear and finding military artifacts was not such a frequent occurrence.

Some thought the turning point was when the largest trove of relics was dug up during the 1819 enlargement of the Birmingham Meetinghouse and the construction of an octagonal schoolhouse on the property the same year (42).

Another relic was added to the collection the following year, when a grave digger uncovered what was described as the scarlet remains of a British uniform that had turned "a light snuff color" with age. In the early 20th century, Chris Sanderson was credited for reviving the tradition of Brandywine Day, but incredibly, no record can prove how the event began. At best, the first mention of the event can be traced to a Wilmington resident named Eli Crozier who appeared in one newspaper story in 1840 as the leader of an anniversary party.

Routinely described as an amateur historian and battlefield enthusiast, Crozier was known for donning re-enactment attire and rounding up Wilmington residents to travel to Chadds Ford (in later years, by train) to commemorate the battle. In due time, area newspapers reportedly tracked the patriotic climate by recording the number of "celebrators" Crozier attracted.

For 40 years, he rarely missed the anniversary with the exception perhaps of the year 1859. On that year, one newspaper reported, (perhaps condescendingly) an estimated 600 to 1000 people arrived in Chadds Ford by special railcars, only to find that Crozier and his entourage decided to stay home and "observe the Sabbath."

Coincidentally, in Sept of 1846, the same time a reporter wrote that Crozier's party and several camp cooks ended the day by frying up a tub full of catfish, a group of historians arrived in Chadds Ford on an important mission. One member of the group was J. Smith Futhey, who in 1881 became co-author of an important book: the *History of Chester County*. Intent on accuracy, the group may have wanted to bolster a first-hand account – known as Joseph Townsend's account – published a few months later by the Historical Society of Pennsylvania.

A reporter noted that the group planned to explore the battlefield on foot using a "rare and valuable" map dating to 1778 (most likely the Fagen map) and "kindly loaned" to them by officials at Philadelphia's Franklin Institute.

In reconfirming what they called the *"Plan of the Battleground in 1777,"* they marked areas of the historical landscape where burial "pitts [sic]" were evident and where fighting may have taken place in the "woods and forests."

47. The Protective Wall: Douglas Brinton's 1899 photograph of Birmingham's Meeting hardly evokes the place where a Virginian regiment formed behind what the historian Reed called a "natural redoubt made by the heights at Birmingham." However, the photograph does show the stone wall which the Virginians famously used to shield themselves as they fired at the advancing British.

Courtesy of CCHS.

The fact-finding mission was also centered on the creation of a survey of historic structures – one that seems modern in its approach. The "present occupants" (in 1846) of numerous colonial-era homes were interviewed for both battlefield stories and information about the history of their homes and properties.

Not surprisingly, given the long-term occupancy of most of the houses by generations of the same family, only a few of the 1777-era structures were listed as "not standing" and those tended to be small buildings such as a blacksmith shop near Chads' Ford.

At the start of the Civil War, news of the battlefield "finds" as well as anniversary celebrations, understandably came to a virtual halt. If the battlefield was mentioned, it was usually news of a military encampment, suggesting that any open land was considered a common area or public ground.

Among the visitors in 1861 was the First City Troop – a national guard unit organized in 1774 as the Light Horse of the City of Philadelphia aka Philadelphia Light Horse – who arrived by train and stayed 10 days in Chadds Ford.

They set up camp west of the Brandywine, on ground described as on a "hill or sloping piece of ground immediately adjoining a fine wood with two springs" and near the railroad station.

The description was detailed in part because of what was found on the site: Members of the troop were digging a flagpole when they struck two six-pound cannon balls. No mention is made of the First City Troops' connection to the American Revolution, only that the artifacts were later displayed in the West Chester offices of the *Daily Local News*.

In 1874, one reporter bemoaned the fact that no one was celebrating the 97th anniversary of the Battle of Brandywine; only Crozier's small camping party appeared as usual in what was described as "Nathaniel Ring's meadow. 47 Still, Crozier managed to round up enough celebrators each year until 1884,

48. Taylor's Monument: Erected in 1877, it was a memorial to Generals Pulaski & Lafayette. *Author's collection*

when a newspaper reporter pronounced the historian as too "decrepit" to make an appearance, setting off fears that it was the end to the annual Brandywine Day celebration.

It wasn't until nearly a decade later, in 1893, that a lengthy newspaper notice announced a new requirement for all Chester County public schools: Teachers had to recognize Brandywine Day with a special anniversary event or curriculum.

One of the more interesting developments in the promotion of the battle occurred in 1899 – the year marked extensive visual documentation. Prints of a c. 1872 engraved battlefield map were published that year, as well as polychromic prints published by a Philadelphia shop called The History Company.

Perhaps the most impressive visual study, however, was the photography series begun by Douglas E. Brinton, an amateur photographer born in 1859 in the small Southern Chester County hamlet of Oxford. Many of Brinton's photos of the Brandywine battlefield (50,54) are found in this book, all taken in 1899, coincidently only a year after Howard Pyle, an art instructor at Drexel University, began summer courses in the former Ring/Turner mill in Chadds Ford.

Much like Futhey and other historians before him, Brinton made a point of tracing the colonial routes on foot to see the Revolutionary War sites. In one series he even traveled to Maryland to document "Elk River Ferry" (Elkton) and then proceeded to the Brandywine in Chadds Ford. 48

Brinton promoted colonial history by producing his prints for the public and issuing them with his own pre-printed grey mounts with the legend: *"Brinton Photographic Collection of Revolutionary & other Historical Landmarks in Pennsylvania, Maryland, Delaware by Douglas E. Brinton, Oxford, Penna."*

A National Trend

Despite the early interest in exploring the Brandywine battlefield – and the occasional unearthing of a military relic – preserving the actual battlefield seemed to hold little interest with the public. Indeed, judging from some of the battlefield literature – much of it published after the founding of the Brandywine Battlefield Park in 1949 – preserving any more than the park grounds seemed like a distant goal.

Perhaps people felt no pressing need since most of the battlefield farms were still owned by the same families, and it was inconceivable that any change would come to a landscape, then parceled into large dairy farms and interlaced with cow paths and unpaved roads.

A similar outlook occurred among residents living within other Revolutionary War battlefields. For instance, Congress appropriated money for a monument at Bunker Hill in 1825, but most commemorations occurred between 1876 and 1887, the centennial of the Constitution. Those years also saw federal funding for monuments at Yorktown, Saratoga, Monmouth, and other major Revolutionary War battlefield sites. Still, this was just a prelude to the battlefield preservation movement. Chester County saw an earlier example for using physical objects such as monuments to express feelings of nationalism or patriotism.

In 1817, a long-guarded but neglected gravesite known as the place where 52 "brave fellows" were buried in a "trench" was finally memorialized with a marker. They were victims of the infamous Paoli Massacre that took place the night of September 20, 1777, in present-day Malvern. The dead were buried in a centralized location in farm fields where it was believed the fiercest fighting took place.

Preservation efforts did not resurface until years later, in the 1890s, an era now known as the "Golden Age" of battlefield preservation in America. Congress was said to have a major representation of Civil War veterans within its ranks, and naturally all five federal parks established during that decade were sites recognizing the Great War between the States.

Veterans' associations were generally behind every battlefield preserved during this era and soon erecting monuments was a national trend. In fact, by 1890, every major Civil War battlefield had gone through the process of being protected and then preserved officially, often in the form of a "military park" maintained by a group of veterans supporters.

This pattern was true of the Paoli Massacre site, although it was another generation of veterans – from the War of 1812 – who were responsible for the region's first military monument placed at the "trench" burial site. (49) [49]

Perhaps the most interesting veterans group at this time was a local group called the Centennial Minute Men of Chester County. In September of 1890, the Minute Men were seemingly on every newspaper reporter's mind.

The year was not a major anniversary – merely the 116th anniversary of the Battle of Brandywine – but the activities of the group were so closely covered, it seemed that the Minute Men were stand-ins for the national quest to honor one's heritage with monuments and historic plaques. Certainly, the time had come: the country was on the verge of its second industrial revolution, and battlefields everywhere were being threatened by railroad construction and road expansions.

Even though it was not until 1900 that a national policy was in place for protecting those military parks already established (and not until 1933 that the battlefields were overseen by the National Parks Service), the first steps in battlefield protection were typically pursued on the local level.

Groups such as the Minute Men were committed to the idea of honoring the early patriots, especially if a monument inspired the "contemplation of youth," as one reporter put it.

Bizarrely, one event organized by the Minute Men in 1893 was hardly a symbolic commemoration of fallen patriots – it was the re-internment of a Revolutionary War soldier. The remains were accidentally dug up a few years before by a Chadds Ford farmer named Eli Harvey. One reporter noted that Harvey kept the soldier's remains in a custom-made glass casket so one could see the "jagged hole through the skull" and the only remains of his clothing: silver shoe buckles.

No mention was made of Harvey's residence, but it was not surprising that he had discovered many military artifacts over the years – Harvey lived at Washington's former headquarters. He had purchased the Benjamin Ring farm at a public sale in 1805 and lived there till his death in 1863. (Harvey's sons also lived on the property but it was Eli who gave his name to the nearby Harvey Run.)

Harvey was a well-known figure even without his Revolutionary collection. He was said to have run a tavern at the Ring House, being part of the Harvey family that were maltsters for several generations. 50

The historian Henry Graham Ashmead describes the Harveys of the "east side of the Brandywine," as living in the c.1774-1799 homestead that still stands on Harvey Road. Thus, family members may have seen Stephen's and Stirling's advance troops gallop by the house on their way from Chads Ford to Birmingham.

Indeed, the race to "Birmingham Hill" or the "Heights" has been described by generations of historians. Yet it has only been in recent years that a timeline has been pinned down. It is now known, for instance, that only an hour before the Crown Forces began its descent from Osborne's Hill, Stephen's and Stirling's divisions were waiting orders, halted in the fields on Nottingham Road near the present-day Brandywine Drive and Painter's Crossing Road.

In 1777, there was no direct route to Birmingham Hill, so at around 2:15 p.m. the divisions had to go slightly out of their way. They initially headed west for one mile on the Nottingham Road before cutting through the Harvey Run watershed and taking Harvey Road north to what is now Oakland Road (once part of Harvey Road) and onto Birmingham Road.

Ashmead's 1884 *History of Delaware County* describes the Continental's route in terms of landowners in 1777 and also indicates the term "Sandy Hollow" was then in use. The history describes Harvey Road as follows.

> It wound "up the ravine from William Harvey's house, past the barn, over the hill to and across Dix's Run, up the next hill to and across the road from Dilworthtown to the Brandywine, at a point between the James Brinton and Darlington residences; thence nearly northeast across the Bennett land to the Sandy Hollow road which led to Birmingham meeting-house."

One wing of Greene's command is said to have been guided cross-country by a man named George Hannum, who piloted them across the "Gilpin" lands and along a road then known as the Philadelphia to Chads' Ford Road. This early road follows the roadbed of the present-day Oakland Road past the 1704 Brinton House. (31)

During the five day encampment after the battle Howe headquartered in the George Gilpin's homestead; until this event changed the course of the family's history, the Gilpins were best known for developing an apple called the "Gilpin" or "winter red-streak." | Another equally well-known Harvey homestead was found on the west side of the Brandywine. (43)

Community lore as well as a family history say that the structure was nearly destroyed by cannon fire during the mid-morning attacks of Sept. 11, 1777. The family patriarch, a Quaker farmer named William Harvey, 2nd, was famously opposed to leaving his home even though his property was on Brinton Bridge Road, and extended to the Brandywine where Knyphausen's artillery was posted.

Writing in retrospect, Joseph Townsend wrote of the general's decision to post there: General Knyphausen "arranged his artillery on the lands of William Harvey, Jacob Way and others adjoining, as the most eligible spot for the intended purpose, having the principal part of his troops under armies in full view of the Americans, who occupied on the east side."

The Harvey house had also received incoming fire for most of the morning from Proctor's batteries across the Brandywine at Brinton's Ford (67). [51] At one point, Jacob Way reportedly came to plead with Harvey to flee the premises when a 12-pound cannon ball suddenly tore through the kitchen, from one wall to another, before dropping to the floor and barely missing Harvey's legs. Only then did he abandon his home. [52]

Harvey later claimed more than 562 pounds sterling in damages —nearly as much as West Bradford Township's total damages —and he personally cited Howe as a "falsifier of his word, and plunderer of private property."

This story was not cited in the 1893 newspaper story about the Minute Men celebration even though it might have clarified Harvey family's ties with the Battle of Brandywine. [53] The reporter simply noted that Harvey placed several of artifacts with the soldier's remains such as a "rusty bayonet, [and] a ponderous horse-pistol" as well as a bucketful of "continental pennies and English pence and shillings" that were "turned up by the plow."

It was also reported that the burial ceremony, complete with a headstone, would still take place, despite the fact that an identifying button had been lost and thus it was unclear if "the bones were that of a Colonial soldier or that of a red-coated Britisher."

While Harvey's actions were exceptional to the times, he wasn't the last local Quaker to acknowledge the losses of the Battle of Brandywine. A turning point that led to more memorials and historical markers was the formation of the Birmingham Lafayette Cemetery Association in 1891. A West Chester resident named John G. Taylor was a birthright Quaker, but he had amassed enough stock in the cemetery to change the all-Quaker burial ground to a non-denominational one. [54]

In a curiously biting news item headlined, *"Peculiar fad of Chester County Quaker,"* Taylor was described as a retired broker who lived fugally in West Chester's Turk's Head Hotel where he was known as the "Monument Man" for spending "his fortune erecting monuments." One of Taylor's first monuments jointly honored two Brandywine Battlefield soldiers: his great grandfather, Colonel Isaac Taylor, and

49. Paoli Massacre Monument: This is one of state's first memorials to the American Revolution. It was created when veterans of the War of 1812 as well as a local militia group called the Republican Artillerists passed a resolution on July 4, 1817, promising to dedicate a memorial on September 20th, the 40th anniversary of the "Paoli Massacre."
Author's collection.

Colonel Joseph McClellan. 55

Another marker recognized four distinguished officers including Count Casimir Pulaski and General Lafayette (48). It was unveiled eighteen years before the Lafayette Monument of 1895 (58), and although an earlier plan to include a bronze statue of the Marquis was dropped, the design matched the substantial weight of Taylor's previous monuments – it was made of granite on a pyramidal base dedicated to more than one war hero. The main monument honored Lafayette and Pulaski, but there were also tributes to the French officers Gen. Rochambeau, Gen. St. Simons, and Admiral DeGrasse.

At the time of Taylor's death in 1913, it was widely reported that he had spent more than 100,000 dollars on the construction and placement of several monuments honoring American Revolutionary War heroes.

While Taylor helped to bring attention to the Battle of Brandywine, but no one had any luck in preserving what was seen as the sacred ground of the battlefield. A case in point was Colonel F.C. (Francis Carpenter) Hooton, a birthright Quaker and Civil War veteran of the 175th Pennsylvania infantry who devoted his final years to promoting the history of the battlefield.

50. The Distant View: The 1899 image (above) by Douglas E. Brinton is believed to have been labeled by him. Osborne Hill, where he stood to take the photograph, is labeled #2.

Some of the landmarks he labeled are not community landmarks today, such as the properties of "Dr Norris Robbins" and "Mrs. Biddle." The label "Lafayette schaft" may have been the 1895 monument to Lafayette at Birmingham Road.

Courtesy of CCHC.

1. Birmingham Meeting House
2. Osborne Hill
3. Road to Schonelltown from Birmingham
4. Mrs Biddle
5. Dr. Norris Robbins
6. Street Road
7. Road to Dilworthtown
8. Direction of Chadd's Ford
9. Lafayette Schaft

In 1900, Hooton (right) successfully advocated for a state appropriate bill that would raise funds for a study of the battlefield, but it was soon vetoed by Governor William A. Stone. It seems that that objection was based on Hooton's extravagant ideas: he went so far as to propose that a national park to be established in Birmingham and that it be similar in scope and importance as Valley Forge.

Judging from the surviving newspaper coverage, however, Hooton received little attention on that topic and, in fact, with the exception of the handful of reporters who covered his planning activities as the chair of the "Brandywine Day" committee, Hooton was often billed as an eccentric member of the Chester County Bar who dabbled in local history and was an inventor of several household devices such as a nonexplosive kerosine lamp.

On at least one occasion, when the Brandywine Day committee convened on the Birmingham battlefield, Hooton dressed in his Civil War colonel's uniform and traveled the distance by horseback from his home on North Matlack Street.

Before turning to battlefield preservation, Hooton's first mission – as chair of a committee connected to a local chapter of the Grand Army of the Republic – was to verify the first use of the American stars and stripes. The committee determined it was at the Battle of Brandywine and held a ceremony that may have been part of a larger anniversary event that took place on Sept. 11, 1915.

According to a long illustrated story in the *Philadelphia Public Ledger,* the anniversary event drew 4000 people including the state Governor, a French Ambassador, a British "attaché," and several U.S. Congressmen and representatives such as Thomas S. Butler of West Chester. The day included the unveiling of 16 bronze tablets scattered throughout the region and Chadds Ford. 56

Hooton wrote a book on the flag's use at the Battle of Brandywine (still in print today) and even though he was later criticized for placing a flagpole near the Birmingham Meetinghouse – a site deemed by reporters as "the wrong place," since it was not at Sandy Hollow – he later received favorable newspaper coverage for his subsequent preservation efforts. 57

Before getting in enmeshed in unrelated financial troubles, Hooton may have been the first to push for state legislation in advancing the idea that a park was needed in a region that the average American knew little about. This was not to be in Chadds Ford, but a place where one newspaper called "the Continentals' last heroic stand at Sandy Hollow."

Early Preservation Efforts

Perhaps it's understandable that before the preservation of the battlefield could happen on the grand scale, residents needed to understand what happened – and where – a process that is still unfolding in the Task Force's research into what is essentially three battlefield regions, such as the "Southern Strategic Landscape" of Kennett Township. In other words, after battlefield anniversary celebrations, monuments, and driving tours, the next step in preservation rested on a broader understanding of the significance of the Battle of Brandywine.

That didn't happen until 1920s when Chester County was enjoying economic stable times, and a few devoted individuals may have wanted to capitalize on the prosperity and good will of the people. Shortly after Sanderson was forced to leave his home at Washington's former headquarters, his friend, John A. Farrell, a West Chester physician, began a campaign to urge the State House to take over the property as a public park.

In an article published on Nov.11th, 1923 in the *Philadelphia Public Ledger*, the headline read "*Brandywine Battlefield to Be a National Shrine,*" and cited both Sanderson and Farrell as the leaders in a movement to recognize the battlefield, then "neglected for more than a century and a quarter, and largely forgotten."

Sanderson and Farrell selected Armistice Day to bring together several World War 1 veterans and members of a West Chester chapter of the American Legion, urging them to join forces to begin what was termed the "big push" to preserve Washington's Headquarters and the surrounding land.

A resolution was later passed at the Legion's State Convention in Reading, Pa., but it was reported that Farrell was not successful with the state policy makers in Harrisburg. Despite this disappointment, Farrell was said to have continued his campaign years after the headquarters was converted into a tearoom and caught fire on Sept. 16, 1931.

As all the newspapers related, a woman named Helen DuBois had operated a tearoom there for a few years when the fire took place at night. It may have begun in a blocked chimney - the newspapers mainly reported that DuBois was awakened by her barking dog and that despite the help of neighbors and the Cleveland family who owned the building, the entire structure burned to the ground so that only the stone walls remained. (39)

Sanderson and his mother learned of the destruction but could not bear to see it until that October 13th, the 25th anniversary of their first night at the former headquarters. Still, it was Sanderson, and not Farrell, who is credited for dedicating his life to activities that would commemorate the Battle of Brandywine such as lectures, bat-

51. Unicorn Block: An undated view of the c.1877 commercial block named for the former Revolutionary War landmark, the Unicorn Tavern. In 1777, the tavern was operated by Peter Bell, who suffered considerable damages when Gen. Knyphausen took over the tavern as his headquarters. A marble plaque is still evident on the building, marking the site. The Unicorn was destroyed by a fire in the months before the British occupation and was rebuilt using an unusual black stone called horneblende, quarried only in a few places including Kennett Township.

Top: The Kerr paper mill once stood at the same site as the mill along present-day Rt. 322.

51. The Kennett Hotel: Two views of the former brick building that remarkably, was built soon after the town's founder, Joseph Musgrave, began laying out land parcels in 1767. It was expanded by the grandfather of the novelist Bayard Taylor and was occupied until the 1950s when it was destroyed by an electrical fire. The son of Philadelphia's second mayor, Col. Joseph Shippen, purchased the Musgrave home around 1776 and saw it used as Howe's headquarters the day before the battle.

Interestingly, Shippen was a Princeton graduate, a veteran of the French & Indian War, and a government official, but he had two unusual connections to spies. His wife was the daughter of Joseph Galloway and his niece was the wife of Benedict Arnold. *Author's collection.*

tle tours, and organizing anniversary events such the annual Brandywine Day (30).

Farrell died in 1939, but amazingly, major steps toward battlefield preservation continued in the midst of the Great Depression – not only lead by Sanderson but a state senator from Farrell's hometown named William Hannum Clark.

Sometime in early 1933, Clark pushed for the state's approval in condemning a large territory around Birmingham Meetinghouse and Sandy Hollow (5) and obtaining the land for public use. News stories of the period are unclear about the intended use for the land – one suggestion was that it could be used as a camping ground for the state National Guard – but it was decided that a state commission would be formed to examine the battlefield land and to determine its boundaries. Individual properties were not discussed, only that the condemned land would "not exceed 300 acres."

According to the scant newspaper accounts, Senator Clark fielded concerns that the proposed park would become a tourist destination and "devalue" the surrounding properties. That did not happen with Valley Forge Park, proponents acknowledged, but the state park had been established long before, in 1893, and was then under the management of state's Department of Forests and Waters.

To preserve the Brandywine battlefield, Clark estimated that 25,000 dollars was needed to seize the land so that a market price could be paid to each property owner (all of them farmers) in Birmingham where, one reporter wrote, the "battle was fought. "

The second bill asked for another thousand dollars to be used by local historical societies to excavate the land for soldier remains. Clark's hometown newspaper, the *Daily Local News*, reported that the "chief complaint" in the senate was "lack of funds," which was understandable given the economic hard times. But both bills passed in March of 1935.

The support reflected a particular Depression-era allegiance and a national interest in private home museums and battlefield sites, although some historians trace the movement back to the creation of colonial Williamsburg that was made possible in 1926 with the help of John D. Rockefeller, Jr. Even if Clark had secured a similar patronage, a short news item published in 1937 suggests that he faced a local community that was largely indifferent to the history of the battlefield mainly because people were so overwhelmed financially.

The article included an interview with a local historian, Charles W. Heathcote, who then chaired a newly formed park-creation commission. Heathcote, the author of the first public school textbook (in 1929) to include the Battle of Brandywine, now expressed disappointment that there was little public interest in basic preservation. He pointed to Washington's Headquarters, still "in ruins," and perhaps worse, the building still described as Lafayette's Headquarters now housed a tearoom. While Heathcote's committee eventually moved forward to create a state park at the former headquarters, Clark's hope for additional battlefield protection went nowhere and he retired from the State Senate at the end of 1935.

It was not until the flush years following World War 11 that Clark's ideas resurfaced, and the State Congress had the funds to consider a battlefield preservation effort led by two Pennsylvania senators: George Scarlett (above), a former Burgess of Kennett Square who was elected to the Senate in 1937, and Weldon Brinton Heyburn, (below) a birthright Quaker from Concordville who served from 1949 to 1957.

Once again there was a move to implement support from the Department of Forests and Waters to secure what was described as "lands lying within the area of the battlefield" in Birmingham Township and to determine "the amount of appropriation required" so that the battlefield land "may be preserved as a park of major historical importance."

In the words of one reporter, the senator pushed for a bill that proposed that the park be comprised of 1,570 acres. The project was endorsed by several historical- minded groups including the Chester County Historical Society and a local chapter of the Sons of the American Revolution.

Most wanted to save the land as a place where Gen. Washington "most skillfully executed strategic retreats" such as at Sandy Hollow and Greene's Rear Guard Defense near the Brinton 1704 House, according to one newspaper. However, the legislation was eventually turned down by the newly elected governor, James H. Duff, and the bill was abandoned. Senators Scarlett and Heyburn then introduced two bills that ruled out condemnation. The first bill called for the purchase of 175 acres in Delaware County that included Washington's Headquarters and nearby land that the owners wanted to sell. The second bill called for $150,000 to purchase 500 acres of the "battle site in Chester County," primarily in Birmingham Township.

Judging from the scarcity of newspaper accounts, the senators wanted to keep any discussion of purchasing property in and around Sandy Hollow under wraps; in fact, no specifics about the location of the acreage was given.

Sadly, the senators were met with major opposition and public outcry. Indeed, years later the period would go down as the "second battle" of the Brandywine, when local farmers, fearing that they would lose their land to eminent domain, were joined in their fight by members of the Birmingham Friends Meeting.

At the time, there were still vast stretches of untouched battlefield land, but few people knew that the Brandywine Battlefield was the only major battle site of the American Revolution that remained unprotected by either state or national laws.

Unfortunately, public consensus in Chester and Delaware County reaffirmed the debate among Quakers and the senators were told to look elsewhere to build their park. The Friends of Birmingham, it was thought, had the right to oppose what they considered to be a war memorial in their backyard.

Warwick Cannon, one of several cannons excavated in 2022 at the Warwick Ironworks. *Illustration by Ann Bedrick.*

The park-planning commission subsequently decided that the proposed Brandywine Battlefield Park would be centered on the American headquarters in Chadds Ford and they raised funds to negotiate a fair price with the landowners. The negotiations were complicated by the fact that the land as well as the two headquarters were owned by two extended families who were reluctant to give up the properties they had owned since 1906. 58 Working with the estate of Richard M. Atwater and the family members of Arthur H. Cleveland, Sr., the commission finally reached an agreement, and the properties were acquired with mostly privately raised funds in 1949. 59

Still the sale was not without controversy, but not because the properties saw no major military action. Coming up with a good reason to buy the property was deemed problematic since Washington's Headquarters had fallen into even more disrepair, and the park commission faced community skepticism concerning the validity that Lafayette even stayed in the house owned by Gideon Gilpin in 1777. Acquiring Lafayette's headquarters also meant displacing Cleveland, Jr., who was living there with his wife, newspapers reported.

Finally in the fall of 1949 about 50 acres of land was dedicated as a state park – albeit one that was considerably smaller in size from what Senator Clark had envisioned. The Clevelands remained living in Lafayette's Headquarters and for a few years, the property looked like any other local farm.(36) 60

State grants eventually funded the restoration of both headquarters under the direction of architect G. Edwin Brumbaugh. A committee was formed to oversee the furnishing of the houses, much of it coming from member Henry F. DuPont and his Winterthur estate. The first donation, in fact, was said to be DuPont's; he gave two 18th-century figurines to the park in honor of Farrell, the West Chester physician who had tried to preserve the battlefield years before. Donations continued to be made until 1954, when the houses were pronounced "finished," although the park had been dedicated on Sept. 11, 1952.

Today the Brandywine Battlefield Park is owned and operated by the Pennsylvania Historical and Museum Commission, and at 52 acres, remains close to its original size in 1949. Even though Washington's Headquarters is a reconstruction and the Gilpin house underwent major changes in the 1950s, the park property is still considered to be historic grounds. Indeed, the all-volunteer group that manages the educational mission of the park, the Brandywine Battlefield Park Association (BBPA), is known for its authentic colonial re-enactments and living up to the tagline *"Keeping The Story Alive."*

In 1997, the park and surrounding the battlefield landmark became the state's first historic site to be named a Commonwealth Treasure, in part because of the park's educational efforts in promoting the history of the Battle of Brandywine. A historic marker explaining that designation was placed the same year at the intersection of South New Street and Birmingham Road.

Part Two

Historic Narratives & Community Anecdotes

[There was] a most infernal fire of cannon and musket — smoak — incessant shouting — incline to the right! Incline to the Left! — halt!—charge! ... the balls ploughing up the ground. The Trees cracking over ones head, The branches riven by the artillery — The leaves falling as in autumn by grapeshot."
British Lt. Richard St. George on the deafening sounds of battle.

War Comes to the Brandywine Valley

When a line of supply wagons rumbled into the Royal Army camp at Kennett Square (51) on Sept. 10, 1777, they were emptied and set aside for further use. The veteran soldiers certainly knew what these wagons would be used for — to carry wounded and dying soldiers from the battlefield. After an uneventful spring, several weeks at sea, and 16 days of uncomfortable, ceaseless marching, the first battle of the Philadelphia Campaign of 1777 was to begin.

A wave of fear and community gossip reportedly swept through Chester County, but it was the residents of nearby Downing's town – named for Thomas Downing, who had several mills there – who were especially concerned with the British landing at the Head of the Elk in Maryland.

Much like Kennett Square, Downingtown was in danger of being in the path of the British if they traveled north and sought out either one of the three probable targets: the settlement of Lancaster, the nation's largest inland town with more than 5,000 residents; the iron furnaces of Northern Chester County, then in full blast to produce the army's artillery; and the military complex known as the Continental Powder Works on the French Creek near Phoenixville. 61

The citizens of Lancaster feared that their hamlet would be occupied by the British – not Philadelphia – especially since in 1777, Lancaster had many forges, furnaces, rifle shops, and mills. If the British came north to occupy the settlement, Downingtown would be a natural stop via the Horseshoe Trail (Rt. 322) and it was also in easy reach of Reading, Pennsylvania.

The manager of the Powder Works, Peter DeHaven, wrote of his concern to government officials on Sept. 10th. Using the common name "magazine" for the gunpowder and ammunition complex, he wrote of hearing that the Crown Forces were in Kennett Square. "We have got sum information that thare is Part of Hows' army Within four Miles of Downins Town [Downingtown] & I believe they intend for our Magazine, and Wee [sic] are in a very Poor Situation for defending it, I should be very glad if you Would send a Proper Gard for this Place."

DeHaven, who eventually obtained his guards, as did Downingtown, was equally concerned that enough wagons were procured to move barrels of gunpowder and other supplies to safety elsewhere. Writing that he could only obtain "8 or 10" wagons so far, he mentioned a settlement north of Downingtown that was also in danger – Reading.

In 1777, Reading's iron production, together with that of the iron furnace country in Northern Chester County, exceeded that of England. Much like Downingtown, Reading was also a forage depot, a hospital site, and a military magazine and supply center. Ironically, none of these settlements were occupied – nor were they part of a deliberate plan of attack if one considers the 1778 British map described as the *"one dramatic sequence of events as they occurred from August to December 1777."* 62

The Delaware historian Walt Chiquoine has compared the map with present-day maps to document the routes the Crown Forces may have taken into Pennsylvania The map, also described as *"A plan of the Progression of the Royal Army from their Landing at Elk Ferry to Philadelphia, 1777,"* is illustrated with landmarks that, until recent years, were not considered to be part of the route to Kennett Square.

The Samuel White Tavern, for instance, once stood at the Toughkenamon crossroads and what is now the circa 1710/1733 Newark Road. It appears on the 1778 British map and reinforces the idea that part of Knyphausen's division may have entered Kennett Square by way of Avondale.

One Hessian of a musketeer regiment may have been on the Newark Road near Avondale when he wrote that his column "resumed its march at 5 o'clock in the morning and joined the First Division at 9 o'clock in the morning at Kennett Square."

Howe's aide-de-camp, Captain Friedrich von Muenchhausen, also records that Howe and Cornwallis made good time on the "bye" roads, having departed Hockessin, Delaware, around 5 a.m. They reached Kennett Square around 8 a.m., long before Knyphausen's rear guard that was encumbered with "many wagons and cattle."

Howe's column may have even arrived sooner, it was suggested, had they not fumbled through the Red Clay Creek Valley and, as the sun set, were forced to halt five miles from the troops' destination. Muenchhausen records the event as follows:

> At six o'clock [p.m.] General Howe marched with the division of Lord Cornwallis and General Grant on another road to Kennett Square, to the right of von Knyphausen [sic] route. The road that we took was so bad, and it was getting so dark, that the General [Howe] halted five miles from Kennett Square."

Few accounts are clear about the specific location of the halt, but those by a few Hessian grenadiers indicate the general direction. One writes of a short march northeast through New Garden Township before stopping.

A member of the *Dincklage* Hessian regiment writes of a roundabout route through New Garden as follows: "We had to make a big detour and arrived in camp in the morning of the 10th near a small town by the name of Kingssquare [Kennett Square]." Another Hessian grenadier suggests a halt was made "after we had covered 6 miles, we made a rendezvous."

One temporary resting area may have been west of Kennett Square, near the present-day New Garden Center and modern Cedar Spring Road. The area is flat and open due to the presence of the Scarlett Run, a tributary of Red Clay Creek, and so it may have been considered an ideal place for an encampment.

Another part of Howe's nearly debilitated troops may have rested from about 5 a.m. to sunrise, when they resumed their march into Kennett Square via modern Kaolin Road which becomes South Union Road (now Rt. 82) at the modern-day Five Points intersection.

Ewald's diary suggests that the troops did not halt so much as to make temporary encampments. Arriving in darkness, two divisions set up camp "in unequal

52. Jones' Ford: Named for William Jones, whose serpentine homestead still stands on Street Road, this postcard is one of few postcards that didn't identify the crossing by name. At least 250 soldiers in the 1st Delaware regiment were stationed here for most of the morning. By the late afternoon, Jones' Ford became a rendezvous point and the crossroads became jammed with American troops on their way to Birmingham.

53. Long Gone: This covered bridge carried Brinton's Bridge Road across the Brandywine. Sullivan was posted on the right. The area received a heavy "cannonade" after the British first brigade, and about 1,300 troops, were ordered from an area near Fairview Road to this ford, marching past the homestead of William Harvey.

lines ... on the heights beyond" and west of Kennett Square. "The right wing" of Howe's army, Ewald explains "ran toward Louis [Lewis] Mill and its left [wing] toward Marlboroug [sic] Meeting House, [and] the *Jäger* [sic] occupied the road toward Chester" [The Great Road to Nottingham].

The mill Ewald mentions may have stood on the foundation of what is now Clifton Mills, at 162 Old Kennett Pike, south of Kennett Square. Ewald used the name of its former owner, Ellis Lewis, whose estate in 1776 sold the 100-acre mill tract (it included two mills, a dwelling house, and a barn) to Gavin Hamilton, a wealthy Scotsman who operated a tobacco exporting business in Philadelphia. Hamilton may have purchased the property for its grist and snuff mills; the latter was used to ground tobacco into snuff powder.

Ewald was evidently aware of the Lewis mill, but he is believed to have misidentified the Meetinghouse. Howe's second column under Cornwallis traveled at least an hour beyond Kennett Square, placing them near the London Grove Meeting, part of the New Garden Monthly Meeting in 1777. The meetinghouse on Newark and Street Roads is just over five miles from Kennett Square.

Washington's Officers

Today some historians see the Battle of Brandywine as the last major battle where top commanders—George Washington and Lafayette and their British counterparts, Howe and Cornwallis – came close to combat instead of following the action from a safe vantage point. 64

Others tend to point out that Washington and most of the American commanders were relatively unprepared to fight the British, who were not only better trained, but they also had more accurate maps and prior spy information. Compared to the British commander Howe, who was known for his ruthless assaults at Bunker Hill and the 1776 New York Campaign, the officers who led the Continental forces seemed to have merely dallied into battle.

At least two members of Washington's War Council that gathered at the Ring House in Chadds Ford on September 10th had to overcome serious shortcomings such as not being fluent in English. They included Brig. Gen. Casimir Pulaski who arrived on the scene dressed as a Polish hussar, or Hungarian light horseman, having escaped a death sentence in his native Poland.

A 1972 marker placed near the entrance of the Brandywine Battlefield Park along Baltimore Pike describes Pulaski as the "Polish volunteer," who later commanded what became known as Pulaski's Legion, which is now considered the first

The Untold Story of Its History and Preservation | 121

The Center of the Action. This c. 1910 postcard acknowledges the John Chads' House as the scene of the battle. *Courtesy of CFHS.*

cavalry regiment in the American Continental Army. The Chadds Ford marker credits him for helping to cover Washington's retreat from Sandy Hollow to the colonial county seat of Chester. However, some historians would consider that to be an understatement since without Pulaski's reconnaissance mission to find an escape route, Washington could easily have been killed or captured.

Another officer with an aristocratic bearing, Maj General William Alexander Stirling, was born in New York but his Scottish lineage gave him the right to use the title of Earl of Stirling. Despite his preference for being called "Lord" Stirling or "Sir" he was hailed as an esteemed "patriot," especially after he survived being captured by the British while serving as a colonel in the New Jersey militia.

Interestingly, he was part of a prisoner exchange and immediately returned to Washington's Army. His loyalty during the now famous Crossing of the Delaware and the Battle of Princeton led to his promotion to Major General in February,1777.

The Brandywine Battle became a proving ground not only for Washington and his generals but for many of his associates including the future president

James Monroe who was a young aide-de-camp in Lord Stirling's American division. Lafayette had no combat experience, but he traveled to America at his own expense (learning English on the long sea journey) and became a volunteer Major General in a little more than a month before the Battle of Brandywine. At the time, it was rumored that Lafayette was allowed to join the troops at the Brandywine mainly because of his immense wealth and social connections (he was related by marriage to King Louis XVI), but attitudes soon changed after the battle.

A French officer, Chevalier Dubuysson, was officially Lafayette's Aide-de-camp but also a caring observer. He was among several French officers who followed Lafayette on the battlefield, but it was Dubuysson alone who wrote about Lafayette's first encounter with "severe fire."

Lafayette had celebrated his 20th birthday only five days earlier during an important time when Washington had gathered his Council of War at the home of a Quaker named Rev. Daniel Byrnes, now a preserved house museum known as the Hale-Byrnes House near Newark, Delaware.

The birthday celebration was no doubt brief, considering that the Continentals had fought the Battle of Cooch's Bridge and now needed a emergency exit plan. Ordered to convene "at 5'oclock..at the brick house by White Clay Creek, and fix upon proper picquets for the security of the camp," Washington's Council stayed from Sept. 6th to the 9th. The strategy they developed ultimately led to what the authors of a booklet on the house have called "the flawless overnight evacuation" of the Continental Army from Delaware to Chadds Ford.

From the start, Lafayette was not expected to do anything but accompany Washington and perhaps observe the Council's debates on strategy. Indeed, Lafayette could have easily avoided any kind of military action if it were not for one incident—one that led to his participation at Sandy Hollow. As Dubuysson writes, Lafayette "always accompanied the general [Washington]," but for some reason he "obtained permission to join Sullivan." 65 It is believed that this happened at a crucial time when the American forces faced an onslaught of advancing British and Hessians, especially at Brinton's (53)and Chads' Fords.

Characteristically, Lafayette uses the third person when he wrote about joining Sullivan's troops in his memoir. "At his arrival, which [Sullivan's] troops appeared to appreciate," Lafayette wrote, "he found that the enemy had crossed the ford, and Sullivan's corps had scarcely had time to form one line in front of a wooded forest."

Lafayette does not mention the "severe fire" until Sullivan's troops left Brinton's Ford around 5 p.m. and were heading toward Birmingham Meeting.

55. Linden Farm: The photographer Douglas E. Brinton identifies this crossroads as being near Sandy Hollow, although he doesn't name the crossroads only that the home of Samuel Jones was to the left.
Courtesy of CCHC.

It is believed that they may have encountered part of the British flanking party as it crossed Radley Run, moving south as a column toward Street Road.

Lafayette later recalled in his memoir both the abrupt encounter and the subsequent American cannonade along what may have been the open farm fields below Birmingham Hill ("the plain"). He writes as follows:

> "Lord Cornwallis's men suddenly emerged from the woods in very good order. Advancing across the plain [sic], his first line opened a very brisk fire with cannons and muskets. The American fire was murderous, but both their right and their left wings collapsed."

Dubuysson also wrote of Lafayette's subsequent gallant behavior at Sandy Hollow, although it may have been his return to the field after he was shot, and his bravery in leading the American retreat that made him a national hero – one honored in the form of towns, counties, colleges, and streets bearing his name. As the historian McGuire wryly observes, "barely out of his teens, one of the most popular and romantic American heroes thus was created in the midst of a collapsing battle line.

Although the wounding of Lafayette was recognized in several ways — one was the planting of a tree and the placement of several cannons near Sandy Hollow (54) — a different site closer to the Birmingham Meetinghouse was selected for another monument in 1895 (58). The change in location was due in part because residents recalled that during Lafayette's visit to the battlefield in 1825, he had reconsidered the "true location" after "coming in sight of that building," as one reporter wrote.

The second monument was the biggest celebration to date, and when the unveiling occurred on September 11, 1895, an estimated eight thousand people were in attendance. They were there to commemorate Lafayette's actions and to mark the place of his wounding, "on rising ground a short distance south of this spot," as the monument reads.

In one telling speech, an official spoke of the "widening and deepening interest" in local history and the work of area schoolchildren who raised funds for the "simple and graceful" monument – one that was deemed a "silent protest against extravagance and show in monuments."

Even though the date has never been verified, it is believed that a separate group spent part of the afternoon working to place what turned out to be Civil War Naval cannons at a location now at the intersection of Birmingham and Wylie Roads (34). One account reported (rather vaguely) that the cannons were donated by "the citizens of Pennsylvania."

The newly formed Chester County Historical Society was later part of a movement to bring what was termed "special exercises in local history" to the public schools. An extensive history of the Battle of Brandywine soon appeared in school textbooks and the annual anniversary celebration, "Brandywine Day," was recognized as a holiday by school officials overseeing the region's one-room schools.

It wasn't long until the battle's heroes and major generals were widely known by the following nicknames: "Mad" Anthony Wayne; Nathaniel Greene, the "Fighting Quaker;" Peter Gabriel Muhlenberg, the "Fighting Parson;" "Light-Horse Harry" Lee; and Alexander Hamilton, the "Little Lion," a nickname given to him for what we would now call his multi-tasking ability, not his physical strength, and "Squire" Thomas Cheyney, the "Paul Revere" of the Brandywine Valley, among them.

Washington's Multicultural Army

The troops that fought at the Brandywine were truly diverse, ranging from free Blacks and Irish working class to German farmers and English colonists. The first group of solders were an anomaly, however. Pennsylvania had more free Blacks than any other colony, but they were not actively recruited for the 1777 Philadelphia Campaign. Indeed, the first unit to allow former slaves and free Blacks in their ranks was the First Rhode Island regiment. These men fought alongside Native Americans and together, they contributed to the American victory at Red Bank, a Continental fort on the banks of the Delaware on October 22, 1777. But the Rhode Island unit did not become an official or authorized regiment until 1778. Even so, Black soldiers would only make up about five percent of the entire Continental Army during the war.

The handful of former slaves who did serve in the Campaign of 1777 were assigned to a Maryland regiment and promised their freedom after an honorable discharge. These African Americans included those who served as soldiers, messengers, and waggoners, such as Edward "Ned" Hector of Proctor's artillery. Many came from established Black communities such as Logtown, near the present-day Concordville, and "Hanging Rock" at Gulph Mills, where the American troops had their last prolonged encampment – from Dec. 13 to Dec. 19, 1777 – before settling at the winter camp at Valley Forge.

Another group of unlikely warriors were the German American soldiers. Although some were recruited from Lancaster and Berks County (and parts of Maryland), many were late-arriving immigrants who settled on less desirable lands in Northern Chester County where they spoke German among themselves.

The German recruits were considered ideal additions to the Philadelphia Campaign since it was assumed that they would counterbalance the German segment of the Crown Forces—all of them conscripted soldiers — known as the Hessian *Jägers* (aka Yeagers or Yagers), a green-uniformed group that carried swords and rifles and whose name literally means "hunter."

Hired by the British from German-speaking regions of Europe, the Hessians were described in Thomas Jefferson's early draft of the Declaration of Independence as "foreign mercenaries," who were destined to bring "death, desolation, and tyranny" to America. (By the time war broke out, the Continental Congress had a different attitude and Hessian soldiers were offered 50 acres of land if they deserted.)

Another major component of Washington's Army – the Scotch-Irish– were not only fiercely patriotic, they were known as the most openly rebellious group, at least in Chester County. The West Chester historian Douglas R. Harper writes that Washington was initially skeptical of their loyalty, but once he arrived in the Brandywine Valley, he "wisely chose," the feisty Scotch-Irish who were typically volunteer "irregulars," meaning they were not members of a regular class of militia.

About 200 residents from "Scots-Irish townships," Harper writes, were selected to escort Washington's troops, presenting a more free-spirited look than the more "formal militia regiment of Chester County men." In 1777, the townships where the late-arriving Scotch-Irish prevailed were in the central and western parts of Chester County. They included the Fallowfields and Caln Townships, where the Brandywine and its tributaries flowed through a countryside of steep and rocky hills. The first group of escorts, which numbered about 200 men, found a similar terrain in the lower Brandywine region.

Some of the men were also experienced in warfare, having been part of a group that responded to Congress's first requisition in Pennsylvania for troops in June of 1775. Outside of Chester County, Washington was said to have relied on the Irish citizenry of Lancaster who were particularly notorious for their anti-English sentiment. One of Washington's officers, Edward Hand, an Irish native himself, had no difficulty in recruiting a Lancaster County militia unit early in the war. Hand was deeply rooted in the community in and around the settlement of Lancaster and his success as a farmer and physician can be seen today in the house museum known as the Rock Ford Plantation. 66

The final addition to Washington's Army was one hundred men "suitably officered" – and primarily selected for their experience as dependable marksmen – to form a special corps of light infantry. Informally called Maxwell's Men, they were to assist the army's militia, a group that had little training in scouting. The man selected to lead this brigade of handpicked riflemen, sharpshooters, and "hunters" was Brigadier General William Maxwell of New Jersey.

"Scotch Willie," as he was nicknamed, was given the job in August and asked by Washington to garnish men from each of the 11 brigades to form a twelfth brigade of American Light Infantry thereafter known as Maxwell's Brigade. Composed of about 800 men (including a group from the Chester County Militia), the brigade was considered a separate entity from the main army in that they rode ahead and scouted, screened, and skirmished in advance of any military action.

Along with the Continental light dragoons under Theodorick Bland ("Bland's Horse"), Maxwell's men were regarded as Washington's elite troops. The American dragoons (mounted troops whose name derives from a type of firearm) were especially independent at the Brandywine; there were three other dragoon brigades besides Bland's but there were no other commanders and so the dragoons reported directly to Washington.

Most members of Bland's Horse, such as Major Henry "Light Horse Harry" Lee, were present but not engaged in the Battle of Brandywine. Maxwell's men were also the first troops of Washington's Army to experience the rough terrain of the Brandywine Valley including its roller-coaster hills, wooded areas of dense vegetation, and wetlands known as the "swampy morass" of the Brandywine. (40)

Curiously, the troops excelled as a light infantry corps, but their use was short-lived. The troops formed on August 28th – only a week before the corps' first battle - they existed for about a month until after the Battle of Paoli on Sept. 17th.

Spies & Traitors

In the weeks and even months leading up to the Battle of Brandywine, the British sought out information from a network of spies that included residents who could tell them how to navigate through the Brandywine Valley, a region they assumed to be chock full of natural obstacles.

The names of many of the spies are now lost to history, but others are well documented as the recruits of Joseph Galloway, a former Chester County resident and Philadelphian attorney. Galloway became the notorious assistant to Howe during the 1777 Philadelphia Campaign, recommending residents, for instance, to serve as spies, scouts, or guides. 67

At least three of the guides were Quaker residents from different regions of Chester County. The Loyalist guide Richard Swanwick, for instance, owned extensive properties in West Caln and Charlestown Townships. He wrote in a compensation claim to the British that he was approached by Galloway after the Sept. 11th battle "in the name of Sir Wm. Howe who requested [his] services in pointing out the Roads and obtaining Intelligence of the force and situations of the American Army."

Two of the recruits were specifically selected to guide the British on the day of the Battle of Brandywine, having been endorsed by Galloway as Loyalists who could suggest the best route for the British Flanking Column through the Bradfords, where the Upper Fords (10,11) were located. They were John Jackson, a clockmaker from East Marlborough, and Curtis Lewis, a blacksmith in West Bradford who owed large tracts of land in East Caln Township and the Bradfords.

In Lewis' compensation claim, he stressed the usual "knowledge of the Country," but also wrote of his long employment, acting as a guide beginning in Maryland, at Elk Landing. He also led the flanking party right from the start in Kennett Square.

Not much is known of Jackson except that he may have later escaped to Nova Scotia. Lewis' downfall can be traced through the minutes of the Bradford Friends Meeting in Marshallton. Lewis was not only disowned by the Meeting, but he was also forced into exile after the Continentals assumed control of his extensive West Bradford lands. In 1779, he fled with his family to Long Island and lost his lands a second time for working again with the British. He contracted a disease and died penniless within the year.

While most of the Loyalist recruits had a similar fate, Galloway may be the best-known spy, mainly because he made such a dramatic turn at the start of the Revolution. A former delegate to the First Continental Congress and a close ally of Benjamin Franklin, Galloway later rejected all attempts at American independence and abandoned both Congress and the Pennsylvania Provincial Assembly, where he had served as Speaker of the House.

Galloway became an informal adviser to Howe sometime in the summer of 1777 and perhaps did the most damage to the American cause by suggesting the route to the Upper Fords. The Hessian *Jäger* captain Johann Ewald was so impressed with Galloway, he pronounced him a "Real geographical chart." Even though Ewald encountered an American patrol during the flanking maneuver, he still considered Galloway to be an astute guide, recalling that he "constantly judged so correctly that I always found the enemy where he presumed him to be."

Knyphausen's Diversion

> *"[Knyphausen] kept the enemy amused in the course of the day with cannon and the appearance of forcing the ford, without intending to pass it, until the attack on the enemy's right should take place,"* as reported to Howe concerning the Hessian general's mission during the British flanking maneuver.

Generations of historians have studied Knyphausen's infamous "diversion" as one driven by Howe's command that the Hessian troops "amuse" or divert attention away from any region but the fighting at hand. There were clashes at Welch's Tavern at 6 a.m. (62) and at Kennett Meeting (8) beginning around 6:45 a.m. that distracted the Americans and bought time for Howe and Cornwallis to make their flanking maneuver.

Washington's late-day reports indicate that the ruse worked – he believed he was facing a weakened Royal Army when he ordered Maxwell's, Greene's, and Sullivan's infantrymen to cross the Brandywine. Writing under the dateline, *CHAD'S FORD, September 11, 1777, 5 O'Clock, P.M.*, Washington's secretary (and de facto chief of staff), Robert Hanson Harrison, penned a letter to Congress.

Harrison gave the highlights of the battle including the observation that the British [and] "their advanced party was attacked by our light troops under General [William] Maxwell, who crossed the Brandywine for that purpose."

The result was that Maxwell "pushed over with his corps," smashing the British troops and seizing their equipment. In one of the few occasions in which casualties were recorded, the fight with Maxwell resulted in "thirty Men left dead on the Spot, among them a [British] Captn' of the 49th, and a number of Intrenching Tools with which they were throwing up a Battery." Harrison, who was known for being able to perfectly capture Washington's plans and opinions, did not mention the fact that the British had stormed Proctor's artillery lunettes, although it happened around 4 p.m.

In a report Knyphausen himself wrote six weeks later, he praised the fearless actions of a Hessian brigade that crossed Chads' Ford and, together with other troops, launched an assault "in a manner [to] force them [the Continentals] to quit [the batteries] notwithstanding the uninterrupted Fire of round & Grape Shot which continued ever [since] the Troops pass'd the Creek...."

The sudden change in tactics was not lost on Washington, who updated John Hancock on the action he described as " a Scattering loose fire between our parties on each side of the Creek, since the Action in the Morning, which just now became warm." Surmising that the intensity of the gunfire was a prelude to a "very hot Evening," Washington's reference to the battle "just now" may have been a crossing undertaken by both armies at Chads' Ford and Brinton's Ford (66). Still, it was the raid of Proctor's artillery batteries that was especially surprising for all involved – the British were astonished at the ease in which they took possession, and the Americans were thoroughly disturbed that it happened.

Historians now believe that Knyphausen not only encouraged his men to abandon the recently seized battery, but he also did not immediately counterattack having stayed with his mission to hold the Americans in place until he heard from Howe.

The signal did not come by messenger; Howe was told to listen for the firing shots of two cannons indicating that the Crown Forces had successfully crossed the Upper Fords (see the map in this book). Until that happened, the Hessian defense line managed to remain in place until nearly 3:30 in the afternoon. The troops numbered only about 5,000 men and they faced nearly half of the Continental Army, or about 8,000 American troops.

The numbers were evidently not an issue for Knyphausen, who followed orders to postpone any direct attack and to create the allusion that numerous regiments were moving in place. This was especially true of the Hessians positioned in a wooded elevation above Chads' Ferry. They were ordered to conduct what recent historians have called "marches and counter marches up and down and in and out of the hills."

The awe-inspiring long British baggage train parked on nearby Hillendale Road was also visible at different places along the road, with camp followers burning fires and no doubt milling around as if they were residents of a small village. The combination of hidden troops and the open display effectively created the allusion that the Crown Forces had all the manpower and equipment. It was a scene one New Jersey soldier called "a sight beyond description grand."

Up at dawn, Knyphausen's forces left Kennett Square and had only gone a few miles when they encountered Maxwell's men posted at Welch's Tavern. Knyphausen himself documented the encounter here when Ferguson's small group of British riflemen, along with 300 American Loyalists with the Queen's Rangers "fell in with about 300 Riflemen of the Enemy, who were posted in the Wood to the eastward of the Tavern." The shots were fired at 6 a.m., but a string of skirmishes and major clashes including one at the next American post at Kennett Friends Meetinghouse, meant that the fighting continued for nearly two hours.

At the tavern, the Continental light infantry famously used what is now known as "shoot-and-scoot tactic." With each volley of musket fire, a group of soldiers withdrew further down the road, drawing the Queen's Rangers and Ferguson's green-coated riflemen closer and closer to Chadds Ford.

Ferguson was said to have been mystified by this American tactic and later concluded that the rebels were "base runaways." "In the course of two hours," he recalled, "my lads underwent the fire of 2000 men who were kind enough to fire in general in the air and run away." Peppered with Scottish vernacular, Ferguson's account may now seem amusing, but it also contributes to the recent understanding that the skirmishes along Nottingham Road involved thousands of soldiers and hours of time before any of the regiments even reached Chads' Ford.

Ferguson himself recalled the encounter as a running battle along the road, noting that his "Lads were so fatigued with dashing after the Rebels over all surfaces," that he had to leave some troops behind. As a result, by the time he neared Chads' Ford, the manpower was greatly diminished ("my whole detachment was under 90 men"). Admitting that it was "no great command," he nonetheless found success with various tactics. He writes "by avoiding the road (U.S. Rt. 1), gaining their flanks, [and] keeping up a rattling fire from the ground or by bullying them we still got on."

Despite the hours of brutal fighting on the run, Knyphausen's "feint" was successful. When he finally made his main frontal attack at 4 p.m. – nearly at the same time the *Grenaldiers' March* was being played during the troops' descent from Osborne's Hill (2,50) and into battle – he did so reportedly without a signal from Howe. The signal, "a sudden burst of cannon so loud it was heard in Philadelphia," as historian Gregory T. Edgar described it, came around 4:30 p.m.

Waiting For The Crown Forces

> *The hilltop above the John Chads House may have been the place where Washington, as Lafayette later wrote in his memoirs, spent the better part of the morning of September 11th —hours before "the enemy crossed the ford."*
>
> C. Quillman

Washington Headquarters at the Ring House served him well, but it was a distance from the Brandywine and was not conducive to observing the enemy from a distance. Therefore, Washington temporarily moved to "the heights" – the area behind the John Chads' house (18)– after he heard the first of several warnings that the Royal Forces were moving forward on the Nottingham Road. Perhaps in nervous anticipation, Washington was said to have paced the ridge, presumably high enough to see above the morning fog and river mist, as he listened for the sounds of distant guns.

Another account describes the tense atmosphere the day before the battle, on September 10th. It is a diary entry written by James McMichael, a newly commissioned 2nd lieutenant of the 13th Pennsylvania. Here he conveys the troops' feelings of uncertainty, not knowing when the enemy would arrive.

> "Septr. 10th at Noon the alarm Guns were fired, and the Army drawn up in the Usual manner, and march'd to the height near the Brandywine where we took post and remained under arms till Evening but the Enemy not comming on we posted large Picquets and remained all night in the woods, for my part my rest very unquiet."

The 19th-century writer J. Smith Futhey was not one for descriptive writing, but he does give a sense of immediacy to an event involving Washington near John Chads' House. The story was based on an interview collected around 1800 from the nephew of Aunt Elizabeth "Betty" Chads, who had the unusual name of Amos House.

He was with his aunt just as Washington was spotted by the enemy since "cannonballs from the enemy's artillery began to drop in the field quiet [sic] near to the company thus collected," House recalled. He also suggests that Washington was actively engaged in recognizance and considered the placement of troops to block the British. In his words, "General Washington, with a few attendants, rode up into the field about Mrs. Chad's dwelling and was engaged, with the aid of glasses, in reconnoitering and endeavoring ...the character and position of the hostile forces."

A Parker family history brings up more questions than answers in explaining House's connection to the John Chads' house. [70] For instance, it suggests that House lived with his aunt, although he was also described as a widower with five children. His wife, Sarah Townsend House, died unexpectedly the previous winter after taking care of a "sick soldier."

The oft-quoted Joseph Townsend, House's brother-in-law, does not offer any clarifications; he only states that in the days before the battle, House frequently left the aunt's home to observe the area around Sconnelltown (65) where his Friends' Meeting had temporarily relocated. [71] It is Townsend who suggests that Chads' House briefly served as an American headquarters. Townsend writes of House's bravery as follows:

> "Amos House, who had left his dwelling near Chad's Ford, and was succeeded therein by Lord Stirling and his attendants, was in the practice of visiting the premises almost daily to see what discovery he could make, went down on the morning of the eleventh, after the can-

nonading had commenced, and rode under the cannon-balls that were discharged from the artillery on the hills, on each side of the creek, without receiving any injury therefrom."

House recorded Washington's calm reaction to enemy fire: the general was heard addressing his "attendants" as "gentlemen," and explaining that they should "retire" or step away to safety since "we are attracting the notice of the enemy."

Other accounts suggest that the ridge behind the Chads' House was not only Washington's preferred viewing station, it may also have been the place where he was nearly shot by the Scottish Captain Patrick Ferguson, and where he later braved a shower of cannon fire.

Thomas McGuire has even traced the British perspective of the former scene to James Parker, a native of Scotland who emigrated to Norfolk, Virginia, and later joined the British Royal Forces. Parker wrote that his position in a battery "on the far heights," across the Brandywine, where he "commanded a Very fine prospect of Rebels ground."

Parker writes that they came to the assistance of Fergusons' troops and "drove the Rebels till [sic] within a half mile of the Creek, where they made a stand behind a breast work of some logs they had made." (See "Washington's Sniper.")

Proctor's Artillery Brigade

Although the Continental artillery batteries are not well documented – in fact, the majority of references are by the British – it is believed that there were substantial ones made of log-and-earth located on both sides of the Nottingham Road, as well as on both sides of the Brandywine.

On the south side of the road, a four-gun battery stood on a ridge later known as Rocky Hill (the steep terrain is still noticeable beyond the Harvey Run fields, off of South Creek Road), that was then to the left of Greene's position at Chads' Ferry. Proctor's battery (called Proctor's Hill in this book) above the present-day Sanderson Museum, was positioned to defend Chads' Ford.

The guns here were long-range French brass field guns and included a howitzer that was cited by name by Robertson, the Royal engineer. In fact, he mentions the battery twice in his narrative; in the first mention, he seems to lump two batteries together (perhaps one behind the John Chads house) by drawing a lunette labeled "c."

In a first reference describing Knyphausen's march along the Nottingham Road (road "H"), he cites a region, "B" that on his map is roughly just beyond the Barns-Brinton House (15). He explains, "having the Rebel Army in their Front on the other side of the Brandywine, nearly in the Position b, besides Numbers conceal'd in the Woods, and the two Batteries c in their Front. A cannonade immediately ensued on both Sides [of the Brandywine]."

At first glance, the second reference to the batteries seems to repeat the Hessians' march on the Nottingham Road, but a close reading reveals the movements of Knyphausen's forces leading up to the capture of Proctor's guns. Citing the wetlands or what Knyphausen called the "swampy morass" still evident today, Robertson wrote of the Hessians' movements as follows:

> "[They were] obliged to advance in Column along the Road h [Nottingham Road] on Account of the Morass on their Flanks, [and] they were galled by Musketry from the Woods on their right and by round and grape Shot from two Pieces of Cannon and an 8 inch Howitzer from the Battery c in their Front, however they advanc'd Briskly and very soon took Possession of the Work and the 3 Pieces of Artillery."

Contemporary historian Michael Harris is especially detailed in explaining what happened when the advancing Hessians were "faced with a swampy morass" (40) Robertson identified it as being 200 yards wide.

The troops became "stacked up as they were on a causeway-like road until the land was dry enough on both sides for the [British] officers to fan out their commands in proper lines of battle," Harris writes and then quotes an unnamed British foot soldier who offers a rare look into the kind of pre-battle preparations the Americans had made; the soldier believed that his position on the road was "half mile in front of the trenches." Harris clarifies that the site was not so distant but likely the fortified lines, or trenches, Wayne's division had set up "beyond the morass."

In addition to the onslaught of guns at Proctor's Hill, smaller artillery units may have showered the "grape Shot" from positions around the John Chads House. A plaque placed near the front door in 1915 is characteristically vague, stating that *"Proctor's American Artillery occupied several redoubts near this house at the Battle of Brandywine, September 11, 1777."*

According to artillery historian Boyd T. Dastrop, this was in keeping to Proctor's method of placing his heavier field pieces on high ground as guns of position such as at Proctor's Hill and the "lighter ones in line with the infantry as battalion guns." The latter description fits Wayne's infantrymen who were part of the Fourth Division of 2,000 Pennsylvania Troops posted near Chads' House. [72]

Again, the exact location of the redoubts is not known, but it's likely that the description on the 1915 plaque was including another redoubt manned by Proctor's men above Brinton's Ford (66,67). Just as Wayne's troops worked with Proctor's men at Proctor's Hill to protect Chads' Ford, Sullivan's troops supported Proctor's redoubt and spent the entire morning posted in the open area that is now part of the Andrew Wyeth estate.

In British and Hessian accounts, Proctor's two-gun artillery battery was perched on a knoll that is still visible off Brinton's Bridge Road, nearly directly across from the British artillery on the other side of the ford.

Sometime after Washington received Ross's dispatch stating that the British were spotted too far to the north to assist the Hessians at Chadds Ford, he ordered an attack across the Brandywine. Greene's and Maxwell's Men crossed at Chadds Ford around 12:15 and got as far as Hillendale Road south of US 1, where they attacked Knyphausen's troops.

By late afternoon, from a timeline estimated to be about 5:15 to 5:30 p.m., the majority of Kyphausen's troops crossed the Brandywine. Much of the major fighting occurred with regiments such as the Queen's Rangers attacking Maxwell's Men near Chadds Ferry, before joining the Highlanders in a raid on the American batteries and forcing Proctor's men to flee.

At Proctor's Hill, the British may have un-spiked the guns to fire on Wayne's position near Chads Ford, while they found the battery at Brinton's Ford was nearly abandoned. For the Americans, it had been a difficult afternoon with not only the nearly constant cannonade coming from British artillery across the river, but the fact that Sullivan's artillery was stretched thin, tasked with the job of covering Proctor's two-gun battery at Brinton's as well as three additional upper crossings as far as Buffington's Ford, as well as a temporary bridge. [73]

By 4 p.m., only one American gun was still working, and most of Proctor's men had been ordered to assist in the artillery elsewhere. Those who remained fled the site by the time Wayne was making a final stand in the Harvey Run fields. This left only a few key men to save what had been left behind.

Gibson's Ford (17) was also the site of a heavy cannonade, but little is known about the redoubt there, only that it was established by Armstrong's troops somewhere near the corner of present-day Rocky Hill and Creek Roads. The troops posted there were largely inexperienced, so it's likely that the battery was not substantial since a direct attack on the ford was not expected. Ironically, that view changed early in the morning, when a "cannonade" erupted in the Ring Run Valley.

As soon as it began, Washington ordered the troops at Gibson's Ford to fire a warning shot across the Brandywine around 10 a.m. Instead of being discouraged, Knyphausen's main column moved forward on their side of the water and engaged the Americans just as a smaller British force moved south and crossed the Brandywine at what may have been both Chads' Ferry and Gibson's Ford.

Armstrong's forces were said to have rallied and instead of merely guarding the fords, they used their artillery to support a brief American flank attack. [74] The firing was designed as a wakeup call to Knyphausen's troops, but the attack also under-

Entrenchments: This 1905 Rotograph card depicts the still-visible trenches built at the Valley Forge encampment.

Remarkably, no photos were taken of any similar sites in Chadds Ford. *Author's collection.*

scored the long reach of the American guns at Rocky Hill. The path of fire crossed over the Brandywine, blasting beyond the present-day Fairville (21) and Stabler Roads where some homeowners later claimed damages. 75

On the west side of the Brandywine, another log-and-earth battery was positioned to face Chads' Ford. Its exact location is not known, but it may have been built just southeast of the present-day Chadds Ford Elementary School. This battery was supplemented by a physical barrier in the form of a long breastwork made of fence rails angling towards Kennett Square.

South of this battery, another Continental artillery battery was strategically placed to cover Chads' Ferry. According to Task Force research, it can be visualized today as the open area where modern Sunny Ridge Lane and Fairville Road now form a triangle with U.S. Rt 1.

The hot, dry weather left much of the Brandywine shallow, but steep embankments and thick stands of trees along the riverbanks made it nearly impossible to cross any area except the fords. The limited access also meant that it was easier to anticipate troop movements across the Brandywine and thus to construct the batteries the day before. As a result, on the morning of Sept. 11th, it was Greene's and Wayne's primary mission to protect the two crossings on either side of the Nottingham Road.

In tracing the Continental batteries, Robertson's map (aka the Windsor map) documents relatively few Continental movements let alone artillery positions in Chadds Ford. However, one citation on the map as well as in the narrative is most striking: it seems to indicate the batteries in the Ring Run Valley, perhaps the breastworks at Chadds Peak (the modern ski site), with the label "**e.**"

As mentioned previously, the so-called "Bombardment of the Ring Run Valley" was a brief victory for Maxwell's Men, but naturally Robertson only presents the

Rangers as having the upper-hand.

The cannonade or bombardment lasted only an hour and half – and abruptly ended at 9:30 a.m. – but there is no mention of enemy fire, and only a hint that the Queen's Rangers seized numerous American artillery pieces and pushed Maxwell's out-numbered men off the hills of Chadds Peak and back to the east side of the Brandywine. Instead, Robertson summarized as follows:

> "The Rebels pass'd the River with a Corps and drew up at d, and in the Breast work e, upon which the Queen's Rangers, Fergusson's Riffle Men, and the 49th and 28th Regiments were sent to dislodge them, which they soon did and drove them across the River."

Faden's 1778 map is similarly marked with the letters "d" and "e," although the latter is described more succinctly as being established by the same "Rebel Detachment" (Maxwell's men) encountered earlier. The words read that "e" was a "small Fleche [fortification] raised by D (meaning the Detachment)." Curiously, much like Robertson's map, the 1787 map depicts the c. 1743 Nottingham Road as located south of the Ring Run Valley, not north of it.

Even if one considered the belief that Old Baltimore Pike, reached by McFadden Road near the Gables restaurant (27), more accurately follows the roadbed of the old Nottingham Road, as well as the changes to the road over the years, there is still a wide discrepancy between the road today and how it's portrayed on the 18th-century maps.

A Record of the Day

Although the narrative account of Joseph Townsend – the Quaker boy who witnessed much of the destruction of September 11, 1777, – was published decades after the American Revolution, it has a remarkable immediacy to it. It captures the horrors of the day while also offering a non-judgmental and even journalistic point of view, especially in examining the different attitudes among the local citizens.

Most residents had never experienced any kind of military conflict, but they seemed to anticipate what was in store. Recalling the typical reaction among the Quaker residents, Townsend indirectly defended their perceived passivity. "They generally believe it was right to remain at their dwellings," he wrote, "and patiently submit to whatever suffering might be their lot and trust their all to a kind protecting Providence."

Unlike the local Quakers who hid or stood their ground according to their "fatalistic brand of pacifism," as one historian put it, Townsend spent nearly the entire day on foot following the Crown Forces. He first encountered the British troops (specifically the "flanking party") in the early morning at Sconnelltown (65) and remained with the troops until the end of the day at Birmingham Meeting, when it was converted by the British into a field hospital. What he saw there, and the surrounding farm fields, prompted him to say that "it would be difficult to describe the many cases of horror and destruction of human begins that came under our notice."

By the time Townsend's 1846 account was published in *The History of Chester County* (1881), residents had endured the Civil War and were more likely to appreciate the significance of the Battle of Brandywine. The earlier romanticized accounts such as the 1846 novel *Blanche Of Brandywine* by George Lippard soon fell out of favor.

Even though Lippard claimed to have visited the battlefield and interviewed "elderly men" he met by knocking on doors, the book's subtitle, "*On September The Eleventh, 1777: A Romance,*" clearly revealed to the reader that the book was not a straightforward account of the battle.

Decades later another acclaimed writer, Bayard Taylor, created a runaway bestseller when he expanded on his earlier successful story concerning area Quakers and penned the novel *The Story of Kennett* (1866). [76]

Although there are only a few hints that the "healthy, pastoral community" of Kennett Township (as one reviewer put it) was set in the years after the American Revolution, one of the central figures in the novel is a former Continental soldier named James "Sandy Flash" Fitzpatrick, who deserted the army after he was flogged for a minor infraction.

Taylor often based his fictional characters on real people, but in this case, he may not have even used an alias. His character was based on James Fitzpatrick, a blacksmith who grew up in an Irish Quaker household in the West Marlborough village of Doe Run. Paradoxically, for a man who would later be associated with turncoat activities, the village and the surrounding region was a well-known enclave for the Scotch-Irish, a group that was a dominant force in the county militia in 1777.

In keeping with what one contemporary critic called the romantic but "credulous" style of the mid-1800s, Taylor's Sandy Flash is painted in broad strokes and focused on his Robin Hood-like highwayman activities and the possibility that he left his "plunder" behind as buried treasure.

Taylor also depicts Sandy Flash as a brawny red-haired young man who galloped his horse through the neighborhood, traveling in a flash and avoiding capture. In real life, Fitzpatrick was credited for being one of the guides on the British flanking maneuver and, after his capture in 1778 (and several escape attempts), he was hanged for treason in September of that year.

A String of Dispatches

"Intelligence is the life of every thing in war," Gen. Nathanael Greene, writing to Major John Clark, November 5th, 1777.

One of the mysteries of the Battle of Brandywine is why Gen. Washington seemingly refused to believe the reports of enemy sighting from several experienced Continental officers including Lt. Col. James Ross, whose patrol went down in history as the one that skirmished with part of the flanking party just north of today's village of Unionville. Instead, Washington had faith in what historian Douglas Harper called a "low-level militia officer's report" namely an early morning dispatch from Major Joseph Spear. 77

Spear was the first of at least five scouts who reported to Washington; he was also the first on the road. He left Martin's Tavern at dawn, under the cover of a morning fog and traveled south, following the course of the West Branch of the Brandywine, presumably on the same road – the Great Valley Road – that the Flanking Column would take. The column comprised more than 9,000 British troops, plus countless camp followers, wagons, and livestock. Yet the column escaped detection until late in the day.

The Great Valley Road was mostly narrow and twisting and went through a heavily wooded and marshy area along the Brandywine. This, along with the abrupt hills, may have served to screen the flanking party, according to McGuire.

All dispatches were to go through Major General John Sullivan, then posted at Brinton's Ford (53), but unfortunately that meant that any added comments could lead to confusion or misinterpretation. For instance, Spear wrote his own report, which was said to have been forwarded by Major Lewis Morris, Sullivan's aide, but then Sullivan wrote his own report to Washington, stating that he saw Spear "who came this morning from a Tavern called Martins in the Forks of the Brandywine."

While the region of the tavern was often wrongly assumed in 1777 to be near the junction of the Brandywine's two branches, that would mean Spear scouted the region around Buffington's Ford, a crossing just below the Forks, where the northernmost American detachment (under Col. Moses Hazen) was stationed. In his report, Sullivan mentions that Spear also traveled to Welch's tavern, but that was not located along the Great Valley Road (9), the route of the Flanking Column. Still, Sullivan indirectly quoted Spear, stating that he "is confident that they [the enemy] are not in that quarter." 78

Washington received Spear's message around 12 noon but took no action – for reasons that are still debated today. The Commander-In-Chief later claimed that many of the reports were of "a very contradictory nature" and that he wanted his

Light Dragoons to be specific or "particular on these matters." The historian McGuire explains this misstep as follows:

> "At one point sometime in the middle of the day, having received specific information of the flank movement from someone credible, possibly Squire Cheyney, Washington sent a terse and an impatient note."

The note was addressed to Col. Theodoric Bland, an officer, Washington lamented, who had "not sent him any information at all." According to McGuire, Bland's lack of communication forced Washington to rely on reports passed on by Sullivan, who fearing repercussion, eventually sent his own scouts to look for the Crown Forces upstream. Bland, the commander of the 1st Continental Light Dragoons, had been given the duty of patrolling the right wing.

One of Bland's patrollers, Maj. John Jamison, also traveled as far as Hazen's post at Buffington's Ford and later reported to Sullivan, who wrote Washington as follows: "Maj. Jamison came to me...at nine o'clock [and said that he had] come from the right of the army, and I might depend there was no enemy there."

Jefferies' Ford was only a mile and a half north of Buffington's Ford, but apparently Jamison just missed seeing the front of the Flanking Column which began to cross the Brandywine there around 9 a.m. Bland's patrol was said to have remained in the Forks region (10) for much of the morning, and although intelligence continued to trickle into Washington's Headquarters all morning, most were from sources who knew neither the fords nor the terrain.

The Sighting

> "*Since I sent you a message...I saw Major Joseph Spear of the Militia who came this morning from a Tavern called Martins in the Forks of the Brandywine [sic] he came from thence to Welches Tavern & heard nothing of the Enemy ....*"
> From a Sept. 11th dispatch from Mj. Gen. Sullivan to Washington.

The exact location or the exact time where Thomas "Squire" Cheyney and Col. John Hannum first glimpsed the head of the British Left Hook is not known but they reportedly left Martin's Tavern sometime after Mj. Joseph Spear had departed and were soon close enough to see a distant cloud of dust rising south of Trimble's Ford. (59)

Cheyney was said to have galloped onward to warn Washington that the "British were coming." Cheyney may have initially reported to Sullivan at Brinton's Ford (53,66) – some estimate that the message was received at 11:45, or right before

Spear's report – but in the words of one historian, Sullivan "was not inclined to take the word of a civilian," so Cheyney asked for permission to deliver the report in person to Washington at his headquarters. [79]

There are numerous interpretations of what followed, including one that quotes Cheyney as saying that the British "fired at him, but he'd got away." A 19th-century West Chester attorney named John Hickman mentions a pursuit and shooting, but not that Cheyney spoke to Washington about it.

According to Hickman, who gave speeches about the battlefield while serving in the U.S. House of Representatives (he preceded William Everhart of West Chester) Cheyney was initially denied entry into the Ring House headquarters and Washington, hearing a commotion, stepped outside and spoke to Cheyney, who then pleaded with the Commander-in-Chief to believe his story. Hickman even offered a visual flourish to his account, noting that Cheyney got down from his horse and drew a crude map in the dirt so that Washington could see the British route for himself.

In his book *Brandywine,* Harris includes other problematic accounts such as one by the historian John Reed, who wrote in 1965 that Cheyney pleaded with Washington to put him "under guard until you can ask Anthony Wayne or Persie Frazer if I am a man to be believed."

Cheyney never documented his encounter with Washington, but it's likely he may have brought up Frazer who was not only a respected officer and patriot, but a man Cheyney knew personally. Frazer's wife, Polly, was the niece of Cheyney's wife and they were close neighbors in Thornbury, Delaware County.

It is believed that Cheyney reached Washington about 2 p.m., but Harris writes that no mention of Cheyney is found in any official dispatch, nor any report issued from Washington's Headquarters, not even those by Sullivan, who had been diligently forwarding reports from the scouts all morning.

A more likely source of information was suggested in Townsend's account. In Sconnelltown, he recalled, it was rumored that Bland's scouts had sighted the British "between the dwelling of Richard Strode and Osborne's Hill."

Bland himself had reported that the Crown Forces were moving toward the homes of the "Widows" Davis, who lived on neighboring farms north of West Street Road in Birmingham. Bland does not cite their late husbands, the brothers Amos and James Davis (as Townsend did), but Bland's report was typical of dispatches in citing property owners. For instance, he told of the widows "who live close together on the road called Fork Road [now Birmingham Road], about a half mile to the right of the [Birmingham] meetinghouse."

Harris writes that Bland was a Virginian "with no knowledge of the area," but he was dedicated to reconnaissance work as one of the "many prescribed roles of the dragoons." Bland's report – dispatched first to Sullivan around 1:15 p.m. – was the first to give any specifics about the location of a British sighting.

In addition to citing the "Widows" on Birmingham Road, Bland described both the location of Osborne Hill (2) and Birmingham Heights; the former was "about half a mile to the Right of the Meeting House. There is a higher Hill on their front." Unfortunately, Washington did not receive Bland's report until about 2 p.m. when the flanking column was about to convene at Osborne Hill.

A panicked Washington quickly ordered troops under Alexander Stirling and Adam Stephen from Chadds Ford to Birmingham Hill, a three-mile journey they were said to have undertaken in record time, most likely by way of Harvey Road. 80 Of all the previous reports, Bland's included the most telling line: "I have discovered a party of the enemy on the Heights."

The report was also in keeping with Washington's direct appeal to keep "vigilant attention" and to give "the earliest report not only of their movements but of their numbers and the course they are pursuing." Bland's report included an estimate of the enemy forces moving toward Osborne Hill, (2, 50) noting there were "about two brigades of them."

Another report by Sullivan provided an interesting visual detail that suggested an even larger size as the Crown Forces marched not in one or two but in three columns from Strode's Mill. As Sullivan wrote of Bland, "he also says he saw dust back in the country for above [sic] an hour."

Sullivan was said to have personally delivered the news to Washington. He galloped to Chadds Ford and found Washington just as he was sitting down to dinner with his staff at the Ring House. Timothy Pickering would later recall that the entire staff left what remained of their meal at "Head Quarters & briskly started from thence." Fortunately for the Americans, it would take several hours before the British flanking party came together and were ready to advance from Osborne's Hill.

Storm Above John Chads' House

> *"Proctor's American artillery occupied several redoubts near this home at the Battle of Brandywine, Sept. 11, 1777."*
> From a 1915 plaque posted at John Chads' House.

Today the John Chads' House (18) is not only intact, but its hilltop location is also relatively unchanged and still suggests how the region's steep hills were good lookouts for the dozens of American pickets scattered in Chadds Ford on Sept. 11, 1777.

Although Chadds Ford was sparsely populated in 1777, properties such as the Chads' House had open fields that were enclosed by stone walls or by wooden fences four or five rails high. They provided cover for the troops as did the thick stands of trees surrounding the house that shielded the infantry in open formation.

Accounts describing the Continental soldiers cutting down trees to be used as road barriers point to the house's close location to the ford as well as the need to protect the American artillery redoubts that were within walking distance to the house.

As 19th-century writers were fond of retelling, Chads' widow Elizabeth "Aunt Betty" Chads, refused to leave her house and so she guarded "her silver spoons daily in her Packet [pocket] until the danger was over." [81] That turned out to be near the end of the day. Maj. Gen. William Alexander "Lord Stirling" of New Jersey would also utilize the house for at least part of the morning, according to Joseph Townsend's account.

Perhaps it was inevitable, but "Aunt Betty" found herself surrounded by troops, in one of the most fortified areas of the battlefield with perhaps the exception of Brinton's Ford a mile upstream. The nearby hills became part of Wayne's defense line while Chads' Ford (the namesake of her late husband) was protected by artillery batteries, or redoubts made of earth and logs.

The center of the American line is typically described as being at the Chads' House and some historians believe that the high ridge extending along Creek Road may have been the place where Washington visited the troops, encouraging them on the morning of Sept. 11th. Harris quotes an unnamed observer as follows. [82]

> "In the beginning of the action he rode from one end to the other of the line, cheering and encouraging the men. [They] seemed animated by his presence; they could give no other vein to their feelings but by shouts of applause, which seemed to rend the air."

Lafayette was similarly impressed with Washington's leadership ability, judging from his description: "General Washington walked the length of his two lines, and was received with acclamations [sic] that should have promised victory."

General Washington's Sniper

Washington may have been standing in front of the John Chads' House when he was nearly shot by the Scottish captain Patrick Ferguson of the Royal Forces. It was also the place where Washington braved a shower of cannon fire. The latter incident was described by Amos House, Elizabeth Chads' nephew, as the place where a "cannonading" commenced, and he overheard Washington calmly tell his officers that they must "retire" since they were "attracting the notice of the enemy."

The same scene was described by the ever-observant Loyalist James Parker, according to McGuire whose use of parenthesis is included here. Parker was in a battery positioned near Chads Ford, which "commanded a Very fine prospect of Rebels ground."

Parker also records the American use of white flags when they needed a break in the artillery fire to plan their next move. In his account, Parker may have wrongly assumed Washington was about to act on a message that the British were crossing one of the Upper Fords, but it's still significant in describing the scene he witnessed.

"About 12, I saw Washington of A farm house [presumably Chads' house]. I pointed him out to the Generals; he had Some of his Officers about him with two White flags.... I was afterwards told by a Rebel, it was just at that time [Washington] got intelligence that Genl. Howe was crossing the B.Wine above him."

The exact location where Ferguson was standing when he almost shot Washington was never recorded. Still, given the fact that Ferguson only took part in the early morning skirmishes, including those at Welch's Tavern, the number of places he could have spotted the American commander is limited.

One set of American breastworks was within view of the Chads' House, and so it might have been the place where Ferguson recalled, with his characteristic Scottish hyperbole, that his men ("my lads") had "dislodged" the enemy embedded in breastworks. Ferguson also remembered he was near "skirts of the Wood" when he spotted Washington with his back turned.

The oft-quoted line of the 33-year-old Scottish captain explains why he didn't fire: he believed it was unfair to fire "at the back of an offending individual who was acquitting himself very coolly [sic] of his duty, so I let him alone."

Moments later Ferguson was shot in the elbow of his shooting arm, and as he later learned, his target may have been Washington based on descriptions reportedly given to him in a conversation during his subsequent hospital stay.

Battle At The Fence Lines

The first engagement at Birmingham Heights may have taken place at what is now a rise in the open fields of Crebilly Farm at the junction of South New Street and Pleasant Grove Road – a site known as "the Crebilly Knoll" among preservationists.

The encounter is believed to have taken place when two advancing columns departed Osborne Hill (50) and formed along Street Road, just east of South New Street. One column was comprised of an elite group of Hessian and Ansbach *Jäger* under Lt. Col. Colonel Ludwig von Wurmb. They were crossing the fields and had just waded through a branch of the Radley Run when their front crested the "Knoll" and they had an intense encounter with skirmishers from Stephen's division coming from the northwest on Street Road.

Sullivan's division would soon arrive from Jones' Ford (52) "at an angle sharply oblique to the British advance," according to the historian Reed, who writes that a subsequent skirmish at Samuel Jones' orchard (now known as Linden Farm) proved difficult for the Americans (55). Reed describes the grenadiers as positioned along a post-and-rail fence to form a "breastwork of their own and laying their muskets on the top rail gave such a heavy fire that the Americans retreated."

However, that Street Road skirmish was nothing compared to the brute force unleased by a division that included 30 grenadiers, who formed along a section of Street Road that borders Crebilly Farm. As a result, some of the Continentals were pushed into some nearby woods on the Crebilly lands, where they briefly skirmished again until they began to flee across the fields toward Birmingham Meeting.

Not surprisingly some of the German troops were encumbered by the Royal artillery that moved with them from Osborne Hill, pulling a pair of 3-pounders and two rampart guns capable of lobbing heavy musket balls several hundred feet.

These troops were not part of the skirmishing Hessians at Crebilly Knoll, but they too were delayed by a series of fences that they had to either climb or tear down, according to Harris who writes "The grenadiers confronted eight stout Pennsylvanian fences between Osborne's Hill and the American lines at Birmingham Hill."

The British engineer's map and narrative are filled with notations and remarks about fence lines but Robertson does not mention the Street Road skirmish – one that the Hessian Capt. Ewald documented as taking place for nearly an hour and continuing on the neighboring Samuel Jones' property. (55) In fact, the closest Robertson comes to acknowledging the skirmish was a notation of "*Rails at F,*" just north of Meetinghouse Road.

Not long after the Crebilly knoll encounter, Ewald's advance guard of foot and mounted *Jägers* encountered the Virginians, who moved back from an area near Street Road (called Samuel Jones' woodlot by some historians) and at one point, switched places with Ewald's troops and fired from the protection of Jones' brick farmhouse and outbuildings along Birmingham Road.

"Unfortunately, for us," Ewald writes of his advance patrol who had inadvertently advanced too far beyond Osborne Hill, "the time this took favored the enemy and I received extremely heavy small-arms fire from the gardens and houses."

Robertson's narrative might have been easier to follow if he had included a timeline of events. The following passage is perhaps typical in recording two seemingly simultaneous movements of the British. He writes that "*two Battalions of Light Infantry being a little in Front and having beat back the advanced Parties of the Rebels, halted in the position of E [Birmingham Hill]*."

Meanwhile the narrative continues, "two Battalions of British Grenadiers go up to the Rails at *F*, when they received a heavy Fire from the Rebels in thier [sic] Front, after crossing the Rails they immediately charged and drove Rebels before them."

The Rebels' position along Meetinghouse Road is also identified as "*Plan C*." They had been at Birmingham Meeting but "*moving and unsettled*" they fell back to C, "*having their light Troops in their Front in the hollow Way.*"

McGuire describes this "*hollow*" or valley as extending from "Lafayette's monument (58) then east along a fence line" or "*along the Fences D*" (marked as several "*D*s" on Robertson's map) across New Street and nearly to Radley Run.

On Robertson's map, the marks denoted as "*Fences D*" are interspersed with the British Light Infantry's formal position at a row of "*E*s." In what seems to be a jumbled timeline, the narrative describes the "First Battn. of Light Infantry" as charging and then seizing "five pieces of Cannon," and thus allowing the 4th Brigade "that followed the Rear" to "gain the *Hill G*" [the second Eminence].

Robertson's narrative makes no mention of what happened at the "*Hill G,*" only that other Crown Forces (including "*5 Companies of the 2nd Battn of Light Infantry*") formed along Birmingham Road ("*H*") directly across from modern Sandy Hollow Heritage Park, and thus "by *that time, had got upon the Flank of the Rebels and so facilitated the Charge made by the remainder of the 2nd Battn.*"

The "Eminences"

In examining the disorder and confusion of the day, historians now see the battles at Birmingham as taking place on three separate ridges the British called "eminences." The first was the ridge at Birmingham Meeting variously described by both armies as the "Heights at Birmingham" or "Birmingham Heights." It was here that Colonel Thomas Marshall (father of future the U.S. Justice) and his Virginia regiment famously crouched behind a stone wall surrounding the Meetinghouse.

The regiment was said to have loaded and fired their muskets as fast as humanly possible. Another Virginian regiment in Stephen's Division had moved there from an orchard on Samuel Jones farm (55) and had the advantage of being on an elevation at the Meetinghouse looking down to the advancing British light infantry.

The official *Jäegers* Corps journal went into further specifics about the deployment of Stephen's and Stirling's forces as follows:

"The enemy had a body of about 1000 men standing on the hill on the other side of the Meetinghouse. [Other men] joined the men on the hill; several battalions were also observed, who marched to the woods on the right and left and united themselves with the above 3000 men presented a formidable front."

Nineteenth-century historians have placed a crucial part of the fighting at Birmingham Hill. This may have been due to the fact that the clamor of Sandy Hollow – some say it was the bloodiest battle of the day – was never fully documented as a battle landscape until recent years.

Historians are now looking into the possibility that part of Sandy Hollow (5) may have extended into the low pastureland on Thornbury Farm, and that the present-day Sandy Hollow Heritage Park region would be more accurately described as "Sandy Hill."

Captain Friedrich von Muenchhausen, Howe's aide-de-camp, wrote of the earlier American line at several "hills" around Birmingham Meeting. He recalled that he and Howe, perhaps from Osborne's Hill, could see that the Rebels had "formed two lines in good order along their heights...We could see this because there were some barren places here and there on the hills, which they occupied."

Quoting Muenchhausen as describing the Virginian regiments' position on the "barren places," Harris identifies it as at the "eastern extension of the rise the Birmingham Meetinghouse sits upon."

This second eminence was considered so strong, it was described in the official *Jäegers* Corps Journal as the Rebels being "advantageously posted on a not especially steep height in front of a woods, with the right wing resting on a steep and deep ravine."

The third eminence, or "Battle Hill," may have been located far beyond the rear of the Meetinghouse, perhaps on an elevated area where a farm market is now located at Thornbury Farm. The pastureland in the rear of the farm's c. 1709 homestead contains deep ravines (believed to be the result of early quarrying) and then rises to another elevation south of Sandy Hollow Heritage Park.

Although some historians dispute the idea that Hessian Capt. Johann Ewald was near the farm, he did describe an attack that may have occurred there sometime after 3 p.m. The collection of farm buildings including a long rectangular spring house which community legend says housed British prisoners, may have looked like the "village" he mentions as follows. (The terrain behind the c. 1709 homestead is similarly bowl-shaped as he describes.) Ewald wrote in his diary that he "caught sight of some infantry and horsemen behind a village on a hill in the distance, which was formed like an amphitheater." 83

While naming these various elevations may add to the confusion, it also underscores the fact that the Americans used these various hills stretching from present-day Street and Brinton's Bridge Roads to their advantage.

Again, it is Hessian commander Karl von Baumeister who suggests that the Americans were consistent in their pattern of attack, as they fell back, then re-grouped, before firing again. Also, perhaps in keeping with Baumeister's habit of promoting the historic actions of his fellow Hessians, he writes that "Howe dispatched some of the Hessian *Jägers* close to the foresaid Meeting House, where they occupied an advantageous post."

Skipping over the battle area, the British captain John Montrésor called "incessant fire from the Rebels out of a wood and above them," Baumeister jumps to "four o'clock in the afternoon [when] the columns advanced to attack, the center column along the main road (presumably Birmingham) and the other two on both sides, through valleys and woods."

Adding that the Enemy "received them with a heavy fire of cannon and musketry," in the end, the Hessians got the upper-hand as follows. "Our men, however, made a spirited attack with their bayonets and drove them [the Americans] into the woods, following close upon their heels. Though they fought stubbornly all the way, they were compelled to escape...towards Chester."

Entrenched At The Second Eminence

The fighting at what is known as the second eminence, or the eastern extension of a ridge at Birmingham Meeting, is not clearly documented, but it seems to epitomize the so-called push and pull of battle. For instance, it's beginning can be traced to Stirling's retreat from Birmingham Hill and into Sandy Hollow. Stirling's troops had no choice—the Grenadiers had driven them five times from the "Hill" which they regained each time— but then it was decided to advance forward.

The move was said to be relatively orderly, but also a withdrawal that had ramifications for the remaining Continentals. Adam Stephen's division, for one, remained in place atop the Hill and its left flank was exposed to surging British troops.

Two of Stephen's brigades — the 3rd and 4th Virginians — were said to have formed on a crest of high ground, with the latter brigade trapped, as Stephen later reported to Washington, since they were mostly "Entrenchd to the Chin in the Ditch of a fence Opposite to the Center of the Enemy."

Things got worse after the American guns were abandoned and the Virginians became overwhelmed and engulfed by a British light infantry unit that at one point held fast on both sides of the Birmingham Road. At the same time, an unit of Hessian and *Anspach Jäegers* attempted to provide support but when they swung east of

Birmingham Meetinghouse, they became bogged down in the marshy low ground between the Hill and Street Road.

In Sullivan's words, the Virginians were soon compelled to "fly" in a retreat that took them down the south side of Birmingham Hill, and into a fighting march across Sandy Hollow and beyond. By then, the American 4th brigade was joined by an additional group of about 200 Virginians, and after the brigade regained its strength, it successfully repulsed another surge by the *Jäegers* who then took cover.

After a regrouping, the British also recovered and flanked the Virginians on both sides. Much like Stirling's troops, the Virginians gained and then lost the Hill. Surprisingly, the first time they withdrew and found themselves nearly in the same formation as they had at the start of the battle.

Another factor that helped the Americans: In an attempt to avoid the swampy lowlands and thickets that had had caused earlier problems for the Hessian and Anspach Jäegers, a British brigade swung southwest of Birmingham Road and away from Sandy Hollow so that they were unable, as Harris puts it, to give " the light troops their promised support." That left the *Jäegers* with the job of trying to turn the American right flank – if they could reach Stephen's position.

By 4 p.m., the Crown Forces had claimed a series of successes and had gained the definite upper hand in a region now identified as Sandy Hollow. However, to get there, they had to push through a low "bottom" valley area in easy view of a Continental artillery battery with two three-pounder guns.

Two Hessian officers would later comment on the regrouping of Stephen's skirmish line. The Americans simply found a better "disposition with one height after the other to his rear." The other Hessian, Lt. Col. Ludwig von Wurmb, seems to describe the landscape between the Meetinghouse and the pastureland of Thornbury Farm when he explains the progression as follows:

> "We drove the enemy…and they positioned themselves in a woods from which we dislodged them and then a second woods from which we found ourselves 150 paces from their line which was on a height in a woods and we were at the bottom, also in a woods, between us was an open field."

Getting closer to what may now be Sandy Hollow Heritage Park, a regiment of *Jäegers* and the British 2nd Light Infantry took the brunt of the attack with Stephen's main line firing "two cannon with canister shot" that rained down on the British troops, and in Wurmb's words, "because of the terrible terrain and the woods, our cannon could not get close enough, and [we] had to remain to the right."

Another Hessian reported that after a half-hour of fighting with grape shot and small arms – and billowing smoke – it was difficult to see the movements of the British light infantry, and so with very few "orders," each "commander had to act according to his best judgment."

At one point, Washington and his entourage including Lafayette finally arrived at Birmingham. They did not witness the hand-to-hand combat at the Second Eminence, but may have seen the collapsing battle lines at Sandy Hollow. Indeed, legend states that both Washington and Lafayette rode back and forth through the region and rallied the men to continue fighting for several hours. In the words of historian Bruce Chadwick, it was a key place where "the Commander-in-Chief was constantly exposed to fire."

When the main attack was made at the Birmingham Meetinghouse, located more than three miles northeast of Chadds Ford, Washington had "faulty" information and had "no idea as to the number of troops or cannons that were available for use," according to Chadwick.

Washington not only didn't know the location of the Meetinghouse, Chadwick writes, "the maps given [to Washington] were not complete... and the terrain looked different from Washington's spyglass than it did on his maps."

As for the Crown Forces, they gained control at Sandy Hollow, but only after they lost many men and horses and struggled to advance through a changing landscape that included plowed fields, old quarries, wet meadowland, and sloping pastureland.

The American Revolution Remembered

> *"It would be difficult to describe the many cases of horror and destruction of human begins that came under our notice…."*
> Joseph Townsend, who famously witnessed the Battle of Brandywine.

What began as a peaceful, hazy morning in September turned into a day that residents never forgot – it was the 9/11 of the era. The regional historian Henry Seidel Canby, who was born into a prominent Quaker family in Wilmington, wrote in 1941 in his book about the Brandywine that generations of Brandywine Valley residents dated things from that day in September 1777, and that obituaries often mentioned if the deceased's relatives witnessed the Battle of Brandywine.

It was a memorable day in part because it was a day full of contrasts. The early morning fog and smoke from the beehive ovens from area homes – it was baking day – was mixed by midmorning with smoke of Knyphausen's artillery blasting into the American troops and Proctor's guns firing in return.

As many historians have written, war came to the Brandywine Valley when it

54. Lafayette's Tree: Douglas E. Brinton's photography series of 1899 centered on known battlefield landmarks, but the place where Lafayette was wounded was based on speculation. The tree shown here was likely the replanted tree in "John Bennett's field," as it was described in 1825. Brinton sold his images with matting, as shown here.   *Courtesy of CCHC.*

was in the middle of harvest season and it prevented residents from preserving food for the coming winter. Not surprisingly, in the subsequent British damage claims, food was ranked the highest in the kind of items seized from local residents.

The reports underscored why it took a generation or two before Chester County residents could recover from what were essentially severe shortages caused by the feeding and supplying of two armies during the relatively short time the armies spent in the region.

From the hot humid days of August until September 22, 1777, when the British crossed the Schuylkill River Fords in and around Phoenixville and went to occupy Philadelphia, Washington and his men traversed much of Chester County. They brought with them long baggage trains and large groups of camp followers.

In addition to food, the British damage reports help to explain why soldiers on the move bothered with raids on homes, often leaving behind a seemingly vicious destruction of a peaceful home. Bedding and clothing were torn in strips for bandages while valuable books were shredded to use the paper for cartridges and many practical household goods made of pewter and lead were seized to be melted down for ammunition.

The 19th-century physician William Darlington, whose birthplace near the Birmingham battlefield is acknowledged with a historic marker, described a more orderly process among some British officers. The men, he wrote, "sent their servants around among the farmers of the vicinity to collect poultry and other provender for their own tables. These marauders regarded as lawful plunder everything they could lay their hands upon and deemed worth carrying away." 84

In hindsight, it wasn't merely residents who experienced plundering and property damage, but what was described as the "desolated" condition of the landscape afterwards that had the greatest impact.

Townsend, the young Quaker who followed the Royal Army, described the destruction as "wanton waste" since it included the unnecessary damage of property on the "peaceable inhabitants of the neighborhood."

It was natural that the army slaughtered one's cattle and seized one's horses, he writes, but it was "not uncommon to see heaps of feathers lying about farms," the feather beds having been ripped apart, along with other linens, for bandages. Fence rails and timber was taken from barns, but this being "enemy's county, inhabited by rebels," the British were also inclined to break up "valuable furniture" that was left "lying about their fireplaces, in the fields, unconsumed," Townsend writes.

While many residents, especially Quakers, reacted by hiding from or ignoring the passing British troops, Townsend was given what was described as "free access" to the advancing British army. In other words, he joined several British officers who were part of the infamous "flanking party," joining the troops in Sconnelltown (65) and following the Crown Forces to Osborne Hill (50) and other sites close to the action.

As a historic document, Townsend's narrative may be slightly flawed in that it was written years after the battle, but few accounts capture a sense of immediacy and the understanding that a momentous historic event was unfolding. For instance, Townsend was initially in awe of the pageantry, the "rich scarlet clothing," found among the sea of gallant soldiers. But he also wrote of the anticipation found in Turk's Head, a place that was not yet the county seat, but the largest settlement in Chester County. News spread that the British had been seen sometime between September 3rd and 6th near Iron Hill (Newark, Delaware), a place Townsend observed was "not much known or spoken of previously as a place of note." 85

Some Turk's Head residents were fearful, Townsend writes, but most either thought that "devastation would be the consequence" or "peace and tranquility" would eventually be restored by the British. Of course, by the eve of the Battle of

Brandywine, the mood was entirely different. The local populace had never experienced war, but they seemed to understand what was in store.

More than a hundred years later, a West Chester physician named Henry Pleasants drew up a list of damages based on the General Assembly's order on Sept. 21, 1782, to register "the damages sustained by the inhabitants of the County of Chester...from the Troops and Adherents of the King of Great Britain during the present war." [86]

The British depredations, or damages, are perhaps the most concrete evidence of the ways residents of the Brandywine Valley suffered from plundering, the result either of having property seized – or less commonly, completely damaged without compensation – by the British and their "Adherents" such as the Pennsylvania Tories.

Lafayette's Tree in John Bennett's Field

Whether or not Lafayette was wounded in "John Bennett's field," as it was termed in 1825, has never been confirmed but there is no doubt that the farm was the center of the fighting. Bennett later claimed more than 400 pounds in damages including 600 pounds of cheese, 80 pounds for his "best wearing appearl" and three pounds 18 shillings for the loss of his vineyard, or "26 yards of grape".

Local folklore claims that the injured Lafayette had his wounds dressed under a tree on Bennett's farm and that he was later taken into the farmhouse and attended there by doctors until he could be taken to Chester. The tree (later replanted) was photographed by Douglas E. Brinton for his Battle of Brandywine series of 1899 (54). Reproduced here with its original matting, the photo is inscribed in the back by Brinton with the following words that border on hyperbole: "This marks the spot where Lafayette was wounded. One of the great historic spots in the county."

Brinton labeled the site as "Mrs. Biddle's" on another photograph of Osborne Hill (50), which was in keeping with another similarly vague description used in a Sept. 16, 1894 news story in *"The Press."* The wounding site was described by the reporter as in "a field between two strips of woodland belonging to Mrs. Biddle and Henry Bennett." [87]

Evidently, the exact site was never determined. Even in Lafayette's 1837 memoir, he suggests that the wounding took place right before the retreat, when he "occupied himself arresting the [fleeing] fugitives" to gain "some degree of order."

In 1877, *Lippincott's* magazine recognized the centennial of the battle with a special issue full of stories. In one story, the writer wrote rather unconvincingly of "trustworthy accounts" that confirmed that Lafayette was with Washington, or "maybe Greene," which suggests that it was at the end of the day during the Rear

Guard Defense near the 1704 Brinton House.

Lafayette himself presented a different view, writing in his memoir that he "ordered his horse to the rear" to show "my comrades that they had no better chance of flight than I." Switching to the third person, he recalled that he had waited for "the generals and commander-in-chief [to arrive]" "so that [he had] the leisure to dress his wound."

Decades later, when ceremony officials gathered near Birmingham Meetinghouse in 1895 to mark the place where Lafayette was wounded, they relied on the memory of an "Old Friend," as George Morris Phillip of West Chester Normal School called him. He had been a 17-year-old bystander in 1825 when Lafayette toured the battlefield and tried to find the spot where he was shot in the thigh.

The bystander recalled when he saw Lafayette point out the likely place where he was wounded. Lafayette was quoted as saying "the exact spot I cannot tell," but he then pointed out a "clump of young chestnut trees" in "John Bennett's field" before changing his mind and selecting a spot near the Meetinghouse.

58. Lafayette's Monument of 1895: Thousands of battlefield visitors came to see its unveiling.

The 19th century historian Gilbert Cope also relied on the same unnamed "Friend," who gave him a personal tour of the battlefield in Birmingham. Later, as a secretary of the Chester County Historical Society, Cope authorized a "temporary marker" recognizing Lafayette's wounding to be placed by the side of the road "from Birmingham Meetinghouse to Dilworthtown, perhaps 50 rods beyond Sandy Hollow."

Cope advanced the idea that Lafayette was close to the Meetinghouse and may have been part of the first action there. According to the published ceremony proceedings, an unnamed speaker expressed "the [disputed] opinion that Lafayette was wounded *before*" Sullivan's division was "forced from" Birmingham Heights aka Birmingham Hill or "Meetinghouse Hill."

"Somewhere upon that slope I was wounded," Lafayette was quoted as saying during his visit to the battlefield in the summer of 1825. The speaker believed that Lafayette's "outspread hand" was pointing to a "piece of land fifty rods below Sandy Hollow." But he concluded Lafayette was unconcerned with finding the exact location since it mattered only that "his blood" mingled with that of the many Americans killed on that sacred ground.

Lafayette's "Other" Tree

In addition to the Gilpin House in Chadds Ford being reconsidered as a landmark connected to Lafayette, historians have steered away from the once popular story that a wounded Lafayette was brought to Gilpin's and had his wounds dressed under the spreading branches of an American Sycamore tree. [88] Lafayette himself was known to have mentioned a Sycamore tree, but he did not include his headquarters in any of his writings let alone in his 1837 memoir.

The historian Michael C. Harris, a former park employee, is one of the few to point to Lafayette's French colleague, François Jean de Beauvoir, the Marquis de Chastellux, who later penned a celebrate travelogue called *Travels in America*," included a revelatory sentence that Lafayette actually stayed at the Benjamin Ring's house – not once but twice. [89]

The first occasion was in 1777 when the house served as Gen. Washington's Headquarters, and the second time three years after the battle, when Lafayette visited Chadds Ford for an overnight stay with Chastellux and other friends. In Chastellux's words, Lafayette sought out the "hospitality of a Quaker named Benjamin Ring, at whose house he had lodged with General Washington the night before the battle."

The community legend about Lafayette's headquarters at the Gilpin House is said to be based on Lafayette's second trip to America in 1824, when he visited 24 states in 13 months. In July of 1825, he came to Chadds Ford, and he paid a visit to the owner himself, the dying Gideon. This written account may have been based on the published writing of Lafayette's secretary who, along with Lafayette's son George Washington Lafayette, were part of an impromptu visit to see the man "under whose roof [Lafayette] had passed the night before the battle." The fact that it was penned by Lafayette's secretary added clout to the story, even though it is full of factual errors such as calling Gideon, Lafayette's "comrade in arms," according to Harris.

Perhaps there is little drama in a shared headquarters. Nor anything like the story of a wounded Lafayette being carried to Gilpin's house and treated for his wounds under not only a tree but a native American species – one that is now possibly the largest and oldest tree in the region. In actuality, the Marquis was wounded miles away in Birmingham. He was said to have refused medical help and famously led the American retreat to Chester.

Lafayette was later conveyed from there by barge to Philadelphia, resting in a local tavern before being taken by carriage on a long trip to Bethlehem, considered the best place to recover aside from hospitals in Reading, Pennsylvania. [90] Yet despite written records about the young general's care, somehow the legend of Lafayette's tree has persisted.

The Lafayette Monument of 1895

The structure now known as the monument of 1895 (58) is perhaps the best example of the kind of community patriotism Lafayette inspired. Described as being the result of a fundraising project initiated by public school children, the monument recognized Lafayette as a young hero or the "[one] who helped to form the third American line near here."

As typical of local memorials, the monument replaced a small marker erected several years earlier near Sandy Hollow. Both memorials commemorated the alleged place where Lafayette was wounded. However, when the site was chosen for the second monument, a committee chose a different site closer to the Birmingham Meetinghouse.

The selection was based in part of the memories of residents who recalled Lafayette's 1825 tour of the battlefield, when he reconsidered the "true location" of where he was wounded after "coming in sight of that building [the meetinghouse]."

When the monument was unveiled on September 11, 1895, an estimated five to eight thousand people were in attendance. They were there to commemorate Lafayette's actions and to mark the place of his wounding, "on rising ground a short distance south of this spot," as the monument reads.

In one telling speech, one official spoke of the "widening and deepening interest" in local history and cited the work of area schoolchildren who raised funds for the "simple and graceful" monument (a "silent protest against extravagance and show in monuments").

The newly formed Chester County Historical Society was later part of a movement to bring what was termed "special exercises in local history" to the public schools. And perhaps more importantly, the history of the Battle of Brandywine soon appeared in school textbooks and an annual anniversary celebration, Brandywine Day, (30) almost guaranteed at least some time off from one's classroom studies.

Fêting Lafayette In 1825

Perhaps West Chester's second greatest connection to the American Revolution —aside from skirmishes that took place in the center of the hamlet in mid-September 1777 – was Lafayette's visit on July 26, 1825.

Local newspapers focused on the unsparing hospitality shown to the Marquis, but particular attention was given to Lafayette's ride to West Chester and his overnight stay at the home of Éleuthère Irénée du Pont at Eleutherian Mills, now part of the Hagley Museum in Wilmington, Delaware.

The next day, Lafayette and his host departed early in the morning (the weather "cool and delightful") and traveled to Chadds Ford by a barouche carriage driven by four gray horses, as one reporter described it. 91 Lafayette's entourage included his son, George Washington Lafayette, and fifteen militia on foot and two on horseback, creating a procession that could be seen for miles away.

While the entire "day was spent as a holiday by a great part of the county," the reporter continued, it was not a time for staying home. Residents did everything possible to catch the attention of the carriage party as soon as it entered Chester County near Chadds Ford, and "the roads were lined with enthusiastic spectators" and "flowers, flags, handkerchiefs greeted the General and his party at every turn." Still, the crowd at Chadds Ford paled in comparison to what the group would find at the county seat of West Chester: an estimated 10,000 waving and cheering spectators lined the streets.

The West Chester historian Douglas Harper quotes one newspaper that reported that Lafayette's approach was heralded "by express riders who came hurrying into town in advance." In his excellent history of the borough, Harper includes an entire chapter on Lafayette's visit, noting that he was "more than just a relic of the Revolution" but rather a war hero and a "survivor of the European Enlightenment, the sister movement of the one that had founded America." Harper also gives a perspective on the 10,000 spectators as follows:

> "The entire borough barely numbered six hundred citizens, and many if not most of the throng had come out from Delaware County and Philadelphia. Even hangings only drew five thousand or so in West Chester in those days."

Considering the size of the Marque's entourage, it is not surprising that it was late in the afternoon when Lafayette's carriage entered the western border of the borough by way of Rosedale Avenue. They had visited all the landmarks Lafayette had wanted to see, especially the possible site where he was wounded near Birmingham Meeting. They had also stopped for lunch at the home of an unnamed host living at the corner of Birmingham and Street Roads, according to newspaper accounts.

The group then headed for West Chester, stopping briefly at Strode's Mill (64) and then "Darlington's Woods" (later Smedley Darlington's estate, Fawnbrook). Crowding in on the plant-filled grounds of the estate, the party was joined by numerous veterans of the War of 1812, who were there to add a touch of military authenticity to the tour – and to fire a 13-gun salute.

The entire day had been set in motion by "Judge" Isaac Darlington, cousin to the renowned physician turned botanist William Darlington, who had extended an invitation to Lafayette's entourage to include West Chester in their travel plans.

The Untold Story of Its History and Preservation | 157

![Trimble's Ford postcard: Trimble's Ford, Route of British, Battle of Brandywine, Sept., 11. 1777.]

59. Trimble's Ford: This c.1900 postcard is an approximate view of the famous crossing on the West Branch of the Brandywine. Note: most Chester County residents knew of the crossing so only the words "Route of British" was needed. *Author's collection.* **60. Below:** Author's photo of Trimbleville taken from Bragg Hill Road, near the Bailey homestead .

They had hoped for a July 26th visit. But as luck would have it, a letter of acceptance was received on July 16th, 1825, and so the Judge's committee had only ten days to plan for the momentous occasion. With nearly all the important local Revolutionary War heroes long dead – namely Gen. Wayne and Col. John Hannum – the group felt lucky to secure the veteran Col. Joseph McClellan, who had fought with Stirling at Birmingham Hill.92

As Harper put it, McClellan "was brought back to West Chester to host the event, in hopes that the old Frenchman would find in him at least one familiar face." It was McClellan, in fact, who met the group in Chadds Ford around 11 a.m., appearing on horseback so that he could escort Lafayette, along with a group of militia cavalry, to the "aged" Gideon Gilpin who was lying in his bed at his home, a structure destined to be preserved as "Lafayette's Headquarters."

The citizens of the county seat were said to have expected an all-out parade, with plenty of militia to add to the pomp and circumstance. For that they needed veteran "Major" Isaac Barnard, a West Chester resident who had become an attorney following his military service. A few years after the War of 1812, Barnard, at the age of 27, worked with Judge Darlington to mobilize a volunteer militia unit known as the Republican Artillerists to raise funds for a monument marking the site of the Paoli Massacre in present-day Malvern. (49)

On that summer day in 1825, Barnard's military escort was the first of 17 different volunteer troops as well as two troops of cavalry that joined behind Lafayette's carriage and his entourage. Their destination was an open field west of present-day East Lafayette Street and Marshall Square Park. Described as the "field of Jesse Matlack, on the hill east of the Friends Meetinghouse," the spot had been selected for its level, expanse of land where Lafayette could perform his celebrated viewing of the troops.

A small flat marble marker can still be seen along E. Lafayette Street; however, it has the wrong date. It reads: *From this spot July 26, 1826/Marquis De Lafayette/Viewed the troops escorting him from a visit to the Brandywine Battle-Field.* A larger historical marker –with the correct year of 1825 – was placed at the park in 1952.

In the Matlack farm fields, Lafayette was greeted by another 13-gun salute. It was one of many tributes that led reporters to write that "the heart of the General was deeply touched," and after reviewing the troops "on foot," Lafayette "expressed his great satisfaction at their appearance and soldier-like behavior," as one reporter observed. That evening, a feast was given in Lafayette's honor at the courthouse with numerous dignitaries in attendance. One newspaper described the attendees, in order of their importance and their roles as organizers, as the town burgess Ziba Pyle, Major Barnard, Judge Darlington, Dr. Darlington, and fellow botanist, David Townsend, and

61. Martin's Tavern: The original structure is believed to have been built as a home in 1750. Today this historic site is named for the first owner, Joseph Martin, who opened his tavern in an addition he built on his home in 1764. During the early days of settlement, when Chester County was a much larger region, the tavern's name reflected its location. It was known as the Centre House throughout the 1880s.
Author's collection

one man whose community status is lost to history named James Tillum. He was simply listed as a "gent" in the 1857 borough directory.

Despite the solemnity of a day spent visiting a former battlefield, the dinner was summed up by one reporter as "by all accounts [it] was a raucous good time with toasts made by and for Lafayette, as well as for our country, and for many of the founding fathers."

Newspapers of the period suggest that Dr. Darlington, who was fluent in French, had encouraged his cousin to extend the invitation to visit West Chester because Lafayette shared a Freemason connection with many of the attendees. Before dinner, Darlington escorted the Marquis on a special walking tour that included Darlington's botanical and native plant collection as well as a stop on High Street to see a colony of Purple Martins that lived in a birdhouse on a tall pole behind the Bank of Chester County.

Decades later a new generation of West Chester citizens would commemorate the anniversary of the Marquis' visit with a display of artifacts that included the mahogany bed Lafayette had slept in. It had been acquired right before Lafayette's 1825 visit when a yellow fever scare changed the hosting venue from the elegant Cross Keys Hotel to Pyle's house across the street, on West Gay

. Perhaps it was a sign of the times, but even though Pyle was the town burgess, he had no suitable bedstead, or one "commensurate with the dignity of the occasion," as one paper termed it, and so a local cabinetmaker "loaned him the carved mahogany one from his own home.

160 | The Brandywine Battlefield:

62. A Landmark to All. This c. 1900 postcard depicts Welch's Tavern when it was known as the Anvil Tavern. In 1777, it was a landmark for both the British and the American troops and it even initially figured into Gen. Howe's pre-battle plans: He thought the entire Royal Force should convene there on Sept. 9th.

Author's collection

Part Three

Historic Sites & Incidents

Martin's Tavern

When the American Revolution erupted in Chester County on Sept. 11, 1777, the members of the Continental Congress were ordered to flee from Philadelphia. They did so, thinking that the colonial capitol was the intended target, and they subsequently ordered the removal of all but one printing press from the city.

One contingent of Congressmen was said to have traveled to the city of Lancaster by way of West Bradford, Chester County. Taking the Strasburg Road, they passed a long-established inn known as Martin's Tavern, named for Joseph Martin, the man who established the public house in 1764.

For weeks since the British landing at the Head of the Elk, taverns throughout Chester County, especially those with patriotic reputations, were crowded each night with residents commiserating about the impending doom.

Martin's Tavern was no exception, but the atmosphere may have been even more politically oriented since its patrons included wealthy Quakers and men with strong ties to Philadelphia such as Humphry Marshall, the colonial botanist and scientist who later dedicated his book, *Arbustum Americanum: American Grove* (1785), to his friend Benjamin Franklin. The book was the first publication and catalogue of native plants, shrubs, and trees that was written by an American and published in America.

On the evening of Sept. 10th, the tavern was the meeting place for several scouts and members of the Chester County Militia in the 1st Battalion. The battalion's commander, Col. John Hannum, was also present and would end up spending the night, although he lived only a short distance away.[93] Another lodger – Thomas "Squire" Cheyney – lived more than a day's ride away in what is now Thornbury Township, Delaware County.

Even though Cheyney was not an official scout, his overnight stay was probably not a random occurrence. He was Hannum's in-law (his brother was married to Hannum's daughter) and therefore he may have wanted to help in the scouting mission.

There were at least four other key scouts including Maj. Joseph Spear of the 8th Battalion of Chester County, but it was Cheyney alone who became a legendary figure as the so-called "Paul Revere of Chester County." In other words, the man who warned Washington that the British were coming. In some respects, Cheyney might have merely been in the proverbial right place at the right time.

One of the largest groups sent to scout the countryside was a detachment of American light infantry under Lt. Col. James Ross – about 70 men in all. They traveled as far north as the tavern and began to scout the area around 9:30 a.m. However, Maj. Spear is said to be the first scout on the road. He departed Martin's Tavern by horseback before sunrise and headed south on the Great Valley Road (41) towards Welch's Tavern.

Cheyney and Hannum rode their horses on the same road a short time later, and sometime after 8 a.m., having traveled to a region that might have been near the present-day Camp Linden Road, in West Bradford, they are able see what Spear had missed. The front of Howe's and Cornwallis' column — Hessian field *Jäegers* corps and a British light infantry battalion — were beginning to cross the West Branch of the Brandywine at Trimble's Ford. (59)

Welch's Tavern

Mainly because of its location on Nottingham Road, Welch's Tavern (62) not only witnessed the Hessian advance, it was the location of the first American position and the scene of one of the first savage skirmishes, which may have taken place as early as 6 a.m. Period records describe the skirmish as taking place in a wooded area east of the tavern. Perhaps the most important of these was Knyphausen's own account. He wrote that he was "Advancing on the Road to Chads's Ford...[and] I had hardly come up to Welch's Tavern when the advanced Corps."

He then cited Ferguson's riflemen and the Queen's Rangers, remarking that they "fell in with about 300 Riflemen of the Ennemy [sic] who were posted in the Wood to the eastward of the Tavern."

Still, other Hessian accounts tell of Knyphausen's advance knowledge of the tavern. In fact, during the march

Trimble's Mill: Author's 2001 photo of the mill site along the Broad Run that dates to 1720.

north from Delaware on September 9th and 10th, the Hessian Maj. Gen. Johann Daniel Stirn wrote of the Hessian column that "marched via Welch's Tavern where the Rebels had an outpost."

Another Hessian officer, Karl von Baumeister, suggests that it wasn't the enemy's presence at the tavern that lead Knyphausen to change his mind and convene at Kennett Square. Baumeister wrote that two Hessian columns – one encumbered with the wagon train, cattle, and artillery – were expected to keep the same pace. In his words, Howe "gave such marching orders that both columns were to arrive at the place of rendezvous, namely, Welch's Tavern, at the same time."

However, at one point during the march through the Delaware settlement of Hockessin and beyond, road conditions made it impossible for the troops to reach c. 1767 Welch's Tavern with what Baumeister called "any semblance of organizational structure or military order from which he could stage an attack."

Throughout the 19th century, postcards of the tavern described it merely as on the "Route of the British Army." The landmark is also featured in Bayard Taylor's 1866 novel, *The Story of Kennett*. Taylor may have embellished or fictionalized his story, but he included the tavern's name at the time – the Anvil Inn at Logtown – and according to community lore, "ancient" Revolutionary War soldiers frequented the tavern and were often seen taking part in a pastime rolling cannon balls in the yard or sitting on the tavern's long porch shrouded with climbing roses.

Although much of the old tavern building was demolished in the 1920s (after serving as a boarding house for the workers at Longwood Gardens), and the site was mostly replaced by the present-day Colonial Revival house, Welch's Tavern has been

The Untold Story of Its History and Preservation |163

63. **Jefferis' Ford:** One of two views of the covered bridge built over the former ford crossing on the West Branch of the Brandywine in 1862. It was said to be Chester County's second oldest covered bridge when it was destroyed by arson in 1952. The current historic iron bridge was relocated to the site from the Doe Run region. .

described by the Brandywine Battlefield Task Force as a "significant landmark not only on Sept. 11th but also the days leading up to the battle." Now part of the Longwood Gardens Historic District, the site is now being considered as a future interpretive center for the Task Force since the property was the place where the "first shots" of the Brandywine battle took place, as well as being a place, in the Task Force language, that "relates to modern warfare in which fighting often occurs in developed areas, and in which professional and non-professional troops fight alongside each other."

In addition, some of the walls of the original tavern are believed to be still standing as part of an existing foundation wall and doorway. The site is marked by an anvil placed at one corner of the wall and because of that, visitors can envision the historic location of Welch's Tavern as well as get a sense of the amount of ground the troops had to cover— a six-mile stretch between Kennett Square and Chadds Ford.

Trimble's Ford

History may had a different outcome if Washington knew of this Upper Ford or if he knew of it, believed it was worth protecting. Evidently Lt. Col. Ross, who gave an early warning, was unfamiliar with it too since he mistakenly called it "Taylor's

Ford" (Cope's Bridge, 33) in a dashed-off report to Washington.

Thomas McGuire imagines the breathtaking beauty of the local landscape as John Galloway, the American Loyalist and Howe's guide, led the flanking party through his homeland of West Bradford. Estimating that the crossing at Trimble's Ford took place sometime between 9 and 11 a.m., McGuire writes that by the time the King's troops reached Trimble's Ford, the fog had lifted, and the sun was shining.

To get through the area's "maze of narrow country roads," the British relied on Galloway's scouts, John Jackson, and Curtis Lewis, who together had "scouted the fords of the Brandywine the night before," McGuire writes. Indeed, thanks to these three men, the Royal flanking party made no errors on the route.

From the Great Valley Road, they took a now vanished road linking the two fords. The road was established around 1754 and thus it was a reliable route in 1777. It followed the roadbed of the present-day Camp Linden Road before proceeding around a so-called "notch" in a large hill, then roughly followed what today is Lucky Hill and Allerton Roads directly to Jefferis' Ford. Several families who lived along the 1754 road suffered damages including the family of George Carter, a wealthy farmer who formed a partnership to build Strode's Mill in 1721.

The Carter family lived more than a mile west of Jeffries Ford, but they may have seen hundreds of soldiers gather on their property as the troops waited their turn to cross the ford.

The troops' march to Trimble's Ford was documented as passing by the house of Humphry Marshall's relative, Joel Baily, a wealthy farmer and grist mill owner whose range of talents were widely known. His skills as a self-taught mathematician, surveyor, astronomer, as well as a clockmaker, led him to be a key member of the team who created the famous "Mason & Dixon" state border survey conducted from 1763 to 1767.

Other nearby sites that were part of the 2010 Task Force study of area historic resources are found in the former colonial settlement of Trimbleville. The structures were very close to the spot where the British troops waded across the Brandywine such as Trimble's Mill, whose Irish-born Quaker owners, William and James Trimble, gave their name to the ford and the now vanished community. The mill still stands just south of the intersection of Broad Run and Northbrook Roads, as does the c. 1709 homestead of William Marshall who, at one point, was one of the joint owners of the mill.

All of these early homesteads contribute to the interpretation of the battlefield landscape in that they offer a glimpse of Chester County's early agricultural history and character of the rural landscape. Before 1777, the farms here were among the

The Untold Story of Its History and Preservation |165

64. **Strode's Mill.** The photo above was part of Brinton's 1899 series on the battlefield. The perspective suggests the mill's crossroads location between an old road (Lenape Road) dating to 1720 that ran from West Chester and the c. 1745 Road (Birmingham Road). Brinton saw the crossroads as an important stop for the British troops to rest and prepare for battle after completing an arduous flanking march that began at 5 a.m. in Kennett Square. *CCHC*

Strode's Mill from Birmingham Road (above): Photographer Ned Goode took this photo and many other landmarks in the area in 1957. Courtesy of Library of Congress,

The Brandywine Battlefield:

Colonial Architecture: Ned Goode's view of the front of the house reveals its sloping dormer, a once common colonial house element as was the shuttered windows and the solid door with a four-pane transom.

Joseph Townsend, who selected the house because of its hilltop location and its sweeping views of the distant Osborne Hill, recalled that while he and his brother were in the house, several of the "principal officers" in the Royal Forces entered the house. It's likely they used this same door pictured here.

65. Old House at Sconnelltown. This c.1750 classic colonial homestead had been converted into a barn when photographer Ned Goode took this image of the rear of the house in 1958. The famous battlefield witness, Joseph Townsend, recalled that he and Richard Strode's son ran to the second story of this home to view the British flanking troops as they continued to Birmingham .

Top left: A side view of the house with a tree blocking the view of the front door. Goode probably wanted to show the steep pitch of the roof and the colonial-style dormer window.

All photos courtesy of Library of Congress, HABS

most prosperous of the young nation, in part because the wheat or flour produced here had a global market and was shipped to Africa, the Caribbean Islands, and to Europe.

The Bailey homestead was located outside Trimbleville but it stood on a high elevation overlooking Trimble's Ford (59). Reached by a now semi-private road called Bragg's Hill Road, (60) Bailey's home was the center of the action for both armies on the day of the Battle of Brandywine. His home was plundered by the British as they made their way down the hill to Jefferis' Ford (63).

Two British officers reportedly stopped long enough to pay Bailey 45 pounds sterling for four horses and various gear. Evidently, there were other losses since Bailey and his wife (the niece of Humphry Marshall) later filed a claim that included nearly 140 pounds sterling in clothing, livestock, and specific losses such as five "fat sheep" and 300 pounds of cheese.

McGuire provides a poetic description of the British flanking party as it "descended the hill from Baily's house, where the Brandywine meanders from the west and loops northward around the hill to the east and south." He also suggests that this region was not a dense wilderness with bad roads that Washington might have envisioned but instead was populated as follows: "Rolling terrain, dotting with farm buildings and mills of stone and brick and log, some bright with whitewash, and rich with emerald meadows framed by rail fences."

That morning several American patrols stopped by Bailey's house but unfortunately, they were too early to spot the British. Capt. Mountjoy Bayly, who led a patrol of Maryland soldiers, found Bailey's home to be a perfect spot for viewing since it was "pleasantly situated on a high hill overlooking the western branch of the Brandywine." The road to Trimble's Ford, aka the Great Valley Road, also passed by the dwelling. Thus, the Bailey home became part of community legend after Futhey & Cope published an incident of mistaken identity.

Bayly's troops wore old Maryland Guard coats that were the same shade of red as the British uniforms, and so Joel Bailey, a "zealous" Loyalist, welcomed them into his house. The historians write that Bailey's error was never corrected and that the scouts stayed for a meal – and long enough to see the head of British column approaching the ford. They then said their goodbyes and left at once.

Jefferis' Ford

> "[We] crossed the Brandywine seven miles up from Chads Ford, where the river is divided into two branches; the bridges were destroyed. The men had to cross these two branches up to three feet of water. We then continued our march a short distance straight ahead."
>
> Howe's German aide, Capt. Friedrich von Muenchhausen.

65. A Village Long Ago. Douglas E. Brinton evidently relied on the public's knowledge of this "long ago" village since he identifies it only as Sconnelltown in his 1899 photography series. In 1777, the village was comprised of only a small cluster of buildings. The flanking troops were glad to reach this safer, higher ground, especially after going through the earlier "defile" along Birmingham Road. *Courtesy of CCHC*

It was nearly high noon when the head of the Flanking Column arrived at the second ford, Jefferis, named for a nearby farm family, and not a ferryman. Writing in his diary, Muenchhausen had been correct about the depth of the fords, but not about the American foresight: the fords had no bridges to begin with. His reference to "straight ahead" may have been modern Lucky Hill Road. It ran a short distance before dead-ending into Birmingham Road, now Allerton Road.

Muenchhausen is believed to have continued on with Howe and Cornwallis while the rest of the Flanking Column may have broken formation and rested in the fields, perhaps under trees away from the sun. Jefferis' Ford had a reputation for stronger currents than Trimble's, and so the troops backed up, waiting their turn to cross single file. 94

Part of the road leading from Trimble's Ford (now only a road trace evident in some fields near Lucky Hill Road) was well used, having been established in 1728. However, it led through a hilly region with sharp turns and therefore it took the Flanking Column about two hours to march from one ford to the other.

Joseph Townsend caught up with the tail end of the British column here, "led by Curiosity" to travel from Sconnelltown (65) and so he decided to stay with the advancing troops "for the better part of the day." In one telling passage, Townsend described a sea of British soldiers, their uniforms dark with wetness from the previous crossing, "coming out of the woods into the fields belonging" to Emmor Jefferis.

As for other legends about the ford, Futhey & Cope were among several early historians to describe the ransacking of Emmor's home by British soldiers (cited as being Hessians in some accounts).

Despite the fact that Emmor is believed to have never filed a damage claim, one popular story of British misconduct focuses on the seizure of brandy and other stores of liquor from the cellar. Ironically, the entire lot had been hidden on the property by "a number of [Wilmington] merchants and others," who assumed the British would never travel that far north, according to an 1845 newspaper account. The writer suggests it was done rather systematically; each cask was rolled out of the cellar, and soldiers "knocked in heads of the vessels, and drank the contents until a great number of them became intoxicated."

In contrast, Townsend focuses entirely on the visual scene and the marching rank. He writes that Cornwallis' column was followed by "horse and foot, artillery, baggage, provision wagons, arms and ammunition, together with a host of plunderers and rabble." Perhaps it was the "plunderers and rabble" who drank the liquor stores. Townsend doesn't say; he only concluded that the troops made it safely across the Brandywine and "their passing took nearly four hours."

Sconnelltown

> "Whoever heard of Sconnelltown? – a village long ago…."
> Excerpt of a poem by James B. Everhart, 1868.

Today there is not much to be seen in the former village of Sconnelltown (65) but that was also true in 1868, when the Chester County poet James B. Everhart summed up its status as one of those enigmatic places in history.

In the opening lines of a long poem about the Revolutionary War site, he asks, "Whoever heard of Sconnelltown? – a village long ago" and then goes on to describe it as an unusual historical landmark, a place where "scarce a vestige can be found/of tenements or tomb."

Named for an 18th century weaver whose surname was Sconnell, the village seems to have existed in memory only: There is no official record – no deed, map, or tax list – that specifically mentions the hamlet. Only tradition places its location on the northern slope of Bradford Heights, an area in East Bradford Township.

It was nearly 1:30 in the afternoon when the head of the flanking party passed through Sconnelltown – an event documented by Joseph Townsend. That morning, the Quaker members of Birmingham Meeting (47) had been forced to relocate their Thursday Meeting and found space in the hamlet's wheelwright and blacksmith shop owed by Richard Strode. Townsend recorded an incident that occurred at the meeting when he famously heard a "disturbance" or a banging on the door, which turned out to be "an alarm amongst some of the neighbouring [sic] women, that the English were acoming."

Unaware that he was about to join the British Left Hook, he writes that he was nearly overwhelmed, especially after the troops moved closer to the settlement and filled the narrow road. Immediately the scene went from the general to the specific and Townsend was able to see the faces of the British, or as he says, "in a few minutes we found ourselves in the midst of a Crowd of Military characters, rank & file...." Most unusual, a neighbor named Sarah Boake, "who had been curious as ourselves," encouraged Townsend and his brother, William, to follow the troops. Within minutes, they were stopped by a British soldier, who inquired where they were going and then suggested that they get permission from a captain.

It was the first of many exchanges during the day, though Townsend's narrative also takes on an impersonal tone, suggesting, for instance, the insect-like swarm of soldiers with the line "in a few minutes the fields were covered over with them."

On their way to Sconnelltown, Townsend recalled that "the space occupied by the main body and flanking parties was near half mile wide" and that "a continual march of soldiers and occasionally a troop of horse [sic] passing: great numbers of baggage wagons began to make their appearance, well guarded by proper officers and soldiery."

While Townsend later sought out other passersby to join him and his brother, 'having "become familiar with" the British but also wishing to have more witnesses to experience the historical day, Townsend suggests that only the two of them left the Meeting, "being disposed to have a better & nearer view of them [the British army] we sat [set] out." They did not go far but ran to a nearby house where Townsend observed the passing troops from a doorway. 95 In his words, he sought out a house with a view, or "we passed through them [the crowds of soldiers) until we reached one of the most eligible homes in the town."

Perhaps the passage of time clouded Townsend's memory—he was living in Baltimore by the time he penned his account—but evidently he considered Sconnelltown to be a community of several homes. At any rate, he continues, noting that "the house we were in was elevated, so that on the first floor where we stood we had a pretty full view of the army as they progressed along."

At one point, William called him to the doorway and they saw "General Lord Cornwallis, who was passing by." "His rich scarlet clothing, loaded with gold lace, epaulets, etc., occasioned to make him a brilliant and martial appearance." (Townsend did not see Howe, a "large portly man" riding a half-starved "English horse" until they got to Osborne's Hill.)

Several "principal officers" also walked into the house and were soon engaged with the "occupants." Townsend concludes this interesting passage by stating that he found the British officers to be "full of inquiries" concerning the whereabouts of Washington's troops and he credits William for answering "modestly and spiritedly."

Interestingly, the answer that Townsend records suggests that General Washington had already received news of the impending flanking attack and had sent troops to Birmingham. William's reply, along with Townsend's use of parenthesis, was as follows:

> "[He]told them that if they would have patience a short time, he expected they would meet with General Washington and his forces, who were not far distant, (the front of his army was then on view on the heights of Birmingham meeting house, though three miles distant from us)."

Respite at Strode's Mill

> "The regiments were stacked up one behind the other and [Ewald's] division rested for about thirty minutes."   Michael C. Harris, *Brandywine*.

Generations of residents knew this crossroads settlement as Strode's Mill (21), but for the Crown Forces it was a much-needed resting place. Having made it through the "terrible defile," or the deep gorge along Birmingham Road (northwest of the crossroads with Lenape Road), the flanking troops finally had time to stop and reorganize the divisions into three columns. 96 Ewald's Hessian troops were among the first to halt, but only for about 30 minutes.

Townsend does not mention the mill property as a resting place; perhaps because he came upon a more amazing site just past the crossroads along Birmingham Road— the Hessians, or German troops, who "wore their beard on their upper lips."

He locates the sighting as taking place "between the dwelling of Richard Strode and Osborne's Hill," a distance of half a mile. Strode's serpentine homestead still stands at 645 Birmingham Road. So that meant the Hessians, a group Townsend called, "an advance guard" may not have stopped to create a formation but marched directly to the gathering point at Osborne's.

Today the Strode's Mill complex is considered to be more than a resting place. Away from the defile of Birmingham Road, the crossroads and open ground around the mill complex gave the Britsh space to maneuever. In fact, historians go so far as to say that when Howe and Cornwallis arrived at Strode's Mill, they used the time to strategize. Howe, in particular, had to change his focus from navigating a successful flanking maneuver to leading men into combat. Within a short time, the troops formed in several columns along present-day Lenape Road.

The three columns were then ordered to move forward, since part of the British forces were already at Osborne's Hill. The marching route was more than a mile wide and can be visualized today as follows: The British Guards brigade extended in a westward direction along modern Lenape Road (Rt.52) to where the road intersects with Edgemill Way.

The British 3rd and 4th brigades formed columns just north of Strode's Mill, extending from Tigue Road to the present-day Osage Lane near Baldwin's Book Barn. All three columns had to cross the Plum Run creek to get to Birmingham Heights, an elevated area near Birmingham Meeting.

The Royal Forces at Osborne's Hill

> "While there were times when a commanding general believed his presence on the front line was needed to resolve a crisis, it was far more common for him to exercise command from a central position in the rear where he could be located, receive intelligence, and issue orders through his aide."
>
> Michael C. Harris, concerning "A Note on Generalship."

It was nearly 2 p.m. when the lead British troops of an estimated 9,000 water-soaked soldiers crested Osborne's Hill (2,50) and were finally able to rest after more than eleven hours of almost ceaseless marching on a scorching day.

Many of the foot soldiers later recalled that the twisting roads made it nearly impossible to complete the task of guiding the horses that strained to pull artillery and supplies. While it might have been a test of endurance, the march to battle was typically described by 19th-century historians as one involving many "lulls" or "respites." Thus Osborne's Hill became part of a community legend that left out the grueling march and highlighted the scenery of open fields high above the countryside where the Crown Forces rested for afternoon tea.

From the British point of view, the "Hill," located about two miles from Birmingham Meeting, was an important military destination. It enabled their commander to plan his strategy from a central position, in the rear of the action, ideally positioned on a high elevation overlooking the enemy's defense line. Certainly, it was command central – Robertson, the Royal engineer, even named it as such, labeling Osborne Hill on his map as the *"high Ground mark'd A in the Plan."*

The historian Harris writes that the British troops "essentially halted," having "earned its rest." The mid-day lull also gave Howe and Cornwallis a chance to discern the American alignment and thus decide that the assault formation should extend for at least a half mile. 97

Townsend also recorded the hilltop as a staging ground. One moment the British officers were "collected together to consult about carrying on the engagement to the best advantage," and the next thing he noticed the "battle had commenced in earnest; little was to be heard but the firing of the musketry and the roaring of cannon from both parties."

Perhaps the most interesting record of Osborne Hill is the suggestion, made by Howe's Aide-de-camp, Captain Friedrich Von Munchhausen, that Howe and Cornwallis risked leaving their viewing post at Osborne's Hill and may have moved closer to see the onslaught of the American troops. For Munchhausen, it became an opportunity to record a glowing account of Howe's valor and bravery on the field. The complete passage is as follows:

> "As usual, the General [Howe] exposed himself fearlessly on the occasion. He quickly rushed to each spot where he heard the strongest fire. Cannon balls and bullets passed close to him in [great] numbers today. We all feared that, since he is so daring on any and all occasions, we are going to lose our best friend, and that England will lose America."

McGuire, on the other hand, offers another viewpoint from an unnamed officer that is more in keeping with the British tradition of considering one's bearings before battle. According to a community story, McGuire writes, the officer admired the landscape from Osborne's Hill. The surrounding farms and rolling hills created a "scenery before him [that] was as familiar to him as the scenery of his native place in Northumberland [in England]; it had come before him at the twilight and in his slumbers over and over again, and [he] added, 'I know I am to die here.' The dream became reality when he was mortally wounded that day." 98

Poised for Battle

When Howe rearranged the Flanking Column just beyond Sconnelltown, the placement of the troops in a three-column formation was well calculated. The commanders could easily keep their troops separated in a specific marching order despite a territory that included the soft ground of the Radley Run watershed.

It took almost an hour for the troops to cross the region. Some troops did not reach Osborne's Hill until about 2:15 p.m., having been scattered along present-day Lenape Road. The Queen's Guards marched on the far west of Strode's Mill, and the British 3rd and 4th brigades posted to the east, near modern Darlington Drive.

After resting at Osborne's Hill, the troops reassembled in marching order so that they could swiftly descend the hill when the command to battle was called. That did not happen, though, until what now seems to be an incredibly late time to begin a battle: 4 p.m. The Royal mapmaker was on hand to record the order of the troops as follows.

The Queen's Guard formed a right wing to attack Sullivan's division, while 1,400 British Grenadiers took up the center of the British line. The *Jägers* and light infantry descended next, swinging to the left in a wooded area and along Cornwallis' left flank, and formed to the west so they could march directly to the Birmingham Meetinghouse. With ribbons of scarlet and shades of red, blue, and green representing different units, the Crown Forces made an impressive sight. Still, only a few Continental soldiers recorded their reaction to seeing the Crown Forces make their descent and march to the lilting sounds of a drum and fife corps playing the lively tune *"The British Grenadiers."*

A New Jersey surgeon named Ebenezer Elmer in General Stephen's division writes that it became a deadly march after the Rebels "formed abt [sic] 4 oClock on an Eminence [at Birmingham Meeting]" and waited for the approach. Then the following happened; in Elmer's words:

> "[A] large Column Came on in front playing yet Granediers March & Now the Battle began [that] proved Excessive [and] severe. The Emeny Came on with fury [and] our men stood firing upon them most amazingly, killing almost all before them for near a hour till they got within 6 rod of each other."

Lt. James McMichael, who was part of the Pennsylvania line, confirms this close range, noting that "our regiment fought at one stand about an hour under incessant fire" and that 50 yards was a "common distance."

Proctor's Hill

> "We remained in presence of the whole Rebel Army from Nine in the morning till after four in the afternoon, [with] constant skirmishing or rather popping & frequently a Cannonade from both sides."
>
> *Major General James Grant, speaking of the action at Chadds Ford.*

The great "cannonade" cited above lasted for much of the day and was largely due to the handful of artillery batteries set up by the Continentals in the days before

176 | The Brandywine Battlefield:

The Untold Story of Its History and Preservation | 177

66. Sullivan's Post: A 1905 view of the mill is by an unidentified photographer. The mill property saw major fighting including a British raid on Proctor's artillery battery and a nearly continuous cannonade from both sides of the Brandywine. The ford here was also an important crossing point undertaken by both armies.

Top Left: A member of the Brinton family, W.C. Brinton, took this 1914 photograph of the former Brinton grist mill, now part of the Andrew Wyeth estate. The stone structure dates to 1717-`20. Edward Brinton purchased the property and enlarged the mill in 1762, the year reportedly found on a datestone when the Andrew Wyeth family renovated the mill.

Bottom Left: A 1934 view of the Brinton Mill when it featured a grain silo. The mill had last been updated in 1824. *All courtesy of CCHC.*

67. Site of the "Aborted Battle": This undated photo reveals the layout of the Andrew Wyeth estate along the Brandywine. For much of the day on Sept. 11th General John Sullivan and his troops were bivouacked in the fields adjacent to the Brinton Mill. A short distance up the present-day Brinton Bridge Road, Proctor's artillery placed a few guns to guard the ford. The subsequent battle was aborted when Washington's troops were diverted to Birmingham. *Courtesy of CFHS.*

the Battle of Brandywine. Proctor's artillery, named for an Irish native, Thomas Proctor, had been preparing for battle since August when his troops were based in Chester, Pennsylvania. Promoted to colonel – the highest field-grade office – in the spring of 1777, Proctor saw the former Pennsylvania-state-run artillery officially become part of the Continental Army as Proctor's Continental Artillery Regiment.

That same August Proctor may have accompanied Washington on a mission to select potential artillery locations in Chadds Ford. One can imagine that both men agreed when a high hilltop above the present-day Sanderson Museum was selected for the main redoubt (French for retreat).

In keeping with the other area batteries, Proctor's Hill was a four-gun earth-and-log lunette, or curved artillery battery. It was equipped with the latest style of guns including a 3-pounder (rebored as a 5-pounder) that had been seized from the Hessians at Trenton.

The battery also had two long-range French brass field guns capable of shooting heavy iron cannon balls, and an early type of howitzer cast in Philadelphia that fired exploding shells or canister shot. As for the placement of the battery, the teenage John Nagle once again provides the best description as follows:

> "The army encamped on the Brandewine on the right of Shads ford on the hier ground....Our artillery was ranged in front of an orcherd. The night before the British arrived, the [American] infantry hove up a brest work, so that the muzels of the guns would run over it."

Nagle was one of few soldiers to describe the view from Proctor's, looking down on an expanse of land filled with buckwheat. He described it as being "a buckwheat field opposite [of] a wood and the Brandywine between them." Nagle writes of a breastwork, made of "some trees cut down", and found in some nearby "skirts of Wood." Here a group of Hessians "got amongst them" and "braved a slew of shots, from a sharpshooter they could not see."

The sharpshooter "crawled on his hands and knees to the fence where he fell in with six more," but then a column of enemy forces seemed to ignore the threat and in Nagle's words, "all rise and crossed the ford and went to the place he [the sharpshooter] had been firing at them, as we suppose to overhaul them."

Brigadier General Edward Hand was one of the few American officers to document the sudden dilemma that occurred around 4 p.m. when Lord Stirling's and Stephen's troop departed for Birmingham Hill and Proctor's men were left unprotected. In Hand's words, "there were no troops to cover the artillery in the redoubt, the enemy was within thirty yards before being discovered; [and] our men were forced to fly, and to leave three [artillery] pieces behind."

The historian Harris quotes an unnamed British sergeant who vividly described the seizure of Proctor's Hill by the British brigade known as the King's Own, the 4th Regiment of Foot. The regiment had barely gotten through the ordeal of crossing the Brandywine under fire, when they had to struggle to avoid the "morass" or wetlands on either side of Nottingham Road. Still, they were able to move, in Harris' words "at a run around the west side of the hill upon which the John Chads house sat to assault the battery from the river side."

Proctor's men could do nothing but abandon the log-and-earth battery, because as the British sergeant observed, "before the Gunners could fire them off, the men of that Battalion [the 4th of Foot] put them to the Bayonets, and forced the Enemy from the Entrenchment."

Among the accounts, Nagle alone documents the struggle to defend the redoubt and to save the guns. Two of Proctor's men were killed and 21 were wounded during the relatively short time the last of the British troops were making their way uphill. He writes that "[al]though our artillery made a clear land through them as they mounted the works, but they filled up the ranks again." Before heading toward Wayne's troops in position south of the road, Nagle "spiked" the guns or temporarily

180| The Brandywine Battlefield:

68. Ring Farm: This historic property, donated by artist Karl Kuerner Jr. to the Brandywine Conservancy in 1999, was the scene of much Continental troop movement along Ring Road. Part of the original home may have served as a hospital after the battle. Opposite the entrance gates in this 1940s photo is Andrew Wyeth's longtime painting subject, "Kuerner's Hill." *Courtesy of CFHS*

disabled them by hammering a barbed steel spike into the touch-hole. That left two guns that needed to be hauled through marshy ground along the Nottingham Road. Nagle recalled the difficulties in a single passage:

> "When we began to retreat, while the infantry covered us, we had a ash [marsh] or swampy ground to cross with the artillery to get into the road, and the horses being shot, the men could not drag the peaces [sic] out. Therefore we had to spike two pieces and a howetor [howitzer]."

Credit in defending the site is now given to Edward "Ned" Hector, a Black private who was born free around 1744 and served in Proctor's Artillery as bombardier, a dangerous but skilled job requiring a thorough knowledge of specialized equipment such as loading cannon barrels, howitzers, and ammunition wagons.[99]

As his fellow soldiers retreated, Hector reportedly was heard to say he would not leave his horses behind. He may have been aware that Proctor's horse, described by the commander as "his best horse," had been shot dead during the raid. What is known about Hector's actions is described in his 1834 obituary; it quotes him as saying "the enemy shall not have my [wagon] team" as he remained visibly calm while soldiers fled and artillery showered down all around him. In the midst of frenzy, the obituary continues, Hector merely gathered up "a few stands of arms which had been left on the field by the retreating soldiers" and then "safely retired with the wagon, team and all."

Hector was a free Black man who served more than three years in the military, much longer than the year's service for the average soldier in 1777. When he applied for a long-over due pension in 1827 and again in 1828, he was denied. Finally, in 1833, the state Congress released some funds and he received an one-time $40 "gratuity" for his military service. That was a year before his death, at the age of 90, in 1834, coincidentally the same year England abolished slavery.

Sometime before 1800, Hector moved to an unsettled area (the first African – American to do so) that later became Conshohocken, Montgomery County. He was taxed there for several years for a small farm as well as "a cow, and dogs."

Hector's farm or post-war accomplishments are not mentioned in his obituary. However, it does gives the most information about his military service. Still, it ends with an unusual detail: that his wife of 50 plus years "expired" an hour after Hector's interment.

Two other tributes followed long after his death. When the borough was formed in 1850, local residents petitioned for an improved transport road for haulers and waggoners and thus Hector Street became named in his honor.

During the Bicentennial year of 1976, a historic marker was placed at the intersection of Fayette Street, recognizing Hector as a symbol of "many Black soldiers who served in the American Revolution, but whose race is not mentioned in the muster rolls." [100]

Washington's Headquarters

For three days beginning on Sept. 9th, the Ring House (16) served as Washington's Headquarters. It was a relatively short time, but Washington's expenditure records suggest that the house was crowded with officers and members of the War Council who met and dined in the Ring parlor. [101]

When Benjamin Ring was finally paid on February 7, 1778, he received 22 pounds and 10 shillings, a fee that was said to have also covered the cost of a special dinner for Washington's staff the night before the battle. [102] Another account shows that Ring was paid 37 pounds and 10 shillings for Washington's entire stay and that he was given the funds from "Col. Hamilton by the general's order." That is more than $2,000 in today's currency.

Washington may have slept in a tent at night (45), but even so the Ring family must have felt displaced. Ring's wife, Rachel, was pregnant at the time with their eighth child. The Delaware County historian John Jordan writes that at one point after the battle began, Ring's wife packed her younger children and valuables into a carriage but discovered the roads were blocked with soldiers and so they abandoned the carriage and belongings and fled on foot to the "nearest" (unidentified) meetinghouse.

Jordan also writes that in addition to the damage done to the property such as the stone walls pitted by shot, and an indentation left by a cannonball on one of the gables, the property was singled out as the home of a traitor, and everything was destroyed including the contents of Ring's mills. The seized items were said to have included 6 horses, 3 cattle, 6 sheep as well as 10 acres of crops and one indentured servant. [103]

After the battle, Benjamin ignored Quaker custom and filed a damage claim, though he wasn't paid until 1795, 18 years after the battle, and he died in 1804 virtually penniless. [104] Historians have documented Ring's financial decline: stating that distinct differences are found between Ring's taxes in 1774 and in 1778. [105]

Today the Ring House is of special interest to military historians since it is associated with both armies. It was a place where Washington's Council of War developed their strategy to defend the area fords, among other crucial decisions.

The structure is also an example of what Hessian commander, Karl von Baurmeister, saw as the Continentals' use of natural and manmade obstacles, noting "they withstood one more rather severe attack behind some houses and ditches." At least one attack occurred at the Ring property, or specifically in an orchard there. (See the Orchard at the Ring House.)

The Gilpin House

As a house museum, the Gilpin home (29) tells the story of the local families who witnessed the battle firsthand. Its historic importance rests more on the fact that the home was surrounded by a battlefield, and the farm, with its cattle and wheat fields, was extensively damaged during the battle. According to his damage claim, Gilpin lost roughly 502 pounds which has a modern equivalence to approximately $87,000.

The trauma of the war and his financial losses resulted in an unusual move for the respected Quaker. In 1778, Gilpin swore an oath of allegiance to the perceived "radical" Pennsylvania government, demonstrating that he was in full support of the Continental cause.

From that year on until 1782, Gilpin actively supported the local militia, supplying them with provisions and other supplies. For this reason and the fact that he opened a tavern to compensate for his losses, he joined many of his neighbors who were excommunicated or exiled from their meetinghouses or places of worship.

After the war, he continued his tavern business until 1789. That same year he was allowed back into Meeting for acknowledging his wrong doings and apologizing. Despite his accomplishments, Gilpin would go down in recent history as the Quaker whose home served as Lafayette's headquarters.

In 19th-century accounts, the headquarters idea is based on descriptions of the Marquis' visit to the house during his accalimed trip to America in 1825, when he paid a visit to the owner, described as the "aged Gideon" "then on his deathbed." [106]

Unfortunately, the sentimental tone of such accounts only served to keep the legend alive and prevented a practical assessment of the basic facts. For one thing, Gilpin may have been one of the last living residents who experienced the battle in 1777 and so, in the words of historian Michael C. Harris, Lafayette's visit may have been merely a "courtesy call." [107] (See Lafayette's "Other" Tree.)

Kuerner Farm or Washington's Hill"

Cannonballs and grapeshot found over the years in the Kuerner farm fields (68) indicate that the farm was in the path of major fighting. The farm was also located on a well-used road –the Ring Road – that led to Benjamin Ring's fulling mill in 1777. It is believed that Washington may have taken the road to get to Chadds Ford from Delaware on Sept. 9, 1777. Armstrong's troops may have also frequented the road since it was the best route to the Lower Fords (17).

A natural landmark now known as Kuerner's Hill, which overlooks Ring Road (7), was identified as "Washington's Hill" on an 1863 map created by the U.S. Coast Guard. The name implies that General Washington used the hill as a viewing station, but there doesn't seem to be any conclusive documentation, only a community legend that area residents watched the battle from the hilltop. [108]

On the afternoon of Sept. 11th, Nathaniel Greene's 1st Division – the 1st and 2nd Virginia brigade and 1st North Carolina brigade – traveled Ring Road, having been called from a resting area near Bullock Road. They were the first American troops to make a major move that morning and they eventually repositioned along the Nottingham Road, opposite of Harvey Road.[109]

Both the 1st and 2nd Virginia Brigades under Brigadier Generals Peter Muhlenberg and George Weedon, were then entrusted with the primary defense of Chads' Ford and Chads' Ferry. Soon after, around 5:15 p.m., Armstrong's troops left the Lower Fords (17) and were resting somewhere south of the Kuerner Farm — perhaps southwest of the crossroads of Bullock and Ring Roads – when they received their orders to cover Wayne's troops along Harvey Creek.

Some of Armstrong's militia were inexperienced and did not move from the Ring Road area until the final Continental retreat around 6:15 p.m. Indeed, many of Armstrong's troops militia may have crossed the Kuerner farm fields and continued (or fled) all the way to Wilmington Pike (Rt. 202) and beyond to the Concord Meetinghouse.

The historian Harris writes that while posted at the Lower Fords, the troops heard "the heavy firing further north at Chads' Ford, [and that] coupled with the initial British thrust across the [Brandywine] river, unnerved the part-time soldiers and their leaders."

Brinton's Ford

> "I had but four Light Horsemen, two of which I kept at the upper Fords, to bring me Intelligence, the other I kept to send Intelligence to Head Quarters,"
> The American Brig. Mj.Gen. John Sullivan, posted at Brinton's Ford.

Although the Continental troops did not see significant action here until around 12 noon – in a battle later termed an "abortive attack" – the outcome continues to be debated today as a study of Washington's strategic planning. If Washington's plans had gone smoothly, he may have directed a flanking maneuver of his own, dividing "the whole Army in two columns" and ordering the "greatest part of the army to cross several fords," as Lt. Col. Jonathan Smith, a militia member of a Philadelphia County regiment, recalled.

Initially Brinton's Ford (66) was considered the central or main crossing area, but Washington quickly repositioned his army so that other crossings would be covered. He ordered six brigades in three divisions to extend an additional six miles in a line that now follows along present-day Creek Road from Jones' Ford (52) (at modern Street Road) to Chads' Ferry, below the present-day Brandywine River Museum. This new course of action was the direct result of Washington's assumption that the British troops spotted near Trimble's Ford were too far north to rescue Knyphausen's troops, especially if an attack was undertaken at once.

Brinton's Ford thus became a key element of this proposed swift action. Historically, the ford was not necessarily easy to cross – it was about chest-high for an average man wading in the water – but an established road (now Brinton Bridge Road) crossed the Brandywine and led directly to the Nottingham Road and the left flank of Knphausen's forces (27). In addition, two columns of Sullivan's American troops planned to cross the Brandywine using both Brinton's Ford and a temporary bridge made of wagons and fence rails, reportedly placed between the ford and Chads' Ford further south. [73]

The peak of Washington's battle strategy did not occur until 12:45, exactly an hour after "Squire" Cheyney first delivered his news and was not believed. At the time, the Continentals had formed a new position in the fields along present-day Creek Road; the defense line extended from Street Road and south past the Nottingham Road. Finally, Sullivan's troops (posted since 9 a.m. at Brinton's Ford) were ordered to cross the Brandywine and attack Ferguson's Rifles and the British 1st Brigade.

The exchange was later called the "aborted" battle at Brinton's Ford, mainly because the troops were called back after only an hour of ruthless fighting. A new dispatch had changed Washington's plans after Bland's patrol reached his headquarters around 1:45 p.m. and he read the news: the British were spotted near Osborne Hill. Their close proximity meant that Washington's troops had been out flanked and they could do nothing but move north to Birmingham Hill.

The "Ravine" in Chadds Ford

The narrative that accompanies the famous map by the Royal engineer Archibald Robertson may be difficult to read by today's standards, but it still reveals some remarkable insights. One is the likelihood that British troops abandoned the fighting at Birmingham Hill. It was said to have happened after Sullivan's troops failed to reconvene with Stirling's troops, and the British took advantage of the weaken American Forces.

Indeed, several battalions of 1st British Guards and Hessian grenadiers pushed the Americans from Birmingham Hill around 5:15 p.m. and pursued them until they came to what was essentially a dead end at a ridge behind what is now the gatehouse to the Roundelay estate on Creek Road.

In the words of Robertson's narrative, having been exhausted, or "blown," after picking through an unfamiliar territory, the guards and grenadiers were still able to pursue an unspecified group of Continentals. The narrative reads that "they pursued as far as S;" however, to identify all the British troops that formed in a column just north along Brinton Run, the map is lined with five "S"s, marking the following: "one Battn. of the Guards [the 2nd Battalion], the three Batts. of Hessian Grenadiers, and the first Battn. British Grenadiers."

The 2nd Battalion was described as a unit that had been led astray in a sweeping movement that flanked the left side of the American defense line, but they now joined the other British forces and headed towards Proctor's battery at Chads' Ford. By that time, the battery may have been abandoned after a raid by a regiment of Highlanders and Queen's Rangers, so it's unclear from Robertson's narrative what happened to the "Rebels" they were pursuing.

With a note that the 2nd Battalion "filed off to the right," (believed to be Roundlay Drive off Creek Road) the narrative seems to leave the remaining Grenadiers halted in place, because only the actions of the 2nd Battalion are cited. Still, when they did move forward, several grenadiers and Guards became mired in a low ravine and rocky ground. Robertson specified that it was a tricky location for the troops, "having in their Front a Ravine, and a woody rocky Hill almost impassable."

McGuire describes the "Ravine" as a "270-foot precipice above Brinton's Run, about half a mile east of the [Brinton's] ford." Robertson then mentions the halted unit by name, "the 16th of Light Dragoons" who "were on the right with the Guards" (the 2nd Battalion).

On the map, the position of the dragoons is marked by a red line extending along present-day Brinton Bridge Road, just north of Creek Road. Two areas of dense woods lie in front of the troops, in addition to winding Brinton Run. These natural obstacles may be one reason why the dragoons did not follow the 2nd Battalion, but instead took Brinton Bridge Road, which still leads today to Dilworthtown (3). In the words of Robertson's narrative, the dragoons "could never have an opportunity to charge from the closeness of the Country, were halted at T, then marched up the Road to Dilworth to the left of the Army."

As for the 2nd Battalion, they eventually crossed Brinton's Run – and encountered the enemy. In Robertson's narrative, it is suggested that soon after the troops were "forming at W," along the Brinton Run (Roundelay Drive), the British "advanced to X by which means they came upon the right Flank of the Rebels who had opposed Lieut Genl. Knypausen's Column." Judging from a recent interpretation of the map, the encounter at X took place just north of Creek Road, near modern Master's Way, now part of the housing development, "The Reserve at Chadds Ford."

In Robertson's narrative, the encounter seems to have occurred by chance. Regardless, the second part of the sentence is especially revealing since it not only skips over the abandonment of Proctor's guns but suggests that, much like the fighting in Birmingham, the troops in Chadds Ford fought until dusk. The line reads: the Rebels "now gave way on all sides, but Night coming on hindered a Pursuit."

The Orchard at the Ring House

The Ring House (16) may have escaped a direct hit by enemy artillery, but that did not mean that it was a distant outpost far removed from the battle. Best known as Washington's Headquarters, the property became part of a late-in-the-day maelstrom. It occurred around 4 p.m., when Wayne repositioned his troops in the fields opposite the house and along the Harvey Run. After the Hessians crossed the Brandywine, Wayne was assisted by the 1st Pennsylvania troops under Col. James Chambers, but they were inexperienced and did nothing to stem the tide of advancing British troops.

Interestingly, a quote from Chambers seems to confirm what Harris has discovered in his research— that a reserve artillery redoubt was located near this area. Chambers recalled the British "advanced the hill, where our [artillery] park was, and came within fifty yards of the hill above me." [111] According to Harris, the 1st Pennsylvania troops "were deployed to protect the guns, to buy enough time to get the artillery out of harm's way."

A few hours earlier, intense fighting took place downstream at Chads' Ferry, with the Hessians facing Greene's division of about 2,500 men who also had been posted along the Harvey Run since early morning. Although popular travelogues of the 1920s insisted that the Americans were able to prevail and that the blood of the Hessians soon tainted the waters of the Brandywine, in reality, at this stage in the battle, it was difficult to discern which side was winning.

At one point, the air was so thick with gun smoke, it was said that a regiment of British Guards mistakenly believed that the American troops were Hessians. It was difficult to discern the color of any uniforms and the advancing "Hessians" appeared as shadowy figures among the trees. Wayne's troops temporarily held them at bay, but there were too many assaults from all sides. One assault took place in a small orchard on the Ring property; the encounter was described by Harris as a "hard, brutal, and short" battle and as a "bayonet to bayonet" clash.

Sgt. Thomas Sullivan of the British 49th Foot, who recalled that his troops were chest-high or "up to the middle in the [Brandywine] River" as they crossed at Chads' Ferry, observed the Americans "who drawing up in the field and orchard just by, rallied afresh and fought Bayonet to Bayonet." The American's use of bayonets must have been unexpected, especially since Sullivan's British foot soldiers had already endured a bombardment by what was described as "four pieces of Cannon" from the "Enemy being posted upon the Hill on the other side of the Road." [112]

A Loyalist with the Queen's Rangers named James Parker gives a different perspective, revealing how quickly one's military advantage could change. He saw Proctor's men fleeing the redoubt (the "fort") as follows. This may have been the redoubt near the Chads' House, or what Harris describes (with his parenthesis) as the "American artillery park, which was about one mile east of Chadds's Ford behind the hills (near the modern-day Brandywine Battlefield State Historic Site)," meaning the present-day state park on Baltimore Pike.

> "Many of them [the Continentals] Ran to an Orchard to the right of the fort, from which they were Drove to a Meadow, where they made a Stand for some time in a ditch."

Parker goes on to explain that the British troops then crossed the Brandywine and routed the Americans from "the ditch" in the "Meadow," and "all afterwards was a mere Chace [chase], so far as I saw."

The Rangers who raided Proctor's redoubt may have then used the captured guns to attack Wayne's defense along the Harvey Run. At least, it is believed that Parker was on the hill near Proctor's battery when he recalled the view. "From the eminence we had a most extensive view of the American Army, and we saw our brave comrades cutting them up in great style."

The British captain John André—a man whose accomplishments were later overshadowed by his hanging, in 1780, for being a spy, at the age of 29— thought to record the victory in his diary, as well as to document the location of one of the seized batteries on a map, describing it as a position where the Guards stood to peer down at Wayne's troops. [113]

André also suggests the Guards crossed the Brandywine well before the rest of Knyphausen's troops did, or at least, long enough to seize Proctor's Hill. "The Guards met with very little resistence [sic] and penetrated to the height," he writes,"overlooking the 4-gun battery of the rebels at Chad's Ford just as General Knyphausen had crossed."

After the battle, the Guards temporarily encamped on the Ring property. Not only were the troops exhausted, but the group also had the most losses than any other unit in the Crown Forces – nearly 20 percent of the soldiers were killed. One member of the Guards, the young Viscount Cantelupe (now known for his watercolor sketch of the action at Birmingham Hill) wrote that his unit waited until the next day, Sept. 12th, when they "marched 2 miles further to Dilworth [Dilworthtown] & there encamped."

Closing Action at The Brinton 1704 House

It was a little after 6 p.m. when the center of what would go down in history as "Greene's Rear Guard Defense" moved to an area occupied by a stately brick home now known as the Brinton 1704 House (31). One of Sullivan's brigade majors described the location as "near the Road, behind a House, to the left of General Green's Division."

Less than an hour earlier, from 4:45 to 5:45 p.m., Washington had gathered his staff in the parlor to plan Greene's defense. With the waning sunlight, this pivotal strategy could only be conceived in a hurried hour after Washington realized that the Americans had no other means of obtaining a safe and orderly retreat to the settlement of Chester. Around 5 p.m. he ordered Greene's division of two brigades to make a hurried trip northeast from their post at Chads' Ferry.

The division numbered about 2,500 troops, all of them Virginians including the first brigade under Gen. Muhlenberg; the speed in which they were able to get into what was termed the "blocking position" was considered the first success of Greene's defense. However, some historians hinge the ease of Greene's deployment to an earlier setback for the British, when Howe was forced to detach the right wing of his advancing brigade to rescue the Hessians from total annihilation, and thus weakened the troops' attack strategy.

Regardless, the American reserve troops under Lafayette were said to have delayed the British advance long enough at Sandy Hollow to give Wayne's division and Maxwell's brigade time to withdraw from Chadds Ford and to assist the retreat. While they didn't make it to Sandy Hollow, part of Wayne's Pennsylvanian brigade played a pivotal role, armed with four cannons at present-day Painter's Crossroads, to cover the retreating troops.

It is not known if the guns were fired, only that they kept the main road to Chester open at a crucial interval, from the time the first group of North Carolinians under Brig. Gen. Francis Nash escaped to the last of Sullivans' rear-guard troops that had fallen back to a property in a movement now called the Dilworth Farm Retreat.

Greene's defense did not end at Brinton House – historians in recent years have examined subsequent engagements some call the "Rearguard South" – but without this initial stand, much of the Continental Army was in danger of being trapped and an orderly retreat would have been impossible.

The fighting nearly engulfed the Brinton homestead and was reportedly savage but brief, ending around 7 p.m. The British then occupied the ground until around 8:45 p.m. That included the Royal artillery that set up a temporary camp right behind the Brinton homestead as well as the left wing of Royal Forces consisting of *Jäegers* and part of the 2nd Light Infantry Battalion that had suffered great losses at what was called the second "Eminence," south of the open fields behind the Birmingham Meetinghouse.

The British officer in charge – Brigadier General Sir William Erskine, then the Royal Army Quartermaster – was said to have made himself at home in the 1704 Brinton House. This was around sunset, or 6:45 p.m., and so Erskine was said to have looked for the first house near Wilmington Road rather than travel the relatively short distance to Dilworth.

Even though there were no more Continentals to fight, an officer with Erskine's light infantry suggests Howe could not fight in the waning light, and that the fleeing Americans left behind a load of supplies and provisions.

> "They [the Continentals] all gave way, leaving 15 [correction, 11] pieces of cannon, 2 Iron ditto, 70 Wagons of ammunition, baggage and provisions 150, with horses completed at 4 for each gun and wagon, but night came on, and brave Howe, not knowing the country, was obliged to halt that night."

A Brinton family history relates that Erskine and the elderly homeowner, Edward Brinton, had a fairly cordial exchange after Erskine "took possession of the parlor and caused his servant to produce some bottles of wine from his baggage" so that the officers present could toast to their victory. 114

The family history gives a positive spin on the home's occupation, but that is questionable since in 1782 the owner, George Brinton, filed for extensive damages – more than 544 pounds, or more than $32,000 today. The homestead's close location to the British encampment likely contributed to the loss of food and livestock including "5 horses, 2 bullocks, 7 cows, 3 yearling heifers, 2 spring calves, and 25 sheep."

British Takeover of Dilworthtown

James Dilworth, a successful blacksmith, built part of the Dilworth homestead, an elegant structure of red brick Flemish bond, in 1758. Today the building is considerably larger with a circa 1770 stone wing and a circa 1800 brick wing. The building served as the Dilworth family home until Charles Dilworth, James' son, inherited the property in 1769 and obtained a tavern license. The Dilworth Inn was a well-known landmark for generations.

During the five-day British encampment after the Brandywine Battle, the tavern served several purposes: it was a prison, a hospital, and a storage area for huge amounts of confiscated property. 115 The tavern rooms were filled with seized items and provisions while the stables housed whatever horses that had survived the battle. Like all encampments, an area was set aside for the slaughtering of livestock and for the chores assigned to the camp followers.

The number of people, including prisoners, who converged on the property is not known, but the damage claim later submitted by the Dilworth family suggests that the tavern was treated very much like the home of a "rebel." The claim totaled more than 820 British pounds, or about $49,000 today. The elder Dilworth, Charles, wrote that he needed to be compensated for the "damage done to my dwelling house by breaking doors, staircase and pulling down an oven, destroying pales [fences] round the garden and yard." Not surprisingly, there were considerable losses of whiskey, brandy, and other spirits. Still, Dilworth's claim stands out: he was also a victim of the Hessian occupation of Wilmington. He notes that a frame house that he owned there was "entirely destroyed."

The number of prisoners that were held is also not known, but it's likely they included not just soldiers but several residents who were thought to have connections to Washington's Army and were held mainly to prevent them from providing intelligence to Washington.

Perhaps the most acclaimed story of a resident being held at the Dilworth Inn was by Henry Graham Ashmead. Writing in the *History of Delaware County* (1884), Ashmead tells of William Harvey (43) being confined with several others in the tavern's cellar, "from which they made their escape by wrenching out the window-frame." Ashmead does not focus on the prison conditions but implies that Harvey's escape was a dramatic end to a saga that began at Harvey's home near Chads' Ford. It was when Harvey stepped outside and suddenly found himself in the middle of skirmish. Ashmead's account tells the story as follows:

"As they went up the hill east of [Harvey's] house, on the brow [the front] of which was a fence covered with bushes, [Harvey] saw the Americans pointing their guns towards him and the British through the bushes and was almost stunned by the fearful flash and roar of their simultaneous discharge. He was astonished to find himself alive, and still more on observing that not a man was killed or wounded. The Americans had fired over [his] head. The British…then rushed up to the fence and fired at the retreating Americans with deadly effect."

A Harvey family history focuses on Harvey's eventual standing with the local Quaker community, noting that "even though Friends did not take part in the battle," Harvey was given "the title of Major the rest of his life, due to his active interest in the revolt." A letter from the Ring family suggests that Harvey, who was part of the family who settled on the east side of the Brandywine, accepted Washington's offer to assist in "the retreat" (either from Chads' Ford or to Chester, it's unclear). He did so after Benjamin Ring declined because of his age.

The Rear Guard South: "The Sun Shown"

Today the terrain of what is known as the Rear Guard South action seems remarkably the same just south of Oakland Road, in an area described in 1777 as "Rising Ground" – the slight rise where Knox's artillerymen positioned two cannons and fired at British troops approaching Dilworth from Sandy Hollow.

Initially they were positioned closer to the 1704 house, but the troops soon decided to reposition the guns further south so that the infantry could form behind them. The first position occurred around 6 o'clock, when Stephen's 4th Virginia formed their rear defense line along present-day Webb Road, near the 1704 House. Their mission was to block a British column that included the 4th Brigade and the 2nd Grenadiers, but as the British troops moved closer, it seemed a hopeless task.

The 4th Brigade alone had about 1,400 men and presented what the British called a "grand and imposing front." In reality, nearly all these troops were depleted from a long day of fighting; in fact, it was said that the entire British brigade and grenadier troops might have been wiped out if it had not been for the Royal Artillery. As Capt. Johann Ewald observed, the advancing lines "received intense grapeshot and musketry fire which threw the grenadiers into disorder."

By the time Greene's rearguard defense was in place, the enemy troops could barely be seen through the heavy musket smoke as well as the blinding setting sun that cast long shadows through the trees. The Royal Army would later report that Knox's men faced the Royal artillery "with two Pieces of Cannon with which they cannonaded the Troops."

The action was ruthless but brief, in part because, in Pickering's words, the American artillery could not get in place until nearly sundown. Pickering's journal not only records the sun being close to setting, it records a following dialogue that indicates Washington's silence in the matter.

> "The sun shone and was perhaps 15 or 20 minutes above the horizon. A few rods in our front, was a small rising in the ground; and General Knox asked — "Will your excellency have the artillery drawn up here?' I heard no answer; [nor] did I see any body of infantry to support it."

Within minutes, Washington did order a final stand – one that took place mainly along what is called a "small rising," or a "clear rise about 100 yards east of and parallel to the Wilmington Rd." Many of the troops involved in this action were, in Harris's words, "survivors from the Birmingham Hill disaster." Others included the 2nd Virginia Brigade under Brig. Gen. George Weedon that, despite their advantageous position in the rising, faced a severe cannonade from the British.

Late in the action, Sullivan was trying to reposition soldiers behind Knox's second location when enemy fire struck and killed his horse from under him. Despite this, Sullivan went on to take part in a reorganization. He commanded his troops to rush forward and to form a defense line on Weedon's right flank, in a thick stretch of woodlands, as well as in a region described by Harris as being on the "reverse" slope of the small rising, one mile southeast of Dilworth.

A member of the American light infantry may have been speaking of this final encounter when he wrote, "the 2nd Battalion of Light Infantry had attacked so far to the right, we stood at a great distance from the army and not until about seven o'clock in the evening, on order, were we rejoined to the army at Dilworth."

In the midst of the violence, Washington may have realized that the defense line was giving way and so he made a last minute agreement to grant Count Pulaski's earlier request: that the Count would take command of an unit that came to be known as Washington's "body guard."

The group had only about 30 horsemen, but they enabled the Americans to buy time for the retreat while foiling the British advance. Indeed, without Pulaski's reconnaissance work in discovering the best route to take, Washington could easily have been killed or captured. The Commander-in-Chief may have recognized this danger; at least, his actions suggest; after the battle, the former Polish "volunteer" was given the commission of brigadier general.

The Retreat to Chester, Pennsylvania

Not surprisingly, there are only a handful of community stories about the American retreat to Chester, while the unfolding story of the British troops who moved through the Aston region of Delaware County is told through the extensive damage reports.

A rare account by an officer in the British Light Infantry (documented by Harris) even suggests that King's Army found sympathy with those residents who housed the wounded. He writes that "[on] the 13th Marched to Chester and on the Road fell in With Several Out houses and Barns full of Wounded men Who [told] us that If We keep on that Night We Should have put a total End to the Rebelion [sic]."

The damage reports, combined with community legends, help to paint a portrait of the hundreds of soldiers from both armies who descended on the region – stories that nearly always mention the wounded, hungry, and thirsty. One well-known story centered on raids—by both armies—on the unsuspecting Mendenhall family, who lived four miles east of Dilworthtown, in Concord Township, Delaware County.

Ironically, the Mendenhalls who lived closer to the action in Chadds Ford were left "unmolested," according to a family history, citing such homesteads as the circa 1748 Springdale Farm on Hillendale Road (occupied until only recently by descendants; The Mendenhalls were among the first settlers on the west side of the Brandywine.)

At the Concord homestead, Phebe Mendenhall Thomas, who was seven at the time of the battle, recalled the events of the day nearly a century later in a published account titled *"Recollections of the Battle of Brandywine."* She wrote of the retreating

Brandywine Day: This undated photo depicts a group of "Redcoats" re-enactors at Hoffman's Mill before it was restored in the early 1970s and housed the Brandywine River Museum.

Open field Re-enactment: This undated photo may have been taken near the present-day Sandy Hollow Heritage Park in Birmingham Township. *Both courtesy of CFHS*.

Continental troops stumbling into the barn yard and the next day, seeing a sea of enemy troops marching towards her Concord home on Chester Road.

Even though Howe had invited Washington to help the wounded left on the field by bringing "any surgeons you may chuse to send," the actual purpose of such a long British encampment was a mystery to the Americans. It was assumed that the enemy was either sidelined by casualties or simply too exhausted to move from Birmingham, but each day of rest heightened the unease Washington's troops felt about Crown Forces' next move.

In fact, the Mendenhall account documents the first departure from the camp. Early in the morning on Sept. 12th, two brigades under General James Grant had been ordered to Concord (now in Delaware County), the reported direction of the American retreat. According to the *"Recollections,"* Grant stopped at the Mendenhall home to get directions so that they could maneuver around a "big hill" that their artillery horses were unable to climb. Phebe later recalled that Grant's troops "had the poorest little horses to pull their big guns," a memory topped only by the sounds of fighting – "a great volley of noise" – that lasted for much of the day.

The day before, numerous American soldiers raided the farm as they made a disorderly retreat to Chester. Phebe recalled getting no supper that night since the bread baked that day went to the soldiers. She creates a visual image of the troops descending on the farm, worth quoting in full:

> "They came flocking into the yard, and sat down on the cider press, trough, and benches, and every place they could find. They seemed so tired. Father said, 'bring bread and cheese and cut for them.' They were so hungry.'"

Today historians cite the raid of the Mendenhall home as a good example of the general despair of the Continental soldiers, especially those who just escaped the battlefield. Other area families suffered a similar fate including the Painter family who gave their name to the present-day Painter's Crossing at the intersection of U.S. Routes 1 and 202.

The 19th-century family historian, William Painter, wrote of his grandmother Jane Carter Painter, a "staunch patriot," who spent Sept. 11th doing her usual baking chores, until "the soldiers, hungry and tired, ate all the dough and drank the well dry."

The historian Thomas McGuire writes that thanks to a great limestone aquifer, the region was filled with natural springs. In 1777, a typical well was 30 feet deep, and stone-lined with three feet of water. Yet "the crush of hundreds of very thirsty men" drained many of the wells on area farms. A long day at war only added to the problem since the act of biting cartridges full of black gunpowder and inhaling "clouds of acid sulfur smoke," McGuire writes, "dried the mouth considerably, to the point of desperation." John Nagle, the 13-year-old American artilleryman, provides one of the best examples of that desperation.

> "It coming on night, I was famishing with drouth [drought or thirst]. Coming to a well, but could not get near it for the mob of soldiers, but paling in with one of the artillery men, he worked his way through them and brought me water in his canteen. Otherwise I should of fell on the road."

Numerous accounts tell of the final throes of battle and the hasty retreat that one British officer, perhaps with a touch of condescension, described as a time when "the Rebels retreated in great Panick taking the Road to Chester."

The retreat was not a surrender, however. The fighting was soon renewed when the British grenadiers and the 4th brigade suddenly faced an *enfilade,* or volley of gunfire that went from one end of their line to another.

The fire came from Brig. Gen. George Weedon's 2nd Virginia brigade, which turned 90 degrees to achieve the firing, although they soon fell back. It was a move that was recorded by several British officers, including one who explained that even though the Americans "formed in a wood to cover their retreat" they were "immediately attacked" by the 33rd regiment and light infantry and were "totally defeated."

Once again it was the American Col. Pickering who records the details of the defeat. He surmised that the British succeeded because of their orderly, tactical movements. While the Continentals fired volleys from the shelter of a hedge and fence line, Pickering writes that the British remained in formation, having been ordered to halt in order to "give time for the Artillery to come up."

Around this time, the Royal Artillery managed to get three 12-pounders in place and then blast so many rounds the Americans were forced to fall back 200 yards to another fence. "A shot from their artillery I saw cut down a file of those troops," Pickering later recalled in horror.

Capt. Ewald's diary reveals that he was certain that there were no other Continentals to fight, but historians now say that the final action of the day occurred along the Wilmington Road (Rt. 202), just south of Dilworth. Here, a little after 6 p.m., Greene positioned his brigade and the remnants of other Continental troops in one formation described as a semi-circular line.

Another formation was described as bisecting Wilmington Road. It included Weedon's Virginians that formed the right wing just east of the road. There is little documentation, but Brig. Gen. Peter Muhlenberg's brigades may have formed west of road, arriving just in time to blunt and throw back the attacking British grenadiers.

The consummate observer, Ewald suggests that it was the guns of the 4th Brigade that presented the final blow and the Americans could do nothing but retreat.

"I certainly believe that the affair would have turned out to be an even more dirty one if an English artillery officer had not hurried up with two light 6-pounders, and fired on the enemy's flank with grapeshot, whereupon the enemy retreated to Chester."

Completing the scene, Ewald then wrote the final line in his diary entry for September 11, 1777: "Night Fell over this story and the hot day came to an end."

Acknowledgments

As always, there are many people to thank when you have worked on a book project that typically spans many months or even years. The encouragement alone often predates the writing stage, so I will just settle on thanking those people whose recent help was indispensable.

The early manuscript readers include Sandi Johnson and Adrian Martinez. They read some of the early drafts so long ago, they might have to be reminded of their helpful input. Thank you, Sandi, for offering suggestions to correct those passages the average reader might not understand; and Adrian, you greatly encouraged me by explaining the long-term value of my book.

Sandi is a staff member of the Chadds Ford Historical Society (CFHS) where board president Randell Spackman often provided me with ongoing insights about the Battle of Brandywine. Both are re-enactors and "living history" type of historians who like to explore the battlefield on foot – in the same way the renowned Chadds Ford resident and historian Christian "Chris" Sanderson and 19th-century writers did in the past.

I also want to cite two historians, Michael C. Harris and Thomas J. McGuire, whose books on the Battle of Brandywine were invaluable resources for me. The author W. Barksdale Maynard was another inspiration in proving to me that historical writing can be more than a conventional genre but can be very visual and lyrical too.

As for my research and photo acquisitions, I could have never completed this book without the resources of not only CFHS, but the Christian C. Sanderson Museum, and the Chester County History Center (CCHC). Most of the images listed as part of the "author's collection," were acquired from the late William "Bill" Supplee of West Bradford, who was a well-known postcard and book collector.

As one can guess from this book's text, I relied on long-term research studies of the Brandywine Battlefield Task Force and of Wade P. Catts, president and principal of South River Heritage Consulting, whose archaeological studies have changed what we know about Revolutionary War history.

Jeannine Speirs, a senior planner with the Chester County Planning Commission who serves as the administrator for the Task Force, was especially helpful in explaining the results of battlefield studies and the content of recently published documents and maps.

And last but not least, thank you Ann Bedrick for your wonderful illustrations.

Endnotes

Part One: Research & Preservation Efforts

1. According to British documents captured after the battle, Howe was most concerned with the American casualties, stating that "about" 300 men were killed, 600 wounded, and "near" 400 made prisoners. A subsequent report stated that 400 American prisoners were taken on Sept. 14, 1777, to a hospital in Wilmington, Del., suggesting that there were many wounded among the prisoners.

2. One report detailed 587 British casualties: 93 killed including eight officers; 488 wounded including 49 officers. It was also estimated that only about six "rank and file" soldiers were missing, and that 40 percent of the Royal Army's casualties were Hessians.

3. The Task Force today similarly has studied 1777 descriptions of key battlefield sites for both armies, operating under the assumption that casualties and therefore burials are likely to be found near combat areas.

4. In a 2016 interview with the author, members of the Brandywine Battlefield Task Force said that about 14,000 acres of battlefield land have remained "undeveloped since 1777." Since that time, the Task Force has undertaken a series of archeological and historical research projects, each one tackling another section of the British route through the Brandywine Valley. The final phase – completed around the time of the battle's 245th anniversary in Sept, 2022 – returns to a region referred to in the 1989 study as the "core" battlefield site, in Thornbury and Birmingham Townships.

5. Brigadier General William Maxwell of New Jersey was recruited for the Philadelphia Campaign to lead a select group of dependable marksmen. Thus "Maxwell's Men" were a special corps of light infantry who reconnoitered ahead of Washington's Army and were tasked with the job of assisting the army's militia, a group that had little training in scouting.

6. As of this writing, the John Hope House is being restored as a joint effort between Pennsbury Township and the Pennsbury Land Trust. It is one of six Revolutionary War era homes on the west side of the Brandywine, and may have also been the site of early morning skirmishes. The process to acquire the circa 1725 homestead began in 2012 when a local developer wanted to demolish the structure. In 1969, the Chadds Ford Historical Society was founded mainly to save the abandoned Barns-Brinton House, which was rapidly deteriorating. The society purchased the former tavern and did the same the following year to save the John Chads' House and springhouse. The latter structures are located across from the society's headquarters at 1736 Creek Road, Chadds Ford.

7. A historic marker placed in 1993 by Pennsbury Township near the township building along Rt. 1 describes the beginning of the running battle. It reads "along this corridor, 800 continental soldiers under General "Scotch Willie" Maxwell engaged some 8000 British Troops. Taking advantage of terrain and cover of woods, Maxwell's light infantry inflicted heavy losses on the British before retreating to positions east of the Brandywine."

8. See the Henry Whiting map cited in this book's bibliography under the National Archives. Titled *"Map of reconnaissance of the valley of Brandywine Creek : including the section from Smiths Bridge to the State Road,"* the map is also available online at the Library of Congress' web site, loc.gov.

9. One area of Rocky Hill can be reached by Camly Lane off PA Rt. 100 aka the "Historic South Creek Road." In more recent years the term "Rocky Hill" was associated with the properties of the N.C. Wyeth homestead and the Andrew Wyeth studio, both now open to the public.

10. Chris Sanderson was responsible for the 1910 marker at Washington's Headquarters. The nonprofit community group known as the Friends of Martin's Tavern acted independently when they researched and raised funds to place the Trimbleville marker near the intersection of Broad Run and Northbrook Roads. The marker highlights the history of the Great Valley Road as well as the crossing at the nearby Trimble's Ford.

11. The signage at the church followed a significant preservation effort to save land that was part of the British route to Osborne Hill, the British resting and staging area. The property was once approved for a nine-lot subdivision, but fortunately, the church recently placed a conservation easement on the land with the Natural Lands Trust.

12. It is not known if any of these "missing" markers were moved. One curious example: the Schoolhouse Road intersection was changed after the construction of the Shoppes at Longwood, and now two markers stand haphazardly right next to each other on the opposite side of Rt. 1. Both markers were erected in 1952 by Pennsylvania Historical and Museum Commission and describe general aspects of the battle such as Howe's "two separate attacks" and the American forces' attempt to "halt a British advance into Pennsylvania."

13. In evaluating potential defense line positions, Lt. Col. Hamilton specifically cited the landscape surrounding Iron Hill (Newark, Del). "This country does not abound in good posts," Hamilton wrote in a Sept. 1st letter to the War Committee, "It is intersected by such an infinity of roads and is so little mountainous that it is impossible to find a spot not liable to capital defects."

14. The elevations or embankments that might have been perceived as defiles along the Nottingham Road are mainly all gone, thanks to modern-day road improvements. It's interesting to note that there were significant elevations at the American posts at the Kennett Meeting house (where the road flowed on both sides), as well as Welch's Tavern, and at the former village of Hamorton. The Nottingham forked at the latter site, but the elevation is still visible west of the modern Rt. 52 intersection. It was here— on a knoll believed to be at least 475 feet high—that a light infantry detachment of about 200 men commanded by Virginian Lt. Col. William Heth fired volleys at Knyphausen's advance guard.

15. John Chads' tavern was located near the corner of the Nottingham Road and present-day Webb Road. Chads obtained his first tavern license in 1736. Another relative, Joseph Davis, who was married to Chads' niece Hannah Cloud, ran the tavern under the name of the "Sign of the Three Compasses." Davis filed his last tavern petition in 1778. (See the endnote #41.)

16. Harris writes of the two considerations Knyphausen made concerning his main push across the Brandywine. When the Hessian troops advanced, they discovered that the Americans had felled trees to block the passage to Chads' Ford. The second discovery, made "that afternoon," was that Proctor's view of Chads' Ferry was "partially blocked by a tree line."

17. One major artillery battle – sometimes called the Bombardment of the Ring Run Valley – took place along the creek that extends south of Rt. 1 from Rt. 52 to the 1960s-era subdivision Chadds Ford Knoll. Although Harris states that no "definitive statistics exist regarding the number of artillery pieces Washington's army possessed at the Brandywine," the location of some of the Continental batteries or redoubts have been traced by the Task Force. The Conti-

nental battery associated with the bombardment was found in a region of steep hills, later known as Chadds Peak, a family-owned ski run built in 1964 off McFadden Road.

18. At the hearing, Fischer used the latest term in defining the suburbs. The word "exurban area" now applies to a region just outside cities, but one where a boom in new housing developments has led to suburban sprawl. The term is often used to describe areas where usually "wealthy" housing developments have encroached on poorer, semi-rural areas.

19. The Civil War Trust is the principal land preservation division of the American Battlefield Trust, the nation's largest membership organization dedicated to preserving "heritage land." Its Campaign of 1776 was a collaborative effort with other groups and to date, has helped to save several key Brandywine battlefield landscapes including 84 acres at Osborne Hill and the 10-acre Dilworth Farm.

20. Osborne Hill Farm is named for Samuel Osborne who purchased the property in 1727 and built part of the current c. 1809 homestead. The property, which includes a historic stone barn, is lovingly maintained by the former longtime owners of the nearby Brandywine Hardware & Farm Center Inc. A marker placed in the stone gate post near the farm's entrance (and near a 1915 state marker) states that the farm was established in 1740.

21. In 2021, the North America Land Trust was able to raise $3.5 million to acquire the 72-acre tract that became the Brinton Run Preserve.

22. Ewald, who had lost one eye in a dual, probably didn't need his observation skills to protect his men. He was the commander of the green-and-brown clad Jäegers riflemen from the Hesse-Cassell region (now Germany). It was a unit much feared by the Americans since they were known to be a deadly light infantry unit and because they carried hunting rifles and were dressed in camouflage.

23. The southwestern section of the Birmingham Road above Strode's Mill still reveals a narrow passage or "defile" between two hills. It was a place Capt. Ewald feared "a hundred men" were waiting for his passage. His account is worth quoting in full: "I was astonished when I had safely reached the end of this terrible defile, which was over a thousand paces long, and could discover nothing of the enemy a good half hour away. Lord Cornwallis, who had followed me, was surprised himself and could not understand why the warning post [Lt. Col. Ross' patrol] with which I had fought from morning until around noon was not stationed here." See the Historic Districts section of this book.

24. The "military map" was probably the 1778 map published by the London engraver, William Faden. There are few words on the actual map (as opposed to the key or narrative) but the phrase "second position" is clearly printed on a region southeast of Birmingham Meetinghouse. The map is available as a download from the web site of the Library of Congress.

25. One study of a suspected mass grave site produced "inconclusive results." Yet because it was a "seemingly unnatural mound of earth," a ground-penetrating radar "sled" was dragged across the area, revealing "a layer of stone or sandy soil near the base of the mound." Dr. Bevan, owner of the geophysical firm called Geosight, concluded that the mound could be an old foundation or related to the nearby stone quarry. However, its location so close to an established area of brutal fighting "adds plausibility" to the idea of a mass grave, possibly a re-internment of bodies that were exposed by heavy rains after the battle. A mound of sandy soil could add another layer of protection, Bevan theorized in his report.

26. The authors of the 2006 study, Mark D. Shaffer and Bruce W. Bevan, repeatedly underscore the purpose of the study: it was not to find human remains but to confirm areas historically thought to be burial grounds. Their findings have also contributed to a greater understanding of the Thornbury Farm's connection to the "second American defensive line," aka "Battle Hill" and "Sandy Hollow."

27. Strode's Mill continued to be used long after its days of grinding grains. It served as theater space for the Peoples Light Theater in the early 1960s; as a longtime workshop and home for a renowned decoy artist, Harry J. Waite, and is currently the Strode's Mill Art Gallery and framing shop.

28. Strode's mill remained operational until 1967. Throughout the 1940s and '50s, it was said to have been used occasionally to grind grain for Pepperidge Farm company in Downingtown. Until recent years, parts of the period stone dam and the original mill raceway could still be found along the Plum Run near the intersection of Lenape and Tigue Roads. As of this writing, an open-air interpretation site, or Heritage Center, was planned for the site opposite the mill, at the c. 1740 Strode barn.

29. The Tigue family actively farmed the property until about 2010. The c. 1746 log cabin of George Entrikin is believed to have been incorporated in a Greek Revival-style homestead, which his son, Samuel, a blacksmith, inherited. Sadly, the homestead was demolished in 2019, along with ruins of a c. 1720 two-story house that featured a well in its cellar. The English-style stone barn, believed to have been built by George, who died shortly after the American Revolution, still stands and was part of a preservation effort by the township working with the owners of the property, Toll Brothers Luxury Home Builders.

30. See the 2017 document, "The Army March'd at Day Break in Two Columns," prepared for the Chester County Planning Commission, by Wade P. Catts, RPA, Robert A. Selig, Ph.D., and Kevin Bradley, RPA, then part of the Commonwealth Heritage Group, Inc.

31. *Excerpts of Letters of Major Baurmeister, During the Phila. Campaign, 1777-1778*, are found in Pennsylvania Magazine of History and Biography, vol. 59. (1935)

32. A biography published in the *Village Record* on Feb. 12, 1861, relates the ironic turn in Townsend's life. He had escaped the trauma of seeing the "devastation of Howe's Army" by moving away with his wife, but he encountered destruction again when the British raided Baltimore in the fall of 1814. Townsend is credited for his work in improving the city while holding various state and local positions including serving on the Board of Health and founding the Maryland Hospital during a yellow fever epidemic. He died at the age of 85 in 1841.

33. The 1778 map was created by the Hessian Lt. Friedrich Werner and published by William Faden, who noted on the map it was "according to an Act of Parliament." Interestingly, Faden became well respected for documenting many important battles of the American Revolution. His professionalism may be one reason why he re-issued the map in 1784, making significant revisions including changing the word "Rebels" in the map's title with the word, "Americans." Both maps stress the first-hand reporting with the line, "engraved from a plan drawn on the spot by S. W. Werner, Leiutt. [sic] of Hessian Artillery."

34. The magazine writer is unclear why Washington was waiting south of the road, but otherwise the narrative does encourage the exploration of the Brandywine Battlefield on foot. For instance, readers were told that they could still see the remnants of a battery of "six guns" that were once located behind the John Chads House (likely "Proctor's Hill") "its location may yet be distinctly traced."

35. The area may have been the "grove" near the present-day Andrew Wyeth Studio. Another Rocky Hill is thought to be the place where an American artillery battery was located in 1777, near the corner of present-day Rocky Hill and Creek Roads, close to Gibson's Ford.

36. The National Archives' online site describes two lower fords in New Castle County, Delaware. Citing a 1777 source, Richling's Ford or "Richland fording place" at "McKims Mill" was about three miles north of Wilmington. It is believed that the second ford was Corner Ford, near the present-day historic covered bridge known as Smith's Bridge on Smithbridge Road.

37. According to an animated 1777 Chester County Property Atlas, the Brandywine Road, established in 1754, roughly followed Hillendale/Fairview Road and was used to cross the Lower Ford, or Chads' Ferry. An unnamed circa 1746 road (also called the "Old Bridle path" on an 1863 Coast Guard map) crossed the Nottingham Road and led visitors north passing behind the John Chads' House. See the web site, chesco.maps.arcgis.com.

38. Construction on the P&BC railroad line began in 1855 at Concordville, Pennsylvania. However, the first section of the line, from Wawa Junction to Chadds Ford, did not open until 1859. A newspaper item in the fall of that year announced that in the process of "grading the Philadelphia And Baltimore Central Railroad in Chadd's Ford, the bones of a large number of soldiers who fell at the battle of Brandywine, have been dug up." The remnants of Hessian uniforms were found including buttons "made of lead," which "were not much defaced. The bones of one man were dug up measuring six feet, six inches."

39. The name Joseph Davis appears on tavern petitions from 1772 through 1776, but the establishment is only named on the May 28th, 1776 petition as "The Three Compasses." It is believed that it was the same tavern that John Chads opened in his family's homestead on Webb Road. Legend states that the tavern continued without a petition through the Battle of Brandywine; it cannot be ruled out since there are no extant tavern petitions issued in the Brandywine Valley other than Davis' last petition dated May of 1777. Interestingly, when Gideon Gilpin petitioned the court in August of 1778 to open a tavern in his home (the "highest house to the creek") he suggested that there were no area taverns open for the past 15 months. It reads that the "inhabitants near Brandywine have been greatly embarrassed by travelers for want of a public house in that neighborhood as Joseph Davis has declined keeping Tavern." Gilpin's last petition was in 1789.

40. One early newspaper described the 150 feet distance as five flagpoles placed end to end. Six years after the bridge's 1860 reconstruction, the big news scoop was the discovery of hand-dug caves along the Brandywine in Chadds Ford. Some accounts assumed, perhaps implausibly, that the caves were dug before the battle to serve as hiding places for residents.

41. Before John Chads moved to a hilltop location (at the present John Chads' House), it is likely he lived in the house along the Nottingham Road that he inherited from his father, Francis Chadsey, as part a 500-acre tract that extended south to the Brandywine. Chadsey built a corn mill a few years after arriving in the area in 1702. (The foundation of the mill was discovered in 1864 when Hoffman Mill was built.) The Chads' house may have stood somewhat northwest of the present-day intersection of Webb Road. It is believed that John Chads operated his tavern there, since he described the location on his 1745 tavern petition as being "where he now dwells."

42. Sanderson's friend, Thomas R. Thompson, who later helped to establish the museum to house his friend's collection, writes in his book that Sanderson typically observed the Sept.

11th anniversary with an evening program at Chadds Ford Elementary School. However, after Sanderson received a half-hearted invitation to attend the opening of the Headquarters at the Brandywine Battlefield Park in 1952 (the organizer told Sanderson "I do hope we can find room for you,") Sanderson made a point of printing cards to the 175th anniversary of the battle, inviting the public to the school. It was one way, he later said, to get over his "bitter disappointment" about not being part of the park commission.

43. At least one of the roads leading to the second crossing was a circa 1754 road that followed what today is Lucky Hill and Allerton Roads. A road trace is still visible in this area, now known as the Worth-Jefferis Historic District, but it is mainly war damages reported by a few households living along the 1754 road that reinforces the idea that the British flanking column took this route.

44. Task Force research has narrowed down the possible site where Ross's light infantry skirmished with the British, who were likely stragglers from the Flanking Column. It was near the intersection of Red Lion Road and a 1742 road now part of Corinne Road in Pocopson.

45. As illustrated in this book's map of the Flanking Column, the route may have included the c. 1775 (resurveyed) East Doe Run Road and the modern Northbrook/Red Lion Roads. The publication, *They Marched at Dawn,* included the roads in a KOCOA analysis. The "observation" point of KOCOA can still be seen today looking east towards the intersection of Northbrook and Street Road (called the "Pre-1707 Marlborough Street Road"). The text reads "Lt. Col. Ross' Patrol's probable observation point & where he sent his message to Gen'l Washington."

46. The former Red Lion Inn still stands on the southeast corner of Rt. 926 and Conservatory Road. Another tavern, also named the Red Lion, still stands in Lionville, Northern Chester County, and is truly an American Revolutionary landmark. It served as a hospital for several years and a rendezvous point for Gen. Wayne's troops in the weeks after the Battle of Brandywine and again after the Battle of Paoli.

47. Ring's Meadow was presumably the meadow surrounding Ring's fulling mill, now the Chadds Ford Township Building.

48. Pam Powell, the former longtime photo archivist at the Chester County History Center, suggests that Brinton's upbringing, from a family of journalists, inspired his reputation for approaching every subject as a "news story." The approach reinforced the idea that a community story about a subject had to be true since Brinton tended to photograph subjects only after "careful research and background information was gathered," according to Powell.

49. The veterans as well as a local militia group called the Republican Artillerists passed a resolution on July 4, 1817, that they would dedicate the memorial on September 20th, the 40th anniversary of the "Paoli Massacre."

50. It's likely that Harvey obtained the property in a sheriff's sale after Benjamin Ring's death left his sons in debt. He is believed to have retained part of the house that had served as Ring's tavern and it was later run as a hotel by Harvey's son.

51. Some historians, including Michael Harris, suggest that Harvey's homestead was likely hit by American artillery since it was in the line of fire from Proctor's batteries at Brinton's Ford. The British position is often described as directly across from Proctor's and that they were fully entrenched there by 9 a.m. However, it is more likely that Knyphausen would have

avoided a direct hit and thus the Royal artillery was placed more to the west of the ford crossing, near what is now modern Chaddwyk Lane.

52. The c.1714 Harvey household at 1401 Brintons Bridge Road was placed on the National Register in 1971. It was also included the 1961 National Historic Landmark (NHL) designation along with the Pennsbury Inn, the Springdale Farm/ Mendenhall homestead, and the Barns-Brinton House.

53. Much like the Mendenhall and Brinton families, the Harvey clan resided for generations in the region. Various historic sources differentiate between the Harveys living on the east side of the Brandywine as opposed to those on the west side. The 19th-century historian Ashmead traces all the Harveys back to William Harvey, "the immigrant," who at the age of 34, settled in 1712 on land "in the Kennett woods," on the west side of Brinton's Ford. His home would later be known as the Brinton Bridge Road homestead.

54. Taylor had begun quietly buying up shares after the board of directors stopped the construction of one of his "war hero" monuments, (perhaps understandable in a Quaker burial ground). However, a new requirement passed in 1890 that all the gravestones be lowered to "aid in the mowing of the lawns," was met with broader opposition. Like the other opponents to the plan, Taylor had loved ones – his wife and daughter – buried in the cemetery. A law suit was filed, public criticism published, and within a year, a board election overturned the old one, ushering in Taylor and his supporters, who promptly changed the name of the organization to the Birmingham Lafayette Cemetery Association.

55. The historian Harris writes that both sides of the monument erroneously state that Taylor's ancestors fought with Anthony Wayne. Harris' research indicates that Isaac Taylor likely fought with John Armstrong's militia in Chadds Ford and McClellan fought with Lord Stirling at Birmingham Hill.

56. One of the nearby markers is still evident today. It marks the entrance to a farm that was part of Osborne Hill at the corner of Birmingham and Country Club Roads.

57. According to a *Daily Local News* item published June 30, 1900, headlined "The old Flag's Baptism of Fire, etc.," a flag committee, chaired by Hooton, had planned to place the flag pole "at Sandy Hollow, on the farm of Henry Bennett." Apparently that didn't happen since an editorial written by Thomas Bennett, perhaps a relative, insisted the "main battle" did not take place in Thornbury Township and that the "errors" needed to be corrected.

58. Richard M. Atwater and his wife Abby Sophia acquired an interest in Lafayette Farms in 1906 and moved into the homestead after six years of living abroad. Their son-in-law, Dr. Arthur Cleveland, also had an interest although they acquired the dairy business after the farm's large stone barn was destroyed by fire on August 5, 1905.

59. A $10,000 appropriation bill was reportedly approved in January of 1947, but it was earmarked for the purchase of Washington's former headquarters and the surrounding acres.

60. During the years Lafayette's Headquarters appeared on postcards in the 1900s, the property was an extensive dairy farm. Today nothing remains of the three-bay stone dairy barn that was razed in 1946, which makes the current stone barn a reconstruction. The house was also reconfigured by the architect Brumbaugh. Other aspects of the farm such as a drinking well, privy, and a corncrib have disappeared over time.

Part Two: Historic Narratives & Community Anecdotes

61. The West Pikeland complex was not only the nation's first powder mill built by an order of Congress, it was also designed with the latest equipment that could quickly turn out gunpowder and feed the war machine in the fight for independence.

62. The map is one of three known maps documenting the Philadelphia Campaign of 1777-78. Commissioned by General Sir William Erskine, it was created by Capt. Charles Blaskowitz, who was considered one of the greatest surveyor-cartographers of the period.

63. Muenchhausen wrote candidly about the poor roads that caused delays – all without hinting that Howe had made a bad decision about the route. Instead, he typically presented Howe as a man of valor and good sense, especially when the general's actions concerned the safety of his troops. It wasn't until 1974, as part of America's Bicentennial's celebrations, that the Hessian's diary was published as *"At General Howe's Side, 1776-1778; The diary of General William Howe's aide de camp."*

64. Lafayette had the same rank as Washington's other five major generals, but it was by special, signed agreement with an army commissioner in Paris. His "counterpart" was not Cornwallis in the military sense, but he spent much of the day assisting Washington as did Cornwallis with Howe.

65. American Brig.Mj. Gen. John Sullivan was posted at Brinton's Ford for much of the morning. The site is now part of the former Andrew Wyeth estate and included Proctor's two-gun artillery battery located on a still-evident high elevation near the present-day Brinton Bridge Road.

66. The plantation, just outside the town of Lancaster, is open to the public with special tours beginning each spring and changing exhibits. Visit: historicrockford.org

67. Galloway's complex relationship with Gen. Howe is apparent in his published writings. A pamphlet published in 1777 at a New York print shop (most copies were later destroyed by a mob) and republished in London in 1780, was a rebuttal to a narrative on the Philadelphia Campaign that Howe presented to the House of Commons. One interesting "misrepresentation," as Galloway put it, was Howe's defense that his troops were forced to fight in dense "forests" when in fact, Galloway wrote, at least "two-thirds" and in many places "five-sixths" of the terrain in the Brandywine Valley was cleared farmland.

68. From material compiled by the Independence Hall Association, a nonprofit organization in Philadelphia, founded in 1942. Published electronically in 1995 at ushistory.org.

69. The phrase, "Knyphausen's Feint," was used on a historic marker placed at the Barns-Brinton House in Pennsbury Township in May of 2022. It reads that the "first shots" were "fired west of this location," meaning at the Welch's Tavern.

70. From the Parker papers at the Chester County History Center. John Parker, whose former home is now the historic homestead known as Ravenroyd along Creek Road, was an early settler in Chadds Ford. He is not to be confused with James Parker, the Loyalist, whose records are known as the "The Parker Family Papers," which were originally published in England and contain about six hundred items concerning the family during American Revolution.

71. Sconnelltown was once located near the intersection of Birmingham and Sconnelltown

Roads, less than a mile northwest from the Strodes Mill Historic District. A historic marker was placed at the site in 1915 by three organizations – PMHC, and the Chester and Delaware Counties Historical Societies. According to an online account, the marker is still found at the intersection of Birmingham Road and Squires Drive, on the right when traveling south on Birmingham Road.

72. The historian Harris provides some interesting details about other possible redoubts near the Chadds House. Writing that there "are a series of hills (or rises and swales) as you move east from Chads's Ford," Harris mentions a little-known redoubt or "park of American reserve artillery" that was among the hills. Harris, who formerly worked at the Brandywine Battlefield State Park and is an authority on its grounds and historic buildings, places the redoubt "about one mile east of Chads's Ford" and nearly in the State Park.

73. Harris writes that there is "contemporary evidence" that a temporary bridge (made of wagons and fence rails) was placed downstream from Brinton's Ford. McGuire also mentions the bridge, which might have been used as an additional crossing point for Sullivan's troops when they attacked across the Brandywine. Perhaps the most interesting reference was one made by Lafayette during his tour of the battlefield in 1825. He reportedly pointed out the bridge's former location to his hosts who thought he was mistaken.

74. Curiously, the Delaware County historian Ashmead believed the cannonade at the "crest of Rocky Hill" marked the beginning of the Battle of Brandywine. Accounts indicate that the brief exchange here, as well as the artillery fire at Chads' Ford and Chads' Ferry involving Greene's and Maxwell's troops, did not happen until after 12 noon – hours after the first exchange with the enemy along the Nottingham Road.

75. One can almost follow the British troops along Hillendale Road by reading the damage reports, sufferings, and depredation claims for several properties in the area, especially where the road meets Fairville Road. They include claims by three wealthy families who lived on separate farms: the farms of Isaac, Thomas, Joseph, and Noah Mendenhall as well as Peter Harvey, and Caleb and Moses Mendenhall along modern Stabler Road.

76. Bayard Taylor published his story, "The Strange Friend," in the *Atlantic Monthly* on January 1, 1867. Its popularity prompted Taylor's publisher to encourage him to continue to write about the Quaker community he knew so well. The result was his novel, *The Story of Kennett (1866).*

77. In explaining why Spear did not have the skills to scout an unknown territory, the historian Douglas R. Harper calls him a "well-meaning but ill-informed Chester County patriot" who did not anticipate the British movements. Unfortunately, Spear may have been destined to be forgotten. By the time 19th-century historians were capturing the heroics of the Battle of Brandywine, Spear was reportedly mistaken for a soldier (with same surname) who left Washington's army to become a spy for the British.

78. The phrase, "in that quarter" has long been attributed to either Spear or Maj. John Jamison of Bland's patrol. However, it's more likely to be from the testimony of Charles C. Pinckney, a Southern aristocrat who had used his own funds to raise one of America's first grenadier regiments. Harris writes that Pinckney was on leave from active duty, but nonetheless attached himself to Washington's entourage. Pinckney later recalled the reports that Washington had received from Sullivan, who was posted at Brinton's Ford. Harris writes that Spear, one of three scouts who spent the night at Martin's Tavern, completed a "reconnaissance report" and was asked by Sullivan to deliver the news to Washington's

Headquarters, apparently accompanied by a light horseman. Harris also quotes Sullivan, who confirms that Col. Moses Hazen, who was in the best position at Buffington's Ford to see the British, sent a report of a sighting around 10 a.m. Stressing that Spear "heard nothing of the Enemy about the Forks of the Brandywine [where Hazen's troops were posted]...," Sullivan concludes, "Colonel Hazen's information must be wrong."

79. Much like members of the Pennsylvania Associators, a group Ben Franklin conceived as a defense unit comprised of pro-Independence civilians, Cheyney was not part of any organized military regiment but nonetheless helped in the early war effort, organizing and equipping the county's militia, for instance, and seizing property from Loyalists.

80. At the time, Stephen's and Stirling's divisions were waiting orders, halted in the fields below the Nottingham Road, near the present-day Brandywine Drive and Painter's Crossing Road. In 1777, there was no direct route to Birmingham Hill, so at around 2:15 p.m., the troops had to go slightly out of their way. They initially headed west for one mile on the Nottingham Road before cutting through the Harvey Run watershed and taking Harvey Road north to what is now Oakland Road (once part of Harvey Road) and onto Birmingham Road.

81. See the Parker family papers held at the library of the Chester County History Center. Folder marked Parker (House) #30 (Vault).

82. McGuire has traced the observation to the Congressman Thomas Burke of North Carolina who was with Washington for at least part of the day. Burke later published a letter that appeared in numerous American and British newspapers. The letter was signed anonymously as "By a Gentleman of Distinction," partly because it "contained criticism of [Gen.] Sullivan" and "led to a second court of inquiry into Sullivan's conduct" on the Brandywine Battlefield, McGuire writes.

83. Harris writes that the location Ewald cited was likely Samuel Jones "farm buildings and Birmingham Meetinghouse, which the captain mistook for a small community." The fighting that occurred first in a "woodlot" on Jones' property (at the southeast corner of Birmingham and Street Road) and later the site a little further south described in many histories as "Jones' Orchard.'"

84. The 1913 marker is one of 8 markers (most concerned with the Brandywine Battle) in the same vicinity as the Darlington marker, which reads "The Birthplace of the Eminent Botanist William Darlington M.D. (1782 – 1863)."

85. Ironically, Iron Hill – named for a now largely vanished mountain in Newark — would have made a perfect Continental defense position but it was only briefly occupied. Made of an iron-rich, bright red soil, the hill rose abruptly 200 feet above the landscape and offered views nearly as far as Elk Landing, Maryland.

86. Henry Pleasants Jr. may have been one of the nation's most unusual military historians. Described as a physician, author, and historian on the national stage, Pleasants compiled his list of British damages in 1960, making it easier for future historians to understand the war's impact on Chester and Delaware Counties. His research resulted in an article titled, "The British Advance on Philadelphia in 1777."

87. The reference to woods is interesting since Bennett's field has also been called "south of Wistar's Woods," the site of fighting. A recent drive tour identifies a cannon beyond the Civil War cannon at the corner of Wylie and Birmingham Road, less than a mile from the 1895 Lafayette monument. The "cannon's muzzle" points to the center of the field, where Birming-

ham "road used to run" and where Lafayette was wounded.

88. Owned and protected by the Brandywine Battlefield Park, the American Sycamore was examined in early 2016 and was estimated to date to the year 1641 or 1650; it had a girth then of more than 25 feet. It is believed that the tree was 100 years old when the battle occurred and therefore was a landmark at the time.

89. The book is based on Chastellux's journal of 1780, written while Lafayette's entourage visited the battlefield in 1774. Chastellux recalled the sleeping arrangements at the time: "it was already late when we came within reach of the field of battle, and as we could see nothing until next morning and were too numerous to remain together, we had to separate into two divisions. Messrs. De Gimat, de Mauduit, and my two aides-de-camp, stayed with me at an inn three miles this side of the Brandywine; and the M. de La Fayette, attended by the other travelers, went on further to ask for hospitality from a Quaker named Benjamin Ring, at whose house he had lodged with General Washington the night before the battle."

90. Lafayette stayed for several months (until the Valley Forge encampment) with the Moravian leader George Fredrick Beckel; the house is gone but a historic marker remains on Main Street, in Bethlehem. The Moravivan town served the Continental Army for six years, from 1775 to 1781. During the Philadelphia Campaign of 1777, it was the site of military hospitals, a munitions base, and a depot for Washington's personal baggage. At one point, more than 200 Continentals occupied area homes and were assigned to guard British Prisoners of War.

91. According to a 1950s park brochure, the carriage was stored in a wagon shed in the Brandywine Battlefield Park and brought out on special occasions.

92. William Darlington had become acquainted with McClellan, a former burgess of West Chester, when the latter retired from banking and sold his West Chester home to Darlington in order to buy a farm in Birmingham – a reverse progression of what was commonly done in the 19th century, especially among retired farmers.

Part Three: Historic Sites & Military Landmarks

93. John Hannum's home, now a private residence, is described by the Task Force as "outside the battlefield" but it is still listed on the group's Historic Resources Inventory at 898 Frank Road, off Rt. 322, near West Chester. Thomas Cheyney's former farmstead is a beautifully restored private home but is surrounded by a township park on North Cheyney Road, in Thornbury Township, Delaware County.

94. An 1851 illustration of an early covered bridge indicates that the bridge was not built at the site of the former ford. Instead, Jefferis' Ford was depicted as being close to the mouth of Blackhorse Run that fed into the East Branch of the Brandywine, west of the covered bridge.

95. The Historic Resources Inventory available on Chesco.org lists the home near Strode's Mill (where Townsend and his brother viewed the British from a doorway) as a circa 1777 house, at 415 Birmingham Road. The property where the Strode blacksmith and wheelwright shop is listed as still standing at 901 Paxson Drive.

96. The northwest section of Birmingham Road near Strode's Mill is still steep, though it's not quite the deep gorge that alarmed Capt. Ewald. As a defense strategy, he had ordered the *Jäegers* to proceed through the defile in pairs, "two hundred paces apart." Ewald knew that they would be greatly outnumbered should they encounter the "van of the enemy." Each

group was told to wait, or "to take post," until all five groups "had reached a point where they could see far around."

97. Some historians have considered the possibility that Osborne Hill changed the course of the battle. The British rested for more than an hour, giving the Americans valuable time to establish their defense lines and to bring artillery from Chadds Ford.

98, McGuire writes about the visual accounts of the Campaign of 1777 (including that of Viscount Cantelupe) in an article titled, *British Images of War at Brandywine and the Tredyffrin Encampment," Pa. Heritage* magazine, Fall 2002 issue.

99. Hector's birthplace is not known other than he was born free in Pennsylvania and this may have helped him to secure his place in Proctor's artillery unit. He applied for a pension in 1827, 1829, and 1833, but was rejected each time. Hector's pension application reportedly does not mention his military rank nor the length of time served, but muster records suggest that he served from Feb., 1777 to Dec., 1780. He may have worked as a teamster at least until 1778, when his work included transporting pig iron for the military stores as well as "42 10-inch shells," (as one order read), working both for Rutters & Potts Furnace and the Brooke family of Hopewell Furnace.

100. The independent researcher John Rees has written about Hector' "demotion" from bombardier to a teamster or wagoner in Proctor's regiment. He suggests that it was based on the idea that "a Black bombardier was superior in rank to a white matross" (the least-skilled position on a gun crew). He also writes that Hector "never applied for a federal pension, and when he petitioned for a state pension, he was denied."

101. Benjamin Ring was one of the wealthiest residents of Chadds Ford. Ring not only had a 150-acre farm, he owned a fulling mill (for preparing woolen cloth), a sawmill, and a tannery. The household included Ring and his wife, their six children, and an indentured servant.

102. Washington's payment is cited in the records of the National Archives (see "general order, Sept. 9, 1777). A "receipt" penned by Ring is said to be preserved in the archives of the Brandywine Battlefield Park. It acknowledges that he received Washington's payment dated Feb. 7, 1778, sent from the encampment at Valley Forge for "30 persons eating at 6 different times" amounting to "22 pounds, 10 shillings." It doesn't mention a special dinner before the battle.

103. According to the web site of the Brandywine Battlefield Park, the indentured servant may have been a German immigrant named Christoph Rudolph, since that name "shows up on immigration papers from Philadelphia in the 1760s." The park also cites the 1859 correspondence of Benjamin Ring's grandson, Samuel Ring, who suggests that Rudolph was in the household in 1777.

104. Ring's damage claims reportedly came to about 737 pounds, or about $130,000 in today's currency. Ring was never banished from his Friends Meeting, as was his neighbor Gilpin who swore an oath of allegiance to the Continentals after the British destroyed his farm. That may explain why Ring received a donation from the Society of Friends; it was the equivalent of about $14,000 in today's currency.

105. Although the Brandywine Battlefield Park doesn't address the property's use after war, Jordan's Delaware County history states that Ring opened a tavern in 1800, four years before

his death, and that his son operated it as a hotel until about 1807. At one point, Jordan writes, the tavern was called "The United States of Arms."

106. Futhey & Cope often recorded community stories as fact, stating that the house did serve as Lafayette's headquarters and that he stopped at the house in 1825, leaving "his procession" outside while he paid a visit to "aged" Gideon.

107. While other historians have addressed such issues as lack of documentation and the fact that neither the Marquis' friendship with Washington nor his ranking did not necessarily give him special privileges, Harris focuses on the 1780 visit and Chastellux's account that states Lafayette stayed at Benjamin Ring's house.

108. Another community legend tells of a Continental cannon placed on the hill, and that the Kuerner farmstead may have served as a hospital. Certainly, the farm was very close to the day's severe action.

109. In 1777, Harvey Road played a key role in getting American troops to one area of combat to another. However, it is still largely unprotected by any scenic easement or preservation plan.

110. McGuire cites an 1863 U.S. coastal topographical map that describes the crossings at Brinton's Ford as the "Point where the British crossed, in force, by a Temporary bridge of trees and rails." It was located near the mouth of Brinton's Run, about a half mile below Brinton's Ford, McGuire adds.

111. Harris includes a chapter in his book on Knyphausen's late afternoon assaults at Chadds Ford. One of the book's appendixes also provides information on the use of artillery in the battle.

112. McGuire writes that this may not have been the expected "Proctor's Hill," but a battery "about 800 yards south of Proctor's position, firing on the British right flank."

113. André's journal was subtitled *"An Authentic Record of the Movements and Engagements of the British Army in America from June 1777 to November 1778 as Recorded from Day by Day."* It has been described as a nearly complete record of the British movements during the Philadelphia Campaign of 1777. His honorable behavior on the field did not go unnoticed and men such Alexander Hamilton and Lafayette later expressed sorrow when André was captured and hanged by the Continental Army after it was discovered that he had joined Benedict Arnold in a scheme to secure British control over the American fort at West Point, N.Y.

114. Erskine went on to lead troops at the Battle of Monmouth and in 1779 was promoted to the rank of Major General. At that time, he was considered one of the most highly regarded commanders in the British Army.

115. Area homes that served as hospitals include the Samuel Painter homestead, owned for generations by the same family, at 38 Harvey Road. The Painters likely received the overflow from Dilworth on Sept. 12th, the same day about 2,000 soldiers – primarily Hessians and Scottish Highlanders – occupied Wilmington, Del. They were ordered to find suitable housing for the wounded but they also spread terror in the city by capturing Governor John McKinley.

Bibliography

André, John. *Andre's Journal*. Edited by Henry Cabot Lodge. Vol. 1 Boston: The Bibliophile Society, 1903.

Ashmead, Henry Graham, *1838-1920: History of Delaware County, Pennsylvania*. Philadelphia: L. H. Everts and Co., 1884.

Baldwin, William C. *Historic Brandywine Guide Book*, West Chester: The Bradford Village Press, 1960.

Canby, Henry Seidel. *The Brandywine*. Illustrated by Andrew Wyeth. Originally published in 1941, reprint by Schiffer Publishing, 1997.

Chadwick, Bruce. *The First American Army: The Untold Story of George Washington and the Men behind America's First Fight for Freedom*. Naperville, IL: Sourcebooks, 2008.

Chastellux, Marquis de, *Travels In North America In The Years 1780, 1781 and 1782*. (Howard Rice, translator) Charleston, S.C.: Nabu Press, 2010. Book reprinted in 1963, but this copy is an exact reprint of the historic 1922 edition.

Cope, Gilbert. *Genealogy of the Baily Family...Descendants of Joel Baily*. Lancaster, PA: Wickersham Printing Co., 1912.

Dastrup, Boyd L. King *of Battle: A Branch History of the U.S. Army's Field Artillery*, Fort Monroe, VA., US Army Training & Doctrine Command, 1992. Digitalized version: University of California, 2016.

Edgar, Gregory T. *The Philadelphia Campaign, 1777-1778*. Westminster, MD: Heritage Books, Inc., 1998.

Ewald, Johann. *Diary of the American War: A Hessian Journal, Captain Johann Ewald, Field Jäger Corps* Translated and edited by Joseph P. Tustin, New Haven, CT: Yale University Press, 1979.

Furst, Karen Smith. *Around Chadds Ford*. Charleston, SC: Arcadia, 2005.

Futhey, John Smith and Gilbert Cope, *History of Chester County*, Philadelphia, PA: Louis and Everts, 1881.

Harper, Douglas R. *West Chester to 1865, That Elegant & Notorious Place*. West Chester, PA: The Chester County Historical Society, 1999.

Harris, Michael. *Brandywine: A Military History of the Battle that Lost Philadelphia but Saved America, September 11, 1777*. El Dorado Hills, CA.: Savas Beatie, Reprint edition, 2017.

Heathcote, Charles W. and Lucile Shenk, editors. *A History of Chester County, Pennsylvania.* Harrisburg, PA: National Historical Association, 1932.

Jordan, John W. *A History of Delaware County, Pennsylvania.* Vol. 1. New York: Lewis Historical Pub., 1914.

Recca, Phyllis. *Chadds Ford, Then & Now.* Chadds Ford, PA: Published by Recca. 2015.

Smith, Timothy B. *The Golden Age of Battlefield Preservation: the Decade of the 1890s and the establishment of American's First Five Military Parks.* Knoxville, TN: University of Tennessee Press, 2008.

Thompson, Thomas R. *The Washington's Headquarters Story: The Eventful Years*, self-published in Chadds Ford, 2002.

_____ . *A Biography of Christian C. Sanderson*. Philadelphia: Dorrance, 1973

Trussell, John B.B. *The Pennsylvania Line: Regimental Organization and Operations, 1776-1783.* Harrisburg, PA: Historical & Museum Commission, 1977.

MacElree, Wilmer W. *Along the Western Brandywine*. Princeton, NJ: Princeton University, 1912.

Maynard, Barksdale W. *The Brandywine: An Intimate Portrait*. Philadelphia, PA: University of Pennsylvania Press, 2014.

McGuire, Thomas J. *The Philadelphia Campaign: Brandywine and the Fall of Philadelphia,* Volume One. Mechanicsburg, PA: Stackpole Books, 2006.

Morgan, Edmund, S. *The Birth of the Republic 1763-89.* Chicago: The University of Chicago Press. 4th edition, 2013.

Muenchhausen, Friedrich Von. *At General Howe's Side, 1776-1778: The Diary of General William Howe's Aide de Camp, Captain Friedrich Von Muenchhausen.* Ann Arbor, Michigan: University of Michigan, 1974. Available on Google Books, 2008 edition.

Pisasale, Gene. *Forgotten Founding Fathers: Pennsylvania and Delaware in the American Revolution.* Chester County: Gene Pisasale-Historic Insights, 2020.

_____ . *Alexander Hamilton, Architect of the American Financial System.*

Reed, John Ford. *Campaign to Valley Forge, July 1, 1777-December 19, 1777.* Philadelphia, PA: University of Pennsylvania Press, 1965.

Booklets, Manuscripts, Digital Books & Online Archives

Bevan, Bruce W. *A Geographical Survey on the Spackman Farm, Brandywine Battlefield National Historic Landmark.* Prepared for the Brandywine Battlefield Task Force, 1999. On file at CFHS and at the Delaware County Planning Dept. Media, PA.

Brandywine Battlefield Task Force. *Brandywine Battlefield Preservation Project, Meetinghouse Road Corridor Properties: Project Costs & Funding Sources, 2000.* Available at the Chester County Planning Commission, West Chester, PA.

———. *Battlefield Protection Strategies: A guide for Brandywine Battlefield Communities,* 2000.

———. *Crown Forces Strategy: The Army Marched at Dawn, Southern Battlefield Strategic Landscapes Plan.* Prepared with the Commonwealth Heritage Group, 2020. Available as a PDF download at the "document center" at chesco.org.

———. *Geophysical Landscape & Battlefield Analysis* (showing results from a 2010 study and a 2013 plan defining the battlefield). Available as a PDF download at the "document center" at chesco.org

Catts, Wade P., Robert A. Selig, Kevin Bradley. *Military Terrain Analysis and Planning Recommendations for two Brandywine Battlefield Strategic Landscapes, Chester County, PA.* West Chester, PA: Commonwealth Heritage Group, Inc., 2017.

Chiquoine, Walter A. *Interpreting the Movements of the British Army out of Mill Creek Hundred, Delaware, Sept. 9-19, 1777- Map evidence,* 2016. Available as download from independent.academia.edu.

Cope, Gilbert and Ellen Starr Brinton. *The Brinton Genealogy…with some records of the English Brintons.* Trenton, N.J.: Press of MacCrellish & Quigley Company, 1924. See 1993 digitalized version.

Delaware County Planning Dept. *Living in a Landmark,* a brochure, 2000.

Galloway, Joseph. *An extract from A reply to the Observations of Lieut. Gen. Sir William Howe on a pamphlet entitled, Letters to a Nobleman. Originally printed in London by J. Paramore, 1781.* The electronic version is available at the New York Public Library's archives at nypl.org.

Heathcote, C.W., *Washington in Chester County.* West Chester, PA: Chester County Historical Society, 1932. Subtitled: Washington Bi-centennial bulletin, 1732-1932. Available from the collection PA's Past: Digital Bookshelf at Penn State, Pennsylvania State University Libraries.

Howe, William. *The narrative of Lieut. Gen. Sir William Howe, in a Committee of the House of Commons, April 29, 1779, … to which are added some observations upon a pamphlet by J. Galloway,* 1780. Digitalized version, 2015. hathitrust.org.

Journal of the American Revolution, a peer-reviewed online magazine found at allthingsliberty.com. A special section is devoted to the Brandywine battle.

Lafayette, Le Marquis de. *Memoirs of General Lafayette : with an Account of His Visit to America and His Reception…from His Arrival, August 15th, … at Yorktown, October 19th, 1824.* Available as a digital book at Kindle Direct, 2015 .

Loper, Joshua Peter and Melanie Kathleen. *The Complete History of the Hale - Byrnes House and the George Washington Witness Tree of Delaware.* Wilmington, Delaware: George Washington Witness Tree of Delaware Museum, 2023.

McGuire, Thomas J. *Brandywine Battlefield Park: Pennsylvania Trail of History Guide*. Mechanicsburg, PA: Stackpole Books, 2001.

_____. *British Images of War at Brandywine and the Tredyffrin Encampment*, Pennsylvania Heritage magazine, 28:4, 2002.

Trevelyan, Sir George Ottto. The American Revolution, 1897-1914; reprint, New York: McKay, 1964.

Webster, Nancy V., Martha L. Wolf, et. al. *Brandywine Battlefield National Historic Landmark Cultural Resources Management Study, 1989*. Available at the Delaware County Planning Commission.

Other Archives

The Chester County History Center, West Chester, Pa.

Collection title: The Battle of Brandywine. As of this writing, the collection was stored in boxes in the library and organized broadly such as listed as documents related to creation of the Brandywine Battlefield State Park. A separate newspaper collection was filed with the same title.

Library of Congress, digital archives at loc.gov.

Collection title: American Revolution and Its Era: Maps and Charts of North America and the West Indies, 1750 to 1789. The archives includes the troop movement map published in London in 1778 and the topographical map of 1863 created by Henry L. Whiting of the U.S. Coast Survey.

Collection title: George Washington Papers . This is considered the largest collection of original Washington papers in the world and includes papers about the Philadelphia Campaign of 177 7. See Military Papers, 1755-1798. Correspondence used included that from John Adams, Alexander Hamilton, John Hancock, and the Marquis de Lafayette

Made in the U.S.A.